COMMUNISM

Classic and Contemporary

Emile B. Ader

PROFESSOR OF POLITICAL SCIENCE
UNIVERSITY OF ARKANSAS

BARRON'S EDUCATIONAL SERIES, INC.
Woodbury, New York

The phenomenon of modern communism has been a disquieting element on the world scene for a century and a quarter. While many earlier theorists had expressed ideas similar to those found in communism, the efforts of Karl Marx and Friedrich Engels constitute a watershed in the history of radical economic and social thought and action. The significant aspects of what came to be known as Marxism were not merely the distinctive analysis of historical evolution and the prescription for novel socio-economic arrangements in society, but the widespread appeal which communism developed and its impact in revolutionary movements around the world. In Lenin's hands communist dogma became a prime tool in forging the Russian revolution and in shaping the new Soviet society. In China, Mao Tse-tung's version of Marxism was a driving force in expelling Chiang Kai-shek's legions from the mainland in 1949 and establishing a new political and economic order. And throughout the contemporary world the influence of communist doctrine and communist political parties continues to be felt.

Naturally an ideology of such import created great interest, attracted considerable support, roused much fear and confusion, and stimulated extensive examination. Since Marxism was subjected to a variety of interpretations and uses by its various exponents, and analysts drew varying conclusions, misunderstanding and dread were compounded. This circumstance, coupled with the development of an esoteric jargon within communist ranks, has cloaked communism in mysticism, made understanding difficult, and generated an unreasoning anxiety in noncommunist societies.

iii

It is the aim of this book to dissipate the anxiety, to clarify the jargon, and to obliterate the mysticism by presenting a factual analysis of the content and intent of communist doctrine and the uses to which it has been put since Marx and Engels. While many works on communism are available, it is hoped that the special values of this volume will be its simplified style, its contemporary assessment of the communist movement, and its brevity. Particular attention is given to the Chinese version of communism, the Sino-Soviet schism, the relations between the Soviet Union and its European satellites, the importance of communism in the cold war, the question of communism in America, and a realistic appraisal of communism in theory and practice.

I am indebted to many individuals for ideas and suggestions which went into this work, not the least of whom are a decade of students whose insight and questions helped to tailor evaluations. Barron's Educational Series provided its usual fine editorial assistance. Special thanks are due to Mariana Ader who typed the manuscript and whose perceptive reading of it contributed significantly to the improvement of the end product.

Emile B. Ader

CHAPTER 1

WHAT IS COMMUNISM?

Fear and Faith

Communism, as an idea, a theory, a program, or a movement, has exhibited the dual capacity—in the contemporary world—of inducing the most irrational fear and the most dedicated commitment. To those to whom communism has appeared as a threat to their way of life, the very word has evoked both dread and compensatory action. To those who saw communism as affording the way to a new and better life, it became the lodestar for the future. In neither case did the feeling produced necessarily reflect the degree of understanding with which communism was perceived. In fact, the very intensity of advocacy or antagonism suggests the extent to which communism was and is misunderstood. Human beings, unfortunately, live with and by labels and the stereotypes which such labels project. As a consequence, emotional depths are frequently stirred on unreasonable premises.

The people of the United States, beginning in the 1920s, are an excellent example of the heightened fear and the intemperate

1

action which communism is capable of producing. Faced with the fact of the Bolshevik revolution and a sizeable propaganda effort by communists in this country, Americans began to feel uneasy about the nature of the threat which communism presented. As the violent aspects of communist tactics became more apparent, as they were related to the activities of individual native anarchists and representatives of such an organization as the International Workers of the World (an offshoot of the socialist movement in the United States), and as the average citizen continued to be unable to comprehend the entirety of communist theory, there developed the first large "Red scare" in the United States. Communism was viewed superficially as a revolutionary operation designed not only to subvert constitutional government but—in some curious way—to redistribute the wealth in such fashion that almost everyone would come out the loser. Therefore, political or economic unorthodoxy of any sort became suspect, and both governmental agents and private citizens moved to a repressive orientation severely restricting the rights of free expression and association. State legislative investigations of "subversive activities" began, and laws proscribing the advocacy of actions designed to overthrow government by force and violence were either enacted or unlimbered for application. Even the Supreme Court of the United States, which, in 1919, had established the "clear and present danger" doctrine as the criterion for the permissibility of free speech, clamped an additional restraint on communist agitation in 1925 by holding that their views were sufficiently incendiary as to permit legal silencing even though their utterances presented no immediate threat to the security of state government.[1]

Following the stock market crash of 1929 and during the depression of the 1930s there was a relaxation of the spirit of anti-communism. For one thing, the feared revolutionary threat had not materialized; for another, basic concern with economic survival took precedence over theoretical speculations and joust-

[1] See *Schenck v. U.S.*, 249 U.S. 47 (1919) and *Gitlow v. New York*, 268 U.S. 652 (1925).

ing with hypothetical menaces. The capitalist system, moreover, had failed to the extent that it had not prevented the economic misery of the depression years. Communism, which rejected free enterprise, elicited a new interest from the American society, and Communist Party membership rose from approximately 7,500 in 1930 to 70,000 in 1939.[2] The Supreme Court adopted a more lenient view of communist activity.

A slight resurgence of anti-communism manifested itself in the late 1930s and early 1940s as economic stability began to return and communism's international aspirations were shown in such events as the Spanish Civil War. The U.S. House of Representatives created the special Committee on Un-American Activities in 1938 to investigate potential or actual subversive activities. World War II erupted in 1939, at which time it appeared that in signing a nonaggression pact with Germany the Soviet Union was aiding in Hitler's conquest of Europe, thus adding a new reason for anti-communist feeling. The resurgence was short-lived, however, as, in 1941, Hitler attacked Russia, and the Japanese attack on Pearl Harbor catapulted the United States into the conflict as an associate of the Soviets. An immediate revision in American thought occurred, and as the stubborn resistance of the Russian armies blunted Hitler's advance, respect grew and ideological fears dissipated.

The post-World War II period ushered in a new era of anti-communism even more virulent than that of the 1920s. Whatever good will had been generated toward the Soviet Union during the conflict was almost immediately dispelled when it became apparent that it had no intention of dismantling its war machine and every intention of dominating the states of eastern Europe. Nor, did it seem, were its expansionist desires to be sated by this prize; maneuvers appeared which suggested that Italy, France, and other nations were viewed as legitimate prey. So concrete was the evidence of new aggression that the United States responded in 1947 with the "Truman Doctrine" of con-

[2] J. Edgar Hoover, *Masters of Deceit* (New York: Henry Holt, 1958), p. 5.

tainment, and the Cold War was inaugurated. The communist victory in China, the Korean "police action," the 1956 repression of the Hungarian uprising by the Soviet Union, Castro's ascendancy in Cuba leading to the missile crisis of 1962, and American involvement in Vietnam served to confirm communist intentions and America's response.

Internally, constraint of communists proceeded apace, nurtured by a flood of anti-communist writings and speeches which, on occasion, were more notable for their lack of moderation than their precision. Such catering to public appetite and prejudice could hardly have had any other result than an intensification of an already inflamed outlook, though to be sure it proved to be profitable either monetarily or politically for its originators. Governmentally, both national and state agencies mounted attacks on the "communist conspiracy." The House Committee on Un-American Activities, as well as various state legislative committees, initiated new investigations. The 1940 Alien Registration Act (Smith Act) served as the basis for the prosecution and conviction of the eleven top communists in the United States for conspiring to teach and advocate the overthrow of government by force and violence.[3] The Taft-Hartley Act of 1947 required a non-communist affidavit of labor union officials. The Internal Security Act of 1950, the Immigration and Nationality Act of 1952, and the Communist Control Act of 1954 placed additional burdens and disabilities on communists and communist-infiltrated groups. Loyalty-security programs were instituted and expanded for government employees. And the infamous era of "McCarthyism" had its inception in 1950.

In the final analysis, it was the very extravagance of McCarthyism—with its callous disregard of personal dignity, with its broadside smears, with its insinuation and innuendo—aided by its treatment in the communications media, which relieved the country of its trauma. Opposition to the Senator and what he represented crystallized, and eventually (1954) the Senate took the unusual step of formally censuring one of its own. In

[3] *Dennis v. U.S.*, 341 U.S. 494 (1951).

the interim Stalin had died and the new Soviet leadership appeared to be more moderate externally and internally. The Korean hostilities were brought to a close, and peace was attractive. This combination of developments introduced a new period of appraising communism sensibly in which emotionalism did not override reason.

None of the foregoing should be interpreted as an attempt to make communism as a theory or movement more palatable. Surely, the United States, as much as any other nation, has an inherent right to defend itself against actions by external forces or dissident internal groups designed to overthrow existing and cherished political and economic institutions by intrigue and violence. It may likewise possess the right to limit speech and publications when such utterances exhort individuals to revolutionary action in the immediate future. But the atmosphere and impact of the eras of anti-communism went far beyond this. Confronted with an idea and a movement which was neither understood nor accurately gauged as to strength, the American public was caught up in a wave of hysteria and found itself applauding restrictive laws and investigating procedures which placed valued individual rights in serious jeopardy. This is the nature of communistically inspired fear.

And what of the other side of the coin—the faith and dedication of communist adherents? In this direction, as well as that of fear, the failure to comprehend fully the ramifications of communist theory, to realize its practical difficulties and inadequacies, has affected its followers. Communism is basically an economic doctrine, and a deceptively appealing one. Its appeal to the "have-nots" is specially attractive, because it purports to offer them a better life as a right—as something which they deserve naturally regardless of status, ability, or motivation. And it encapsulates this promise of improved living standards in an historical analysis which justifies its fulfillment and guarantees its attainment. It then coats the capsule with a methodology carefully colored to guide the way to achievement. To the poor and the underprivileged, to those lowest in any caste system, to those who have little or nothing to lose, this entice-ment is not to be weighed or questioned (and found wanting), it is to be grasped, and the leaders of the movement striving to make the theory a reality are to be followed and supported. Work and temporary sacrifice are well worth the prize to be gained. It is apparently this belief in the promise, this desire for change, for improvement, that stimulates much of the dedi-cation, much of the effort expended in behalf of communist endeavors. When there is added to this the additional entreaty to fulfill independent national aspirations, to overthrow old imperialist domination, some of man's most sensitive emotions are brought into play.

There are at least three other factors which may account for individual support of communist action. First, there are those who, possibly being deluded by their own idealism and sense of humanitarianism, support the communist cause in the interest of the poor. Even when aware of communism's inconsistencies, such backers may still believe that no more suitable path to greater economic equality exists. Second, in the case of Com-munist Party members—as distinguished from casual supporters —the manner of induction and training explains much. In con-formance with Lenin's doctrine, the "privilege" of Party mem-bership is not broadly extended. As a closely knit, highly trained cadre of professional revolutionaries, the Party chooses its mem-bers carefully and indoctrinates them thoroughly before full status is granted. In the course of this experience the new member becomes a fully disciplined and strongly motivated minion of the ruling hierarchy. Third, the top echelons of Party leadership have a further reason for commitment. While recognizing in a more realistic fashion the actualities of dogma and program, the leaders of communism exhibit the dedication of any who view their positions as conferring power, preroga-tive, and perquisites. They are not anxious to relinquish the privileges which Party position permits, and, therefore, they work with a fervor which solidifies authority or assures ad-vancement.

Precursors of Communism

Precisely what is the nature of this communism which can create such faith and fear? It is, of course, that version of Marxism—as modified by Lenin—which served as the theoretical underpinning of the 1917–18 Russian revolution, the establishment of the Soviet dictatorship, and the subsequent developments which caused the movement to be viewed as an "international conspiracy." The characteristics of contemporary communism will be summarized at the end of this chapter and examined in detail in those which follow. But it may be productive here to peruse those ideas and exploits which by their nature served as forerunners for the modern ideology. This survey will not only indicate the theoretical roots of Marxism but will also suggest the differences between communism and the earlier theories.

Communism is a term which inherently implies a commonality of interest, a mutual sharing of that which is possessed in common, a communal life. To some extent, such a "common" outlook exists in any organized grouping of individuals. For modern communism, however, and for many philosophies preceding it, the "communal life" takes on a specific definition particularly with regard to property arrangements in society. Nor is property the only aspect of ideology which is of concern; the total theory of society's organization, social relations, the goals of society's existence, the best road to their attainment, and relationships between rulers and ruled are all examined. In these terms, then, much of communist doctrine can be found in previously expressed human ideas and endeavors.

Plato's *Republic* is one of the earliest works which contains seeds of communist thought. This utopian presentation of an ideal state in which society is to be divided into three classes— artisans, soldiers, and governors—is in many ways non-communist. There is not, for example, the materialist emphasis of modern communism; private property is approved for the majority of the population; class cooperation is urged rather than class conflict; no classless society is envisioned; and no revolutionary tactics are advocated for the achievement of desired ends. Plato's "communism" is most apparent, however, in his plan for the ruling class. Concerned that these men and women should devote all their energies to the proper governing of the state, he decreed the abolition of private property for the group and prohibited monogamous relationships. Breeding was to be regulated, and offspring reared by the state; modern communism does not go this far, though it shares the "community" outlook. The idea of an elite ruling class finds a counterpart in today's practice, and Plato's emphasis on the well-being of the total society as opposed to the enlargement of the individual seems to match the realities of contemporary communism.

Strangely enough, a second source of sustenance for communist theory comes from the dogma of that force which has opposed communism so resolutely—Christianity. Certainly the "godless" nature of communism and its materialism would immediately receive Christian condemnation, and the church through the centuries has surely supported the idea of private property. In some senses, however, Christ's teaching and the practices of the early Christians are reflected in communist thinking. Having a prime interest in man's soul, Jesus cautioned against the amassing of wealth and the temptations to sin which are its concomitants. While stemming from different motives, the parallelism of communism's condemnation of the wealthy entrepreneur cannot be avoided. Even more to the point, the experiences of the early Christian communities, the communal life, the sharing of all material things, and the donations of the more affluent to the welfare of the poor are adequate evidence of a practical similarity to communist theory regarding the ideal distribution of the goods of society.

From the sixteenth century into the nineteenth a host of utopian theorists, especially in Great Britain and France, developed concepts and engaged in experiments which relate to current communist dogma. On the whole, these writers are primarily socialist in orientation and, therefore, diverge strongly from the thinking of their communist cousins.[4] In 1516, Sir Thomas More published his *Utopia*, a severe criticism of English society and a call for extensive overhauling couched in mythical terms. In "communistic" phrasing More exclaims that "as long as there is any [private] property, and while money is the standard of all other things, I cannot think that a nation can be governed either justly or happily." He is critical of the failure to improve the lot of the working classes, and he denounces the societal arrangement which produces poverty, gives rise to crime as a means of overcoming it, and then severely punishes the criminal. His answer is a new society in which production is planned and the focus is on communal living. Products are placed in a common store from which all draw to satisfy minimum needs. Luxury is shunned, and education and experience teach the basic virtues of the common life.

In the seventeenth century such theorists as Francis Bacon, Peter Chamberlen, and John Bellers, together with that radical group known as the Diggers advanced ideas on which communism later built. Bacon saw the advance of science as the key to man's material advancement, and his *New Atlantis* presents the scheme for its application in a utopian society. Chamberlen and Bellers bewailed the plight of the poor in society and advanced such plans as the nationalization of British royal and church property and the establishment of publicly financed cooperative colonies for the benefit of the poor. The Diggers insisted that natural law prescribed an equality of right to land and subsistence and urged that every individual had the privilege of sharing in the produce of the communally tilled land. Their spokesman, Gerrard Winstanley, advocated a society in which the ownership of private property would be severely limited and the selling of land prohibited. All would labor in this commonwealth, goods would be placed in a common re-

[4] For an elaboration of these theories see Emile B. Ader, *Socialism* (Woodbury, N.Y.: Barron's Educational Series, 1966), pp. 19–42.

pository, and each would draw from this store in accordance with his need. The Diggers even attempted to implement their plan, but the effort was quickly halted by government action.

In the same century the Italian Thomas Campanella produced his *City of the Sun*—another utopia which purports to remedy the evils of contemporary society by the substitution of new ideals. Campanella is somewhat unique among the socialist theorists in that he is critical of both man and his environment, and, therefore, his plan of reformation covers both the individual and the institutions of society. Seeing paternal concern with the wealth of offspring as the prime motive in achieving fortune—and detracting from loyalty to the state, Campanella provides a plan of selective breeding and the rearing of children outside of a family circle. Patriotism, moderation, the virtue of toil, and respect for authority are the ideals taught in schooling, and special talents of children are developed for later satisfaction of society's needs. The governing body is an elected aristocracy, presumably chosen for its intelligence and training. The key to Campanella's theory is the emphasis on communal living. Poverty is to be eliminated through common effort, and wealth prohibited. The society, as a whole, is to be the major concern of all of its members, but the perfecting of society will naturally benefit each of its members who will not know want and will not desire the fruits of acquisitiveness.

In the following century, various writers added their ideas to the stream of thought from which communism borrowed. Jean Meslier not only condemned private property but attached both the temporal organization of society and the organized church as institutions whose prime objective was keeping the lower classes in bondage. The Abbé Morelly charged that private property, improper education, and the marital relationship all contributed to society's imbalance, and he sought modification of all three. Gabriel Mably and Jean-Jacques Rousseau voiced their opposition to private property as the chief ill of society, and François-Noel Babeuf claimed that private property contravened the law of nature and urged that those who had enriched themselves at the expense of their fellows should be forcibly dispossessed of their gains. Each of these commentators saw in human equality the index of a satisfactory and happy society.

Other theorists of prominence living and writing in the late eighteenth and early nineteenth centuries, whose works deal with the human relationships on which Marx dwelt, are the Englishmen William Godwin and Robert Owen, and the Frenchmen Etienne Cabet, Henri de Saint-Simon, Charles Fourier, and Pierre Joseph Proudhon. Godwin was so distressed with the decay of his own society with its lopsided property distribution, its classes, and the gross domination of the poor by the rich that he believed piecemeal renovation impossible. A new society based on "reason," founded on moral principles, establishing an equitable distribution of property, and without formal government was, to his mind, the only answer. Owen was a foremost exponent of the idea that man's lot could be improved by the modification of the social and economic institutions within which man exists, and his outstanding contribution to the stream of "radical" thought was his practical demonstration of the validity of his hypothesis. In 1800 he became the manager of a cotton mill in New Lanark, Scotland, and, acting as much the benevolent paternalist as the social reformer, proceeded to establish a working "utopian" society for the laborers in the mill. Improved sanitation, sobriety, religious toleration, enhanced educational opportunities, lowered food prices, shortened hours of employment, and the moderation of child labor all became realities under Owen's direction, without any adverse effect on profits. When Owen left the mill over disagreements with his partners he embarked on a career of education and persuasion for his conception of the ideal societal setting. He envisaged colonies of 500 to 1500 workers established on 1000 to 1500 acres of land engaged primarily in agricultural pursuits, supplemented by a modest manufacturing enterprise. Each unit would be self-sufficing—after an initial private or public financing—and the community spirit would be all-embracing. Owen even went so far as to establish an experimental community of this sort in New Harmony, Indiana, a venture that lasted for three years.

Cabet was the producer of a version of the utopian society obviously modeled after that of Thomas More. In the mythical Icaria, the state owns and directs economic enterprise—as communism requires—and the equality of the citizenry is reflected most clearly in the sharing of economic produce. Newspapers are not permitted, and books must be approved by the government before publication. Cabet also instituted a practical colonial experiment in Missouri, but it never fulfilled the high hopes of its founder. Saint-Simon brought to his theorizing a large variety of experience including revolutionary participation and imprisonment. His background led him to the conclusion that neither the nobility nor the clergy was worthy of leadership in his contemporary society, and that philosophers, scientists, and industrialists should replace them. While distinctly possessed of a moral orientation, Saint-Simon did not plan a revamping of society according to the precepts of organized religion which he thought oppressive. Instead, he construed God's admonition to "love one another" as a command to improve the condition of the poor and to create a society in which the greatest good of the greatest number should be the aim. Though he would vest leadership in the talented and reward labor in accord with productivity, Saint-Simon's "radicalism" embraced the abolition of inheritance, public ownership of some industry, and a deemphasis of the importance of the clerical and military segments of the population. He opposed idleness in any class and believed that each person should labor up to his capacity. He approved primitive Christianity, but he was not an apostle of asceticism. He was an advocate of change through persuasion rather than a proponent of violent class conflict. His followers attempted in various ways and places to implement his principles but with only moderate success.

Charles Fourier, much more a mystic than Saint-Simon, was led to expound his idea of the ideal community after being early impressed with the dishonesty, the waste, and the monopolistic trend of the economic practices of his time. The underlying philosophical tenet of Fourier's plan was a belief that the release rather than the restraint of human passions would lead to the ultimate harmony in society which man desires. Individual passions, said Fourier, might produce anti-social acts, but expressed within the context of carefully organized groups, the free play of passion will result in the greatest harmony because of the dovetailing of the variety of aspirations represented in the group. The ideal society, then, would be comprised of "phalanxes" of 1500 persons in which a wide assortment of talents would be included. Though the inhabitants would be centrally housed and use common warehouses, there would be a formalized distribution of produce to capital, labor, and talent in line with the contribution each made, with the largest proportion being assigned to those doing the most disagreeable work. A unique feature of the plan was to permit laborers to choose those tasks which they most desired and to allow a change every few hours so as to prevent a feeling of drudgery. Fourier and his followers initiated a number of practical experiments along the theoretical lines he advocated, but all, including the Brook Farm in Massachusetts, ultimately perished.

Pierre Proudhon was probably an anarchist more than anything else, but in some respects he was an early Marxist, a socialist, a utopian, and even a democrat. He condemned government on empiric grounds, holding that it was a defender of the rich in their exploitation of the poor. Even "democratic" government was undesirable because "consent of the governed" was never a practical reality. Therefore, he said, revolution was inevitable because the affluent segment of society was generally unwilling to make adequate concessions to the "have nots" even when the masses were no longer content to accept their impoverished condition. Private property, said Proudhon, was no better than theft, except as represented by such an endeavor as the individual farmer tilling his own acreage for his personal benefit. The concept of property in the form of interest, rent, and profit received his unrestrained condemnation. They represented perversions of such practices as division of labor and competition into instruments of injustice and exploitation.

While opposed to government and accepting revolutionary tactics, Proudhon, nevertheless, served in the French National Assembly where he sought to use democratic processes to institute his plans for societal change. He also appeared to reject communism because he saw it realistically as consisting of an oppressive autocracy, limiting freedom and individual initiative, and imposing the "passionless" judgment of the state on the individual's personal judgment. He was a vociferous proponent of human equality and even rejected the notion that natural intelligence and special talent should receive extra compensation because they were products of the total environment from which they grew and in which they flourished.

Proudhon, however, is an unwitting apostle of communism not only in his attack on government and private property, and his emphasis on equality, but in his economic concepts. He predated Marx in devising a labor theory of value which measured the worth of a commodity by the amount of labor which went into its production, and he urged the creation of a state bank— to be capitalized from taxes on property and bureaucratic salaries—from which laborers could borrow without interest in order to obtain the instruments of production. Goods could be deposited with the bank in exchange for "money" which would entitle the bearer to purchase any other products of similar labor value. Though none of Proudhon's theories ever led to pragmatic experiments, his status as a contributor to socialist thought and, indirectly, to the communist program is notable.

Socialism and Communism Distinguished

While all of the foregoing theses are not exactly alike, and while they should properly be classified as utopian or socialist, they do, collectively, serve communist thought to some extent.

They are critical of existing institutions of society; they attack private property; they question the intense profit-seeking of free enterprise; they emphasize cooperation as opposed to competition in economic endeavor; to a degree, they are anarchic—matching communism's view of the "withering away" of the state; they call for the melioration of the condition of the poor and the equality of all; they adulate the communal spirit in society. But such coincidence of criticism and objective should not lead to the easy conclusion that socialism—as represented in the writings of the theorists noted—and communism are synonymous, or so closely related as to be distinguishable only through a process of semantic hair-splitting. Aside from the fact that—as a practical matter—socialists and communists have been over the years bitter political enemies, in both theory and program socialism and communism have evinced significant differences.

In the first place, socialism's religio-moral disposition marks it as distinctly different from the purely materialist base on which communism stands. Ethics and morality, while not totally ignored in Marxism, are relegated to minor positions as considerations for the ideal society. Socialism sees a moral code as an essential part of man's environment and a director of man's actions. As a matter of fact, socialism's concern with man's economic well-being is, at least in some branches, merely a step to permit man to lead the "good life" as prescribed by some ideal ethical concept. For communists, material satisfaction is an end in itself; God is a fiction, and religion is the "opiate of the people" operating to dull their sense of persecution and to insure the perpetuation of the exploitative status quo.

Secondly, socialism and communism differ radically as to methodology. Socialism is basically committed to gradualism and legality in the attainment of its ends; communism is equally irrevocably committed to violence as the only path to success. To be sure, some socialists would not shrink from sporadic violence in the interest of their cause; and Marxism acknowledges the potentiality of achieving desired ends by constitutional means in selected places. But, on the whole, socialism is evolutionary in character, and communism is revolutionary. From the socialist viewpoint, if socialists are unable to obtain majority support through democratic process, the possibility of gaining control of society through armed violence against an entrenched majority is nil. For communists, since capitalists control the state, its political processes and its military might, the *only* way to wrest control from an entrenched *minority* is by overt upheaval.

A third point of distinction relates to the degree of substitution of public for private ownership advocated by the two movements. Socialism views specific branches of economic enterprise as being particularly able to exploit many for the advantage of the few, and it is these areas which are earmarked for "nationalization." In socialist eyes, such endeavors as public utilities (power, transportation, communication) should be transformed to public enterprises by law, and other businesses such as banking, steel production, and the extractive industries —which have such a broad impact on the total economy— should likewise become state activities. The greater proportion of economic activity, however, including agriculture, distributive facilities, and service functions may remain in private hands, though subject to varying degrees of public regulation. Communists, on the other hand, refuse to concede that *any* private economic enterprise is justifiable, since all such areas of activity represent opportunities for exploitation and domination. Therefore, in communist theory and, for the most part, in practice, aside from such exceptions as small private agricultural efforts undertaken by individuals and an occasional trial of pseudocapitalist endeavor, *all* economic facilities are to be owned and operated by the state.

Still another point of contradiction in the two philosophies involves the question of compensation for private property which is socialized. Socialists, in general, agree that nationalization of privately owned facilities should include compensation for the owners. The usual process would be the issuance of government bonds to the shareholders equal to the "fair value" of the industry or enterprise at the time of takeover. Naturally, what constitutes fair value in any assessment of this type, even within a democratic-capitalist society, is always a subject of debate. It cannot be claimed that each national expropriation has been accompanied by a realistic appraisal of the worth of the enterprise, but, in some instances, as exemplified by the British experience, the compensation of private owners could be classified as generous. Communists flatly reject the proposition that private owners should receive *any* compensation for their property. By definition, "capitalists" are exploiters, and, therefore, they have no legitimate claim for any recompense for seizure of property which has been used as a means of personal enrichment.

Finally, socialists do not accept the communist theory of the necessity for a "dictatorship of the proletariat" as a means of inaugurating the new society nor the dictum that the political state will eventually "wither away." For socialists the bourgeois state is not an inherently evil institution which must be utterly obliterated; it is a mechanism which can, under proper leadership, be used for the betterment of society. Therefore, neither a temporary dictatorship nor a progressive disintegration of usual political structures is required.

Characteristics of Communism

To explain communism, more than a general characterization is required. It is, for example, necessary to recognize that Marxism and Leninism vary, that the Russian and Chinese versions of communism exhibit differing idiosyncrasies, that communism is a term used to describe a national politico-economic arrangement and an international movement, and that communism as an economic theory differs from communism as a rallying point for aggressive expansion. Nonetheless, there is some value in beginning this analysis of communism with an outline of basic traits against which to consider the specifics which will follow.

1] Communism represents a *critical commentary on the existing social and economic institutions of the nineteenth and twentieth centuries.* More specifically, communism *levels a vicious attack on the capitalist economic system.* Private property, the profit motive, competition, the gulf between wealth and poverty, the exploitation of the many by the few, the tendency to monopoly, and the boom and bust of the business cycle—all seen as part of free enterprise—are condemned as inimical to the general welfare and fit subjects for popular elimination.

2] *The basic concepts of communism are enunciated as part of a total appraisal of human history.* The tenets of communism appear as the natural consequences of an historical analysis known, as Marx used it, as *dialectical materialism.* Historical progression, according to Marx, is the story of "forces" which, as they develop, generate contrary forces which, in time, modify the original forces so that synthesized new forces come into being. Thus, any movement (a *thesis,* e.g., capitalism) necessarily creates an opposed tendency (an *antithesis,* e.g., the proletariat) which remolds the movement along new lines (a *synthesis,* e.g., communism). An important facet of this development, from the communist viewpoint, is its *inevitability.*

3] In this evolutionary process *economic motives and influences are always dominant.* Communism views man's primary activity as an attempt to wrest a living from his environment and continually to improve his material status. When men combine in groups, certain methods of production and distribution of goods and services will evolve, and these will, in turn, produce *social* classes determined by relative positions in the economic structure. Thus the *economic* base of a society will color its political, social, legal, and cultural characteristics.

4] As the struggle for economic superiority is the driving force for human endeavor, the various economic classes in society are pitted against each other, or, *class conflict is the natural state of affairs* so long as different classes exist. In capitalism, the picture of class conflict is quite clear, as there are only two basic classes—the exploiters (entrepreneurs) and the exploited (the proletariat), the former attempting to retain its position of superiority and the latter (the more numerous) seeking to unseat the other in order to attain its rightful economic return. The conflict between the two occurs not only in the economic arena but in the political as well, where the capitalist class uses the instruments of the state to maintain its dominant position.

5] The degree of exploitation Marx explains in the *theory of "surplus value."* The true value of any commodity, according to Marx, should be measured by the amount of labor involved in its production. The market value of most commodities, however, exceeds this "labor value" because labor has not been adequately paid for its productive role. Labor receives instead only a subsistence wage—far below the value of its real contribution. This surplus value on the market is pocketed by the capitalists. It is against such exploitation that labor, as a class, must rebel.

6] Given the entrenched position of the capitalists, *communists insist that the change in society sought by the masses must be achieved by violent revolution.* Marx concedes that in some few instances where democratic processes are a strong tradition, radical changes may be gained by peaceful means. However, since these cases are few, and even then the ruling class may dispense with normal democracy when confronted with its own overthrow, overt violence appears as the only road to success, and the end justifies the use of any means in achieving it.

7] A Leninist conception is that *the vanguard of the revolutionary movement—the Communist Party—must consist of a hard core of professional revolutionists.* This group would provide both the ideology of upheaval and the leadership in attaining communist goals. Instead of accepting the Marxist contention that revolution will be the spontaneous consequence of labor's own class consciousness and sense of exploitation, Lenin believed that the proletariat had to be led from wage slavery by middle class intellectuals. He felt that the labor mentality would proceed no further than trade unionism and, therefore, labor would have to be inspired and motivated to revolution from outside its own ranks.

8] *Capitalism,* the communists believe, *will make an inadvertent contribution to its own downfall.* In the first place, as the entrepreneurs continue to enrich themselves at the expense of the workers, the gulf between wealth and poverty will be widened and the number of poor will be increased, making more rigid the class structure and contributing to the sense of frustration and desire on the part of the proletariat. At the same time, as the consuming power of the most numerous class decreases relative to the total production which must be absorbed effectively by society, over-production and depression must result serving as an additional spur to revolutionary action. Nor, say the communists, can luxury production and credit sales do anything more than postpone the periodic debacle of the business cycle. Other debilitating factors in capitalism are noted as the monopolistic tendencies which undercut the theoretical advantages stemming from competition and the internecine warfare among capitalist powers growing out of the strenuous competition for external markets in which to dispose of their burgeoning production.

9] The successful communist revolution is to be followed by *the establishment of a dictatorship of the proletariat to inaugurate the new society.* This dictatorship the communists believe to be necessary in order to protect against counter-revolutionary activity and to insure the installation of novel institutions. In this emergency period, the dictatorship is justified in exercising extraordinary powers in the interests of all the people. It should be noted, however, that communist theory specifies neither the manner in which the dictatorial leaders are to be selected nor the duration of their dictatorship.

10] The new regime will have as its prime objective *the substitution of common (public) ownership of the means of production and distribution for private ownership of such facilities.*

Since private ownership opened the door to exploitation, the only way to end this deplorable matter is by permitting all members of society to own all productive and distributive resources.

11] Communists declare that *every segment of economic activity must be publicly owned and operated.* Any economic activity permitted to remain in private hands offers an opportunity for one man to take advantage of his fellows, to amass wealth, to derive a disproportionate share of financial return from the fruits of his labor. Profits are, by definition, evil and an index of inequity in economic arrangements.

12] *The process of nationalization of previously private enterprise is not to involve any compensation for the owners.* This, surely, is not a surprising tenet of those who view "exploiters" with such animosity that they urge violent revolution to unseat them. In the minds of many communists, the uprooted capitalists should receive even harsher treatment—perhaps even execution.

13] *In the new society all will be workers and all will have an opportunity to work.* Economic activity will be so carefully planned that the fluctuations of the business cycle will be eliminated, and unemployment will cease to be a problem. On the other hand, in order to share in the fruits of productivity every person must make a contribution. No one will be permitted to derive the unearned increments of profits, interest, and rents.

14] *The goal of communism is described as a "classless" society.* Only when all are equal and share equally in society's production can the practical utopia be achieved. Only when all opportunities for exploitation have been eliminated and the domination of the many by the few obliterated can real freedom truly exist. Only when the communal spirit has been inculcated in all can the millenium be attained. Of course, the communists do not deny that minor deviations will exist among individuals, but they do declaim that, in comparison with capitalist societies, such differences will be insignificant.

15] The ideal toward which the communists claim to be working in economic relations is epitomized in the phrase *"from each according to his ability, to each according to his needs."* In the communist utopia each individual will be so highly motivated— having thrown off the shackles of economic serfdom, will be so strongly imbued with community spirit, will be so thoroughly dedicated to the welfare of all that he will exert himself to the utmost regardless of his expected remuneration. Whatever the level of his contribution and productivity, he will be willing to be recompensed from the common product "according to his need" (by whom defined, we know not). The communists concede that during a transition period additional motivations may be necessary, and that one such motivation may be additional material rewards for more productive workers.

16] *Communists foresee the eventual "withering away" of the state.* The state, in communist theory, is consistently viewed as a potential weapon of exploitation. With its political apparatus and its military force the state can be a fearsome tool of domination. Unlike the socialists, who believe that the state can be a force for good—when properly directed—as well as the machinery for subjugation, communists hold that the ideal society must dispense with this dangerous structure. In a somewhat cloudy manner the communists propose that with the withering away of the state there will remain only a skeletal structure of administrative agencies necessary to direct the economic activities of society. In what way the "economic" organization of the community, presumably with the authority to enforce its decisions relating to economic planning, will differ from a political organization powerful enough to enforce its decisions the communists do not clarify.

17] *Communism is an international movement in which national loyalties must give way to class loyalties.* Though the instances of communist revolutions to date represent unique rebellions within the borders of single countries, communistic theory has, with few exceptions, trumpeted the international nature of the class insurrection. Exploitation within one national context is simply symptomatic of the much broader exploitation against which workingmen in all countries must unite. Thus, various communist "internationals" were formed from the middle of the nineteenth century—organs which advertised the common broad front along which communism would advance. Three significant deviations from this international outlook, however, should be noted. The first occurred during Stalin's regime in the Soviet Union when it became apparent that there would be no world-wide revolt to parallel that in Russia, and, at least temporarily, all efforts were directed to establishing "socialism in one country." The second appeared in the doctrine of "polycentrism" in the 1950s when the various communist parties of Europe sought and, in some cases, obtained a degree of independence from oppressive Soviet domination. And the third is expressed in the debate, during the 1960s, between the leaders of the Soviet Union and Red China which suggests so strongly the absence of a united communist front and a strenuous competition between the two giants for leadership in the world communist movement. On the other hand, there remains an undercurrent of unity as communists throughout the world strive to gain positions of political dominance in newly awakening areas.

The foregoing sketch of the characteristics of communist theory and practice is, of course, neither definitive nor fully descriptive of its ramifications. It is designed to acquaint the reader with the general nature of this ideology so that the more detailed material to follow may be related in perspective.

STUDY QUESTIONS AND PROJECT SUGGESTIONS

1. Outline the major tenets of communist theory.

2. What reasons can be assigned for the attractiveness and spread of communism in the twentieth century?

3. Trace the evolution of ideas and movements from which communist theory borrowed.

4. In what respects do socialism and communism differ?

5. Analyze the U.S. Supreme Court's decisions in *Schenck v. U.S.* and *Gitlow v. N.Y.* and indicate which decision you believe to be more consistent with the American constitutional guarantee of free speech.

6. Why has communism created such widespread fear in the American public?

7. On what grounds can American legislative enactments placing restrictions on communists be justified and criticized?

CHAPTER 2

MARX AND ENGELS

Karl Marx and Friedrich Engels are unquestionably the progenitors of modern communism. Out of their friendship and collaboration grew the basic theory, the fervor, and the advocacy of that politico-economic system which—in modified form—has been instituted in the two largest contemporary states and a number of smaller ones. Together they kindled a revolutionary spark which produced a conflagration whose ramifications are still to be finally assessed.

Marx was born in Trier, Prussia, in 1818 to Jewish parents who, together with their family, later converted to Christianity. Following a relatively uneventful childhood in which his intellectual talents were shaped and encouraged, he attended the universities of Bonn and Berlin studying law in the former and philosophy in the latter. At Berlin he became an atheistic materialist and was considerably influenced by the philosophic atmosphere created by the deceased Georg Hegel. Eventually, with the intention of becoming a teacher, he attended the University of Jena where, in 1841, he received his doctor of philosophy degree at twenty-three.

Being possessed of radical political views and an irascible and tactless nature Marx was not considered suitable for a university position, so he turned to journalism, associating with the *Rheinische Zeitung* in Cologne of which he became editor in 1842. By 1843 the increasingly radical tone of the paper led to its suppression by the Prussian authorities, the incident prompting Marx to embark on his long exile from his native land. At this time he married Jenny von Westphalen, daughter of a childhood neighbor and counselor. Despite their differences in social backgrounds and experiences the couple appears to have had a happy married life and endured the economic hardships and prolonged illnesses which beset the family.

Marx moved first to Paris where the exhilarating intellectual atmosphere and his association with a number of radical thinkers helped to form his ultimate ideas. The inspiration of the anarchist Michael Bakunin, and the socialist Pierre Proudhon, was especially impressive, and, of course, it was in Paris that Marx began the life-long friendship with Friedrich Engels. Under political pressures Marx next moved to Brussels (1845) where he remained until 1848 and where he first engaged in political activity. The Belgian authorities expelled Marx against the background of revolutionary ferment throughout Europe, and he had brief sojourns in Paris and Cologne. In the latter he was tried and acquitted for sedition, and after returning momentarily to France, finally settled in London (1849) as his permanent residence.

The life of the Marx family in England was far from ideal. The burden of poverty was alleviated only by the charity of relatives and the devoted Engels, and physical ailments affected both parents. However, Marx, a prodigious worker, constantly strove for the achievement of his radical program until his death in 1884, and, despite all handicaps, published his most significant works, among them, *The Class Struggle in France, 1848–1850; The Eighteenth Brumaire of Louis Bonaparte; Critique of Political Economy;* and the first volume of his monumental *Capital.*

Friedrich Engels was born in 1820, the son of an industrialist with textile interests in Germany and England. He has not, perhaps, received full recognition for his contribution to the fruitful collaboration with Marx, but he seemed content to play the role of junior partner in their efforts. Generally acknowledged to have been of lesser intellectual stature than Marx, Engels was, nonetheless, a luminary in his own right as a businessman, journalist, and revolutionary. The relationship between the two was so intimate and so prolonged that it is difficult to discern the origin of ideas and motivation, but Engels' part in the formulation of communist doctrine should not be overlooked. His book, *The Condition of the Working Class in England* (1844), was a strong indictment of the ills associated with the industrial revolution; he was a prominent participant in the European revolutionary action of 1848; and he was an official of the First and Second Communist Internationals. Not the least of his worth to the radical movement was his financial assistance to Marx and his responsibility in publishing the second and third volumes of Marx's *Capital* after the latter's death. One commentator has called Engels "almost the only likable and fully human of all the saints in the entire communist calendar." [1]

The Communist Manifesto

The *Communist Manifesto* was written in response to a request to Marx by the international Communist League (formed in 1848 in London) for a statement of principles. It was authored by Marx and Engels, though Marx is usually conceded as being its principal architect. It is an important historical document not only because of its concise exposition of communist doctrine and the impact it has had as the kernel of Marxist dogma, but as well for its vivid prose and clarity—characteristics not always found in Marx for whom perspicuity was not a prime virtue.

[1] Henry B. Mayo, *Introduction to Marxist Theory* (New York: Oxford, 1960), p. 10.

The *Manifesto* does not embrace the whole of Marxist doctrine, but it is a core from which the broader scheme expands. It contains the dialectic method and the historical interpretation which serve Marx as doctrinal foundation and inevitable imperative; it contains the critical analysis of contemporary economics leading to the violent denunciation of the capitalist system; it contains a castigation of competing critical doctrine (socialism); it emphasizes the class struggle as an essential element in any society; it states the objectives of communism—forcible overthrow of the bourgeoisie, seizure of political power, and abolition of private property; and it entreats the workers of the world—the proletariat—to flock to the communist banner, to unite to throw off their chains.

While the *Manifesto* (published in London in 1848) did not have an immediate impact on the French and German revolutionary disturbances of that year, its stature as a revolutionary exhortation, an indictment of capitalism, a catechism for communists, and a "proof" of inevitable proletarian triumph has grown through the years.

Tenets of Marxism

A general characterization of communism in theory and practice was given in Chapter 1. What follows here will be a recitation—necessarily somewhat repetitive—of those ideas of Marx which form the heart of communist philosophy. Any redundancy, it is hoped, may have the incidental virtue of impressive emphasis.

Dialectical Materialism. This term, which is the foundation of theoretical Marxism, is compounded of two items, both of which have a special usage for communism. Marx is a materialist, not in the sense of a believer in a mechanistic nature of which man is a part, or even in the sense that he believed that ideas are primarily a reflection of matter. Instead, Marx's materialism emphasizes the position of *"material concerns"* (*economic mat-*

ters) in man's life and highlights the *deterministic* nature of such material concerns as they apply to man's existence. Things —material values, economic revenue, according to Marx, are more primal to man than ideas—spiritual, ethical, cultural values. And, equally important, this concern with material matters *dictates* the course of human history.

The dialectic has been, traditionally, a form of discussion or disputation, a process by which truth was sought through the examination of conflicting opinions. In the hands of the German philosopher G. W. F. Hegel, the conflict of ideas inherent in the dialectic became the series of contradictions inherent in historical evolution—each "movement" breeding an opposite tendency which in time distorts and reshapes the original into a novel trend or system. Hegel used this version of the dialectic to glorify the state; Marx, borrowing from Hegel, uses it to rationalize communism's inexorable march.

Dialectical materialism is, then, in the Marxian sense, an historical analysis in which thesis (any selected chronological drift) produces antithesis which warps and amalgamates with the initial movement to eventuate in a synthesis, all being prompted in a basic and deterministic sense by economic concerns. Of special importance is the "inevitability" which attaches to the progression, the inescapability which Marx postulates for his version of historical analysis.

Economics and the Class Struggle. Man's essential motivation and effort, says Marx, is economic—that activity which is necessary to sustain existence. In any society at any time, some system will be devised to produce and distribute goods and services among its members. The nature of this system will automatically create certain economic classes based on the position of various persons in the economic process. In time, social castes will evolve consistent with economic status, and a political structure expressing the viewpoint of the *dominant* economic class will take form. Thus, the total socio-political fabric of any society stems from its economic foundations. Ideals, ethics, spiritual and cultural values, Marx contends, have no real existence apart from their economic orientation. (Strangely enough, with all of this Marx remains something of a "moralist," not simply because he is fired by a sense of the ethical rightness of his stand, but in terms of his personal standards of Victorian morality.)

Each socio-economic class, Marx maintains, is constantly motivated to secure for itself a greater economic return. It follows, therefore, that such classes are naturally antagonistic—competing for shares of the society's production. Such natural competition is initially in the economic sphere, but as it becomes more apparent that politics is an economic weapon, "class warfare" moves to the political arena. The dominant economic class will, of course, utilize every force in its arsenal—economic, political, legal, and military—to resist the advances of its adversaries and to perpetuate its position of privilege. In these circumstances, the "emerging" (dialectically) class has no alternative but to resort to force to secure its demands.

In the capitalist system, according to Marx, the class structure is especially clear. There are only two classes: the capitalist, bourgeois, exploiting class, and the proletarian, exploited class. The former and least numerous derives an affluent economic return from its pitiless exploitation of the latter, far more numerous group. The battle lines are easily seen and the nature of the conflict evident.

Surplus Value. The "surplus value" concept is what Marx advances as a gauge for the manner and degree of capitalist exploitation. The concept views the true value of any commodity as being measured by the amount of labor which goes into its production (land being neutral and machinery representing the result of prior labor). However, the market value of a commodity, says Marx, is considerably higher than its "labor value" because the capitalists have consciously failed to remunerate labor fairly for its contribution in the production process. Rather, labor is given only a subsistence wage which permits it to continue to work and produce but which is not in the least commensurate with its equitable contribution to the end product. Labor as a "resource," then, is consumed without adequate recompense, and the value created far exceeds the cost of the labor power which is used. This excess or surplus value is appropriated by the entrepreneurs as profits, interests, or rents, and equates with the degree of exploitation to which the proletariat is subject.

The Capitalist Anomaly—Thesis and Antithesis. Capitalism, says Marx, may be predicated on the assumption of equal opportunity, competition, premiums for the exercise of initiative and ingenuity, and the operation of "natural" economic principles. But, he continues, the actual functioning of free enterprise deviates considerably from the ideal and, in the final analysis, creates for itself the very conditions which will lead to its downfall. In the first place, as the capitalist class continues to enrich itself by its exploitation of the proletariat it widens the gulf between wealth and poverty, it increases the number of the poor in relation to those who possess wealth, it solidifies the economic class relationship, and it makes the proletariat more conscious of itself as a distinct entity with special characteristics and aspirations. This leads, in turn, to a desire of the proletariat to improve its economic status, a desire which, thwarted by capitalist intransigence, supplies the spark to revolutionary activity which will transform capitalism into a novel politico-economic arrangement.

Not only is this "inherent contradiction" the antithesis of capitalism's thesis, but corollary developments within the structure of free enterprise, Marx states, contribute to capitalism's ultimate demise. So long as workers' wages are kept at a subsistence level—while the wealth of the entrepreneurs increases—there is inadequate consuming (purchasing) power to absorb effectively the total production of which the society is capable. Yet, the capitalist desire for ever increasing profits leads to a constantly burgeoning production. The upshot is that a stage of overproduction must be reached, production must be curtailed, and a period of unemployment and general depression must ensue. The capitalist attempt to forestall this eventuality through such devices as luxury products, credit selling, intricate financing and investment schemes, Marx contends, can serve only as a temporary bar to depression misery.

It may also be noted, as Marx points out, that capitalism seems almost suicidally bent by its reluctance to abide by its own rules or to emphasize its natural virtues. The honest application of initiative, imaginativeness, and industriousness is too frequently replaced by corruption, unethical business tactics, and an unscrupulous pursuit of profits. The healthy competition which supposedly leads to better products at lower prices and improved production techniques too often degenerates into monopolistic enterprise which destroys opportunity and leaves the consumer at the mercy of the producer. On the international scene, Marx observes, competition for external markets in which to dispose of surplus production must result periodically in overt hostilities among capitalist nations in which the working masses are most adversely affected, again serving as an impetus to the capitalist eclipse.

Revolutionary Necessity. Accepting the Marxian dialectic, and assessing the frailties of laissez-faire economics as stipulated, it might be concluded that Marxists are merely chronicling the course of events which must inevitably produce the fall of a decrepit system. Not so, says Marx. Despite all of its disabilities, capitalism can presumably demonstrate a fantastic capability for survival—and the perpetuation of the economic and other inequities with which it is riddled. Therefore, since capitalism refuses to concede that it is fatally ill, and since the dominant class is so firmly entrenched in its position of power, the only course open to the proletariat to secure that which is its right is that of violence. Control of production and distribution can be wrested from the exploiters only by force. Marx is willing to agree that in some few instances democratic procedures may be able to obtain proletarian dominance, but as a rule, violence must be the prevailing motif.

Communism's Goals. What sort of socio-economic arrangement does Marx envision as the successor to the capitalist structure, what synthesis to the conflict between the free enterprise thesis and its antithesis of the proletariat? The basic premise of the new society is that public ownership and common control of economic facilities—production, distribution, and exchange—shall replace the private ownership of economic machinery. The capitalist era was one of exploitation precisely because private ownership of the means of production was possible. The corrective, then, must take the form of joint, communal ownership and direction. And, unlike socialists who limit the degree of public ownership essential to the ideal society, Marx maintains that every aspect of economic endeavor must be removed from private control. To the degree that private ownership remains, to that extent does society remain imperfect, and to that extent does the possibility for exploitation exist. The basic premise of capitalism must be totally uprooted. Marx does not foresee, of course, that every person will be directly involved in the management of every enterprise. "Representative agents" of the people must of necessity direct industrial, agricultural, and distributive pursuits. But he appears to believe sincerely that such agents will be of and for the general populace and will make decisions in the general interest.

In the *Manifesto* Marx gives us greater specificity: Abolition of property in land; heavy graduated income tax; abolition of the right of inheritance; confiscation of rebel property; centralization of credit in a national bank; transportation and communication in state hands; nationalization of production; planned agricultural activity; free education for all children in public schools. It is easy to see that such a list is a combination of ends and means dovetailed for communist purpose.

When the communist society is established, economic egalitarianism will have been achieved. All members of the society will be workers, and all will have an opportunity to work. The business cycle with its fluctuations of prosperity and depression —bane of the capitalist system—will be eliminated through meticulous planning of economic activity. By the same token, however, each person will be required to make a distinct contribution in productivity. No one physically or mentally able can expect to derive a livelihood without exerting himself to his full capacity. Ideally, according to communist doctrine, that stage of human perfection will be reached at which each person will contribute to the society according to his ability and receive from the society's production only that which he needs. This naturally assumes—and Marx seems to accept the assumption—a selflessness in the human character which places a greater value on society's welfare than on egocentricity—a proposition which has mustered only meager support in the past. Theoretically at least, the absence of monetary incentives will not diminish the drive, the initiative, the zest of a worker who will find his motivation in a sense of personal accomplishment and in doing his part for the welfare of the whole society, or, in the crudest sense, in the necessity for working in order to sustain existence.

Ultimately Marx portrays a classless, "stateless" society—a millenial achievement of the maximum in human goodness and cooperation. The ideal of the classless society should not be distorted from the true Marxian sense. It is not one in which the members of the community have been so leveled, so molded in the same pattern that individual distinctions are indiscernible. It is not one, necessarily, in which conformity—either coerced or induced—has been so established as to obliterate pragmatic castes in the intellectual or economic realms. Necessity dictates, in the large complex society, a hierarchy of decision-making and implementation which unavoidably preserves class distinctions. The Marxian classlessness, means essentially the elimination of the class of exploiters, the creation of a system in which, regardless of an individual's position in society, as highest director or meanest worker, exploitation will be neither desired nor possible. Class competition will be replaced by the mutual cooperation of all. Individual selfishness will be superseded by a community spirit; the ruthlessness of self-interest will be sublimated to the goal of the common good. In short, classes will continue to exist, but they will not be tools of personal enrichment.

Coupled with the idea of classlessness, and dedicated to the same end, is a belief in the ultimate "withering away" of the state. In Marx's eyes, the state—and particularly its governmental apparatus—is part of the capitalist machinery of domination. Laws—the rules and regulations of government—reflect the thinking of the economic exploiters and have been directed to the continued suppression of the proletariat. Consequently, this weapon of dominance as well as all others must be removed. The process of "withering away" is not clearly detailed by Marx, and imagination may have to be fairly active to visualize the phenomenon of "no government" in the modern world. Nonetheless, Marx suggests that as the spirit as well as the fact of communism is firmly established formal government will begin to disintegrate and there will remain only administrative structures necessary to plan, direct, and carry out the economic activity on which the society depends. (To what degree this differs from "government" will be examined later.)

There is another sense in which the withering away of the state has meaning for the communist. Marx consistently argued against national loyalties and for class cohesion regardless of nationality. The class struggle was not confined to this or that nation but was a unified conflict which transcended national boundaries. Therefore, were communist goals to be achieved around the world, the "fiction" of the nation would have little meaning and less practicality. Not only government, then, as an instrument of exploitation would be destined for elimination but the nation itself of which government was such an integral part.

Proletarian Dictatorship. The revolutionary process is destructive, its aim is to overthrow, to disrupt, to crush an existing system. When the process is successful the revolutionists are left with the problem of constructing something to replace that which was destroyed. History offers adequate illustrations of the fact that the destructive process is frequently easier than the constructive one.

Marx was not unmindful of the importance of the period following a successful revolutionary effort. He recognized the chaotic circumstances which might ensue and the potential for failure of idea at the moment of physical victory. Being cognizant of the issues Marx postulated a procedure by which the fruits of victory might be gathered in orderly fashion—a temporary dictatorship of the proletariat. Such dictatorship is not, of course, exemplary of the optimum societal organization which communism promised. It is not the minimization of governmental coercion; it is not conducive to the maximum of economic and personal freedom which communism preached. It is, nevertheless, a necessary expedient and a momentary one. The attainment of the destructive revolutionary goal still leaves a possibility of successful counter-revolution especially from a group with so much at stake and so experienced in the use of power. Destruction of the old regime leaves the populace at loose ends and uncertain as to how to install the new system. In order to crush opposition and to initiate the novel institutions a firm hand is required, hence the dictatorship of the proletariat.

The concept is a bit fuzzy, however, because there remains undefined the exact nature of the dictatorship. Can the entire proletariat fulfill the function? If not, what segment of the proletariat will serve in the dictatorial capacity? (Lenin gives us answers to these questions later.) Still more important, how long is "temporary"? The imprecision on this point may give us pause. Whatever difficulties there may be in grasping its exact dimensions, the importance of the period of dictatorship in Marx's scheme is unmistakable, and its practical functioning may be judged to some extent by the example and experience of the Soviet Union.

In sum, Marxism is a scheme of historical analysis in which economic factors predominate, in which capitalism is mercilessly villified, and in which the inevitability of its decline is proclaimed. It is an economic analysis in which the nature and extent of the exploitation of the many by the few is recorded, in which the class struggle is examined, and in which the ultimate victory of the proletariat is forecast. It is a pattern for a renovated society in which common ownership of productive resources, common effort, and common sharing are the goals. It is a call to action; it is a proclamation of economic emancipation; it is a somewhat sketchily drawn map depicting the path to utopia.

STUDY QUESTIONS AND PROJECT SUGGESTIONS

1. Describe the economic and social environment of 19th century Europe which contributed to Marx's theory.
2. Detail the role of Friedrich Engels in creating the international communist movement.
3. A. Outline the major features of the *Communist Manifesto*.
   B. Describe the impact of the *Manifesto* in developing European revolutionary movements.
4. Explain the meaning and import of "dialectical materialism" in Marxism.
5. Discuss the validity of Marxist criticism of capitalist economics.
6. Describe the nature of the communist society which Marxism envisages as succeeding capitalism.

CHAPTER 3

LENIN AND THE RUSSIAN REVOLUTION

Marx expected that the communist revolution which he preached and for which he worked would occur in the more industrialized states of western Europe. Somewhat surprisingly, the first instance of a "proletarian" revolt (if one excludes the Paris Commune of 1871) occurred in the considerably less industrialized, less politically sophisticated nation, Russia (though Russia made remarkable strides in industrialization in the early years of the 20th century). The complexities of the Russian revolution of 1917 were such that to label it a communist revolution is an oversimplification. The sequence of events was such that even the most radical leaders who had been preaching revolution were caught unprepared by the suddenness with which it happened. This is not to say that there had not been many years of conspiracy, revolutionary exhortation, and radical activity. Russian despotism had been criticized endlessly and, on occasion, attacked openly. But the final upheaval cannot be described accurately as purely Marxist, and it became so only through adroit maneuvering at critical moments. To the extent that the revolution was communist inspired, many individuals helped to shape it, but one man above all others is responsible for the nature of the revolution and its sequel, Vladimir Ilyich Ulyanov or, as he is better known, Nicolai Lenin.

Other Russian Marxists

Before examining Lenin's contribution to the theory and practice of communism in the Soviet Union, it may be rewarding to take note of other theorists and activists who shared in developing the Russian revolution and its aftermath. This will naturally be a selective assessment of only the major figures in the movement.

George Plekhanov is one of the more prominent personages in the history of Russian Marxism. Born in 1856 to middle class parents, Plekhanov turned to radicalism in his early manhood but avoided the extremists and formed the so-called Black Distribution, a group demanding land reform. Despite his moderation, discretion urged him to leave Russia, and he did not return until 1917. It was as an exile, then, that he made his theoretical contributions to groups within the homeland.

Plekhanov found in Marxism an appealing precision and scientific approach which confirmed his own conception of the necessary course of events. Marxian emphasis on the role of the industrial proletariat seemed to fit developments in Russia, and Plekhanov agreed that the class struggle had to be carried on in the political as well as the economic arenas. This was not a rejection of economic determinism, but a caveat that economic competition must be supplemented with political activism. He was quite insistent that a "socialist intelligentsia"[1] had an edu-

---

[1] The term "socialist" in this context does not refer to orthodox socialism, but rather to "scientific socialism" or Marxism. This latter usage will be intended when the word "socialist" is mentioned in the succeeding pages —unless otherwise noted.

cational purpose, that of bringing a sense of class consciousness to the working class—a belief expounded further by Lenin on whom Plekhanov appears to have had a considerable influence. To the dismay of some Marxists Plekhanov suggested that communist dogma be viewed flexibly, that peculiar environmental circumstances be considered as dictating the course of working class progress. This was important in the sense that the comparative infancy of capitalism might have meant a postponement of the ultimate proletarian victory unless the capitalist period, as explained by Marx, could be telescoped into a briefer time span. It meant also a reconsideration of the position of the peasantry in any revolutionary picture. On one other point he was distinctly at odds with a major position of reformers within Russia. The Russian group known as the Economists held to the belief that economic action should be the prime realm of concern, that socialism's validity would appear to workers through their own experiences, not through ideological indoctrination and political mobilization; and, most significantly, that on the political plane it was in the workers' interest to support bourgeois opposition to autocracy. Plekhanov stated that this last position would still leave the proletariat a captive of a dominant economic group; a separate political attack by the workers themselves, he demanded, was the only sure path to the true socialist society.

In a practical vein, Plekhanov joined with Lenin in the publication of the famous newspaper *Iskra,* an organ designed as the mouthpiece of radical theoretical direction and opinion. He also sided with Lenin at the Second Congress of the Russian Social-Democratic Party in 1903 which led to the designation of the Leninist group as the Bolsheviks (majority)—as contrasted with the Mensheviks (minority)—though, in the Party, Lenin's faction was actually the less numerous. Though he later broke with Russian communism's famous leader, Plekhanov's temporary alliance, as well as his theoretical influence, represented an important support for the radical socialists' emergence and dominance in the Soviet Union.

Another of the influential apostles of Russian Marxism was Martov (born Iuri Tsederbaum). An associate of Lenin's, Martov was also an opponent of the Bolshevik master. Like most of the communist leaders he experienced arrest, jail, and the life of the émigré. While he participated in the formation and launching of *Iskra,* he began to part with Lenin at the important Second Congress. The basic issue causing the split was the nature of the Party. Lenin favored a closely knit group of active conspiratorial participants. Martov favored a more broadly based Party, and his position carried in the Congress. Subsequently, when Lenin attempted to purge the editorial staff of *Iskra,* Martov again opposed him and, supported by Plekhanov, once more carried the day.

Like Plekhanov, Martov was emphatic about the role of the intellectual in shaping the class consciousness of the workers, but he advised a somewhat different approach. He saw the intellectuals as active participants in the workers' way of life—especially in those activities designed to improve the lot of the proletariat. In this way, Martov felt, the workers could understand more easily the objective sought. This education of the workers fitted Martov's conception of a mass Party, but placed a heavy burden (theoretically) on the learning capacity of the working class. While he was a revolutionary Martov was willing to work with liberal parties—in specific instances—to overthrow the political regime, though trying all the while to convert them to the proletarian cause. His emphasis on consensus led Martov to the verge of supporting democratic processes, a position totally untenable to Lenin.

On other points, Martov was less enthusiastic about the peasantry as a revolutionary force than was Lenin, placing more confidence in the urban proletariat; he opposed Russian participation in WW I as a bourgeois conflict and a deterrent to the revolution; he chided the Bolsheviks for moving too fast and without majority backing at the time they sought power; and he remained until his death much more an internationalist

Marxist than many of his peers—a stand which deprived him of a greater influence in the Russian revolution.

Alexandra Kollontai was one of the few women prominent among the Russian revolutionary leadership. Not only was she a significant contributor to proletarian theory, but, despite outspoken opposition to Lenin's post-revolutionary policies, she was allowed to serve the Soviet Union in a diplomatic capacity for many years and survived Stalin's ire during the purge era. Her stature is further attested to by the fact that she was for a time a member of the Bolshevik Central Committee. As might be expected Kollontai's major theoretical contribution was on the position of women in the new society, though she addressed herself to other issues as well.

The emancipation of women under communism was the theme of Kollontai's concern. Under capitalism women were tied to home and family, they were subordinated to men in almost every respect. Under the new regime women's inferior position was to be transformed to one of equality with men through the elimination of private property and their incorporation in industrial life. This would not only broaden woman's horizon but free her from the economic shackles of monogamy. Kollontai did not condemn monogamy nor advocate free love, but she did see the difficulty of divorce as incompatible with the new freedom of women, and she believed that the concentration of love on a mate deprived women of the broader "social" love of the community. In other words, as emancipation became a reality women should have the same opportunities as men for self-fulfillment in a broader environment than that provided by the home. Even the burden of child rearing was to be lightened through state efforts in this regard. The Soviet state has not destroyed the monogamous family relation, but it did, for a while, simplify the process of divorce and removed the stigma of illegitimacy by legal action—steps which were surely in accord with the concept of looser family ties advanced by Kollontai.

Much more of a classical Marxist and less of a revolutionary tactician than Lenin, she took issue with him on the course of the "proletarian dictatorship," in the years immediately following the revolution. The Party, she felt, had begun to dissociate itself from the proletariat, to lose confidence in the masses, to experiment with bourgeois administrative and productive techniques. She urged greater assimilation between the Party and trade unions, greater emphasis on discussion and democratic processes within the Party, less isolation of the leaders from the proletariat, and greater reliance on truly proletarian committees for management of industry. The failure of her advocacy is an interesting commentary on the opportunistic nature of communist leadership in its deviations from the traditional Marxism to which it is supposedly committed.

Another "old Bolshevik" was Nikolai Bukharin. Following the émigré course of most of the Russian radicals Bukharin eventually became a member of the ruling clique, and, as a competent journalist, served as editor of both *Pravda* and *Izvestia*. He was not reluctant to challenge either Lenin or Stalin on matters of theory and practice, but ultimately paid for his temerity with his life during one of the latter's purges. His devotion to traditional Marxism and his internationalist viewpoint led him to question Russian withdrawal from the first World War which, he believed, could be transformed into a true class conflict, and, like Kollontai, he was dissatisfied with the bourgeois nature of the economy which persisted under Lenin, being willing to sacrifice production in the interest of keeping revolutionary development pure. He differed with Lenin who supported bourgeois revolutions against autocracy as a first step to proletarian success and who wished to "capture" state institutions rather than "crush" them, and he managed to modify Lenin's opinions in the latter area.

Ironically, when Lenin inaugurated the "New Economic Policy" (NEP) in 1921, it was Bukharin who had to justify it in Marxist terms. He then became known as an apostle of the very bourgeois approach which he had previously condemned, arguing that the petty bourgeoisie would grow to accept socialism. Not wishing to lose peasant support, he proclaimed that industrial growth should not outstrip agricultural expansion in the interest of a balanced economy, but the failure of the peasants to conform to the socialist ideal led Stalin to a campaign of agricultural collectivization, coercion, and planned industrialization, and Bukharin's stock fell.

Bukharin's experience is eminently illustrative of the problem of maintaining purity of doctrine in the face of pragmatic political situations. It further illuminates the comparative ease of conversion from one ideological position to another which occurred among communist leaders when faced with practical necessity. The twists and turns in dogma and practice likewise suggest the inadequacy of Marxist theory as a blueprint even for proletarian uprising and the initiation of a communist society. And, finally, Bukharin's fate is a clear comment on the danger of being out of step theoretically when the hierarchical pinnacle of political authority decides on a different course.

The list of prominent Bolsheviks, in addition to Lenin, would be incomplete without the inclusion of Leon Trotsky (Lev Bronstein), outstanding theoretician and activist, and, in the opinion of many, second only to Lenin in making the Russian revolution what it was.[2] Trotsky occupies a unique position in communist history. Without his organizing and leadership abilities the revolution might have foundered. Without his direction the early economic efforts of the Soviet Union might have failed. Without his prophecy and plan the nature of Soviet Russia under Stalin might well have been a different matter. He was the natural heir to Lenin's leadership position. Yet, eventually, he was a prophet without honor. He was too much an individualist, inadequately concerned with the effect of his pronouncements on his personal political future. He was dedicated to the

[2] Trotsky's theory and role, as well as those of Plekhanov, Martov, Kollontai, and Bukharin, are detailed more extensively in Thornton Anderson, *Masters of Russian Marxism* (New York: Appleton-Century-Crofts, 1963). Stalin's role will be examined later, and note will be taken of other outstanding leaders such as Leo Kamenev, Gregory Zinoviev, Alexei Rykov, and M. P. Tomski.

revolution, but he was a victim of the conspiratorial competition for leadership which the revolution spawned. He was highly articulate, but, finally, his articulateness was turned against him. And in the end not even his exile from his native land saved him from the assassin—a vivid notation of the threat he was still considered to be by Stalinists.

Born to a *kulak* family, Trotsky was introduced to Marxism in his teens, became a disciple, was sent to Siberia for his revolutionary exploits, and in his early twenties joined the *Iskra* staff abroad. Over the years he frequently argued with Lenin on theoretical questions and organizational practices, but the experience brought them closer together by the time of the revolution, and out of their debates grew the basic features of the new "proletarian" society.

He was more adamant than Lenin in insisting that the revolutionary leadership should be the industrial proletariat rather than a proletariat-peasant combination which would represent a numerical majority. He was more convinced that a minority could make a successful revolution and that initial support of peasants might be easily lost. He was also an advocate of "permanent revolution"—the concept that a prolonged period of bourgeois democracy and capitalist economics was *not* essential to transform a feudal society into a socialist one. The theory of permanent revolution further implied a continuing effort on the part of the revolutionaries to guard against reaction, and an expectation that the Russian example would stir revolutionary movements in an ever widening circle—especially in western Europe. While Lenin spoke against the validity of Trotsky's contentions, he was subtly converted to acceptance. The 1905 Russian revolution did not underscore the accuracy of his predictions, but Trotsky was, to an extent, vindicated in 1917, though the other expected revolutions did not materialize.

Trotsky's position permitted Lenin to lead Russia out of World War I, and in 1918 Trotsky reorganized the Red Army, achieved internal victory, and repelled external invasions. With peace secured Trotsky led the fight for increased productivity through compulsory labor, revamped the railway system, and fought the trade unions which were insisting on collective management of industry. Though helping to stabilize the economy, these actions made powerful political enemies for Trotsky. Subsequently he proposed that a free market be restored as a production incentive, though he did not fully support the capitalistic aspects of Lenin's New Economic Policy, and that centralized planning be applied to industry. Both plans were initially opposed, but both were later implemented to varying degrees.

Trotsky's brilliance and self-assurance finally brought him afoul of the Party's rule against factionalism, and Stalin was able to maneuver him into disfavor, discredit, exile, and death. His contributions to the cause of Russian communism, however, cannot be denied, and he was prophetically accurate in his analysis of the Communist Party's organizational evolution. In time, he predicted, the "organization" of the Party will supersede the Party as a whole; then the central committee will grasp the power of the entire organization; and then a single dictator will usurp the power of the central committee.

Lenin

Lenin was born in 1870 to a middle class family whose service to the Russian autocracy had little to suggest the revolutionary course of this son. The hanging of his eldest brother for participating in an attempt to kill the Czar Alexander III undoubtedly had a telling effect on his future life. Expelled from the University of Kazan for political activity, he immersed himself more and more in a study of communist works and subversive activities until he was arrested in 1895, spent some time in prison, and was then exiled to Siberia for three years. While there he was still able to continue his study and writing, and in 1900 he went abroad where, as an émigré, he directed revolutionary developments at home until the time of the revolution in 1917.

Lenin's special contribution to the Russian experience was as an organizer and activist, though his theoretical contributions were also important. In his pamphlets and booklets, *What Is To Be Done?, The Development of Capitalism in Russia, State and Revolution,* and other tracts Lenin proved to be an adept modifier, innovator, and inspirer. It was, however, as a conspirator, orator, and leader that Lenin made his impact. As a theoretician Lenin was not an outstanding original thinker. Most of the Leninist principles had been enunciated earlier by others or were shaped in the interchange of ideas among the Marxist exiles. His theoretical genius lay in his capacity to adapt communist doctrine to a different environment—to bring Marxism up to date in the turmoil of the Russian society of the early 20th century. He also possessed the facility of making a seeming inconsistency in theory or a contradiction between theory and event appear as a natural and logical development. He saw in Marxist theory not an ideological straitjacket but a guide to practice—a tentative set of principles to be applied within the context of existing circumstances. This is not to say that Lenin was merely a theoretical opportunist, or that he made no notable and lasting contributions of his own; the theoretical as well as the practical organization of the Communist Party is uniquely Lenin's brainchild. It was, however, his flexibility, his capacity for searching out the most effective political path, his willingness to deviate from broadly accepted dogma in the face of reality, to inspire confidence, to lead that made Lenin the effective revolutionary he was.

Lenin's outstanding theoretical innovation relates to the nature of the upheaval which is to unseat the capitalists and introduce the communist society. In the Marxist view, the emancipation of the working class from capitalist exploitation is the task of the working class itself. Developing its own class consciousness and becoming aware of the degree to which it is being denied its rightful economic return, the proletariat will evolve its own revolutionary credo and unleash the violence required to establish a new society. Not so, said Lenin. Left to itself, Lenin

argued, the proletariat was incapable of developing a revolutionary ideology. Spontaneously, he said, workers were capable
only of expressing a trade union mentality. This palliative would
deprive them of any revolutionary fervor and would still leave
them captives of bourgeois ideology. Therefore, said Lenin,
socialism, and its concomitant of violent action must be brought
to workers from outside their own ranks, must be inculcated in
them by a group of middle class intellectuals who understood
the forces involved and could imbue the masses with the revolutionary spirit required.

That this position was laden with inconsistencies seemed in-
consequential to Lenin. If the dialectic is valid, and trade
unionism is the highest stage of the workers' mental development, why should not unionist tactics be the final proletarian
answer to capitalism? Or if revolutionary socialism must be
consciously fostered, what becomes of dialectical spontaneity
and inevitability? Or, for that matter, why should the middle
class—whose very existence was at stake—produce an intelligentsia dedicated to indoctrinating the proletariat with a revolutionary ideology which must in time destroy the bourgeoisie?
Such quibbles did not deter Lenin from illustrating in the
Russian revolt the validity of his contentions.

Coupled with this contention of ideological indoctrination
was Lenin's conception of the nature and role of the Communist
Party, a conception over which he was consistently at odds with
his Menshevik opponents. The Mensheviks viewed the Party
in this light: 1] it was to be a decentralized mass organization
of trade unions and other proletarian institutions, and   2] it
was to be a mobilization of working class forces for legal political action. Lenin viewed the Party as an underground conspiratorial grouping engaged primarily in extra-legal activities,
and he saw the nucleus of the Party as being an inner group of
professional revolutionists, highly organized and rigidly disciplined. He envisioned this group as an intellectual elite defining
and preserving the purity of doctrine, outlining and leading in
the implementation of policy, and as a moral elite in its devotion

to the cause—an ethical position developed through the careful selection and rigorous training of its members.

In line with his beliefs on proletarian mentality, middle class intellectual leadership, and the nature of the Communist Party, Lenin expounded further on the necessity and desirability of the dictatorship of the proletariat following the successful revolution. The dictatorship, he contended, was necessary to wipe out the last traces of exploitation and opposition and to reorganize society along socialist lines. The bourgeoisie was not easily overcome, and the organization of the socialist society required tireless effort and shrewd leadership. Nor was there any mistaking who were to be the "dictators"; they were to be the inner group of professionals who had fashioned the revolution. It might, of course, be asked in this context to what extent were the workers to have a voice in the shaping of their own destinies?

The advent of World War I came as a rude shock to many socialists, and, in Lenin's case, led to a reinterpretation of Marxism which sought to rescue the consistency of dogma from the contradiction of reality. Revolutionary socialism had preached the primacy of class loyalty over national patriotism. Yet, faced with the war threat and appeals to traditional nationalism, most workers had forgotten class consciousness and joined in what militant socialists described as a capitalist-imperialist war. Lenin, however, did not see in this a reason for despair or the loss of socialist hopes. He had both an explanation and an inspirational call. The explanation was that democratic socialist parties had been too successful. They had become sufficiently large that they could place some faith in parliamentary process as contrasted with rebellion. Trade unionism and legal political activity had made some gains. The economic situation of the workers had distinctly improved, blinding them to the exploitation to which they were still subject. In fact, said Lenin, an influential part of the proletarian leadership had become so successful economically that it had joined the bourgeoisie in the continued exploitation of the mass of unskilled laborers. In this light, he went on, it was understandable why workers might be deluded about the virtues of patriotism and national loyalty. But, Lenin asserted, there was hope to be taken from this apparent betrayal of close ties. The war itself was a clear indication that the highest stage of capitalism had been reached—that zenith immediately preceding the introduction of the socialist economy. Free, competitive capitalism was dead; it had been replaced by monopoly capitalism in which, in the competition for external markets, capitalist nations were led to war with each other. This gave evidence that the dialectic was operating as postulated and that the world was on the verge of universal proletarian revolt. The fact that such event did not occur again seemed to cause Lenin little concern.

One other Leninist theoretical point is worth noting. Marxism stated, in effect, that capitalism as a movement would have to run its full course before its successor system could be initiated. And there was implied in this analysis that a bourgeois revolutionary rejection of feudal autocracy, followed by the development of democratic industrial capitalism, must precede the period of proletarian revolt. In other words, the overthrow of *political* tyrants must occur, followed by an intervening period in which *economic* tyranny flourishes, before the time was ripe for the workers to overthrow their economic overlords. This intervening time, in short, was the training ground for proletarian revolution. Trotsky had argued against this position at the time of the 1905 Russian "bourgeois" revolution, claiming that the communists should convert this event into a "permanent" socialist revolt. Lenin then—and for the next twelve years —rejected the proposition, clinging to the orthodox Marxist view. In 1917, however, perceiving the opportunity presented by the second bourgeois uprising, Lenin proclaimed the doctrine of "interlocking revolutions" diverting the middle class discontent to communist ends. The practical success of implementing this theoretical idea in 1917 must, in retrospect, elevate Trotsky's value as a theoretician—and Lenin's worth as an appraiser of the political situation.

As a tactician Lenin was much more concerned with the political impact of action than he was with effectuating the theory of economic determinism. He saw more clearly than the orthodox Marxists that politics and power rather than economics were the determinants of successful revolution, and he was completely willing to sacrifice theory to practicality—waiting until after the event to attempt a philosophical justification of the action.

In this vein, Lenin—like other Bolshevik leaders—recognized the necessity of seeking peasant support for the 1917 proletarian uprising in Russia. While Marxist theory emphasized the key role of the industrial proletariat, Russian circumstances prompted Lenin to include the agricultural element in his revolutionary plans. After the initial uprising in March, 1917, Lenin, on his return to Russia, decided against any compromise with the existing moderate regime of Alexander Kerensky and moved to translate what had occurred into a Bolshevik revolution—a surprisingly successful maneuver. Subsequently, Lenin was not averse to introducing the New Economic Policy as an impetus to heightened production though this flirtation with capitalist techniques appeared to be the antithesis of socialist aims.

Whatever may be the assessment of Lenin's ideology and goals, there is no denying his success as a revolutionary leader and his installation of his own theoretical design. In Russia, the revolution was made by middle class intellectuals, the Communist Party took the shape proposed by Lenin; the "proletarian dictatorship" was inaugurated in his terms; tactical flexibility was a keynote; and the establishment and growth of the Soviet Union are a testimony to his plans and actions.

The Russian Revolution

Chafing under the corruption and inefficiency of czarist autocracy and sparked by the massacre of hundreds of peaceful demonstrators seeking to present a list of grievances to the ruler, the Russian peasants erupted in revolt in 1905 and were joined by many workers notably in St. Petersburg where a workers soviet took power. The spontaneity of the revolt was not, however, matched by its coordination and organization, and it soon collapsed. It was unable to attract sufficient popular support, and czarist forces restored order, but it was clear evidence of the dissatisfaction which stirred the Russian people.

The period from 1905 to 1917 saw only nominal improvement along democratic lines, and the traditional conservative and aristocratic forces remained firmly entrenched both politically and economically. Some minor land reforms were introduced to minimize peasant unrest, and revolutionary ferment subsided, but the undercurrent of discontent continued. The Bolsheviks participated as a distinct minority faction in the *Duma*—the legislative body convened in 1906 as a superficial concession to demands for constitutional reform—and worried about the abatement of the fever of rebellion.

The outbreak of war in 1914 ended whatever developments might have occurred naturally. The socialist dream of class loyalty was shattered and the czarist position was doomed by the sequence of events. Out of Russia during the war Lenin made his famous optimistic interpretation of imperialist war and planned its transformation to a workers uprising. When it came, the revolt of March 1917 was of a different order and had to be converted to socialist aims.

The March "revolt" consisted simply of a series of strikes and riots in Petrograd which were successful only because of war weariness and the corrupt inefficiency of what remained of czarist administration and military strength. A provisional government was established under Alexander Kerensky, but much political power was exercised locally by the soviets which arose around the country. Lenin, on his return in April, preached radicalism and no compromise with the moderate provisional leadership. In July the government took action against the Bolshevik radicals—and sent Lenin into hiding—only to be threatened anew by the conservatives under General Kornilov who sought to stage a coup in September. Weakened and powerless, the provisional government fell before the Bolshevik uprising in Petrograd and Moscow in November. A new central government was established with Lenin as leader, but with the country as a whole almost in a state of anarchy and with German armies still advancing on Russian soil. The single experiment with democratic elections in 1917 showed the Bolsheviks still in a minority position, so in 1918 democracy was abandoned for dictatorial power as the Bolsheviks made their bid for total power.

Having seized political power, the Bolsheviks were then confronted with a number of problems. The first was what should be done about Russia's position in the war. After considerable debate, the Treaty of Brest-Litovsk was signed taking Russia out of the war at the price of surrender of much territory. Next there had to be settled the matter of internal strife and subsequent external aggression against Russia. The solution to these problems was accomplished under the direction of Trotsky who recreated an effective armed force, defeated the czarist supporters, and then beat off successive incursions by foreign troops. Simultaneously, the new regime had to decide how best to inaugurate the new system for which they had so long propagandized. In view of the chaotic circumstances and being faced with the monumental task of translating a multifaceted theory into practice, the revolutionary leaders launched a program of "war communism" in which land was nationalized, forced labor instituted, and industrial production was dedicated to the purpose of the state. With the restoration of some measure of peace and stability by 1920, debate was renewed regarding the most effective path for the future.

Lenin's answer was the inauguration of the New Economic Policy which existed between 1921 and 1928. In the eyes of orthodox Marxists this was nothing more than an abandonment of socialist objectives and a retreat to capitalist economics. It involved individual land ownership, private enterprise in many economic areas, a "neglect" of needed industrialization, and a reinstitution of exploitation. To the devoted Leninist it represented a shrewd practical maneuver to give the nation a new breath—a relaxation from war pressures and restraints, and an incentive to increased production so badly needed before the next step could be taken to full communism. The central issue was the position of the peasant—dissatisfied and unproductive without land of his own, who, when granted land and freedom, could lose the sense of socialism and revert to the ranks of the petty bourgeoisie. Yet Russia was a peasant nation, and agricultural production lagged. The Bolshevik hope was that, with agricultural production stimulated and further industrialization initiated, the temporary superficiality of free enterprise could be easily replaced with the socialist ideal. As an interim productive expedient the NEP worked, but the peasants were weaned from socialism, and the rapid advance in industrialization which the revolutionary leaders so coveted had not occurred; the experiment had been only partially successful. At this juncture, then, a new episode in the life of the Soviet Union was instituted.

While Lenin was the undoubted leader of the revolt which created the new Russia, he was not fated to see the culmination of his plans. An attempted assassination in 1918 left him partially disabled, and four years later the disability was complicated by a stroke. He died in 1924. His death left two significant questions. Who was to succeed to the position of leadership left vacant? What was to be the future policy to be followed? Two "logical" aspirants appeared as prospective answers to the first question—Leon Trotsky and Joseph Stalin, but with either it appeared that the NEP was due for revision. Momentarily, the Soviet Union entered a phase of "collective" leadership, but shortly, through adroit manipulation and ruthless action, Stalin emerged as the sole political leader. What the Soviet Union became—and at what cost—was essentially Stalin's doing.

STUDY QUESTIONS AND PROJECT SUGGESTIONS

1. To what extent can the Russian Revolution of 1917 be said to have been communist inspired?
2. Discuss the degree to which Lenin's theoretical conceptions were shaped by his relations with other leading Bolsheviks.
3. In a thoughtful essay describe the philosophic and practical contributions of Lenin in creating the U.S.S.R.
4. Outline the manner in which the Leninist version of communism differed from that proposed by Marx.
5. Detail the role of Leon Trotsky in establishing Russian communism.
6. What is the meaning of the terms *interlocking revolutions* and *permanent revolution* as used by Lenin and Trotsky?
7. Should Lenin be considered a determined leader or a political opportunist?

CHAPTER 4

STALINISM
AND AFTER

Even while Lenin lived and was the acknowledged revolutionary leader there had evolved a kind of collective leadership of the Communist Party in which contrary and shifting theoretical positions were expounded and in which competing individual ambitions could be observed. Trotsky, the brilliant theoretician and tactician, was distrusted and feared by the others not only because of his stature but because he had disagreed so violently with Lenin for many years before the revolution. Gregory Zinoviev and Leo Kamenev were "old Bolsheviks" with strong personal followings in Leningrad and Moscow respectively. They were orthodox Marxists who had opposed Lenin on a number of occasions—especially when he sought to transform the revolution in 1917, but they were essentially loyal and influential. Alexei Rykof was of sufficient repute that he rose to be Chairman of the Council of Commissars. M. P. Tomski exercised considerable influence as leader of the Russian trade unions. Bukharin was, of course, prominently on the scene. And there was Joseph Stalin.

At the time of Lenin's disability the first inkling of the subsequent power plays appeared. Possibly wishing to avoid, at least momentarily, a successor dictator, but more likely motivated by fear of Trotsky and by their personal aspirations, Stalin, Zinoviev, and Kamenev joined in a triumvirate which led the Party during Lenin's last days and after his death. Of the three, Stalin at first appeared least likely to press for or attain dictatorial power. Trotsky was a more likely claimant of Lenin's overriding authority than any of them. Yet out of the swirl of politics following Lenin's demise, Joseph Stalin emerged as the unrivaled dictator of the Soviet state. The story of this accomplishment gives an interesting insight into the policies, practices, and motivations of the leaders of Russian communism.

Stalin

Stalin (Joseph Dzhugashvili) was born in the Caucasus in 1879 to parents who were former serfs. With his mother's urging he subsequently entered the theological seminary at Tiflis with the idea of becoming a priest. Though he remained there for five years, Stalin was drawn to radicalism by his disapproval of the condition of the poor and the inferior position of the non-Russian minority nationalities like the Georgians from which he came. Prompted further by his reaction to the rigid discipline of the seminary, he quit his clerical training and embarked on his Marxist voyage. Though he had his share of arrests and exiles —he spent World War I in Siberia, unlike most of the Communist Party leaders, Stalin remained in Russia and worked underground during the 1905–1917 period.

He caught Lenin's attention in 1905 as a leader of the Georgian radicals, and by 1912 he was made a member of the Bolshevik Central Committee. Returning to Petrograd in 1917 he cooperated with Lenin in shaping the revolution, though philosophically he was more attuned to those who favored a broadly based Party. He continued to serve in the Party's inner circle, the Politbureau, after the revolution and was also appointed Commissar of Nationalities supervising the affairs of the minorities. In 1922 he was appointed General Secretary of the Party, apparently a glamorless position involving a great deal of detailed work. Stalin utilized the position for political advantage, however, by inaugurating the practice of *appointment* of lower echelon administrators, so that within two years the hierarchy was largely controlled by his personal selectees. The office of General Secretary was transformed from a purely administrative post into one of great political power, and it was from this bastion that Stalin confronted his prospective competitors.

Moving carefully and shrewdly Stalin first sought to isolate his most dangerous opponent, Trotsky. Trotsky's old disagreements with Lenin were brought up against him, and his insistence on worldwide revolution was treated so as to appear an extremist view rather than orthodox Marxism-Leninism. Any dissent which he lodged brought a claim of "factionalism" on which the Party frowned. With Zinoviev and Kamenev persuaded to his side, Stalin effectively forced Trotsky from power (and eventually into exile) at the Thirteenth Party Congress in 1924 while successfully posing as a moderate restraining Zinoviev and Kamenev. In 1925 came the disposal of Stalin's erstwhile collaborators. Suspicious of Stalin's ambition and doctrinally opposed to the moderate pace of socialization, the trappings of capitalism, and the gentle treatment of the peasants, Zinoviev and Kamenev launched, at the Fourteenth Party Congress, an attack on Bukharin as the symbol of their antagonism. In the end, the attack turned to Stalin himself. Stalin's supporters pointed scornfully to the frustrated ambitions of the critics and lauded his administrative skill and diligence which had raised him to eminence. Stalin was again the moderate disclaiming dictatorial intent. Zinoviev and Kamenev were finished. By 1929, when Stalin was determined to force agricultural collectivization, hurry industrialization, and introduce central planning, it was the turn of the "rightists"—Bukharin, Rykov, and Tomski. Depicted as opponents of progress and theoretical heretics they were read into oblivion. By the mid-1930s, Bukharin, Rykov, Zinoviev, and Kamenev—as well as others less prominent—had been physically liquidated, and Stalin was left in complete control of both Party and state machinery. Any real or imagined threat to this supremacy—as in 1939–41—was again met by Stalin with the most drastic "purge" methods. Intrigue, perfidy, violence, and death became the hallmarks of communist dictatorial practice and police state methods.

Known primarily as a revolutionary organizer, activist, and architect of the contemporary Soviet Union, Stalin was also a sometime theoretician. Whether, in Stalin's case, theory was offered as a rationalization of action, or practice followed from theoretical conviction is, to some degree, questionable. But in either case several points are clear about Stalin's theorizing: it was neither novel nor abundant; it reflected the reality of circumstance; it served as the practical guide to Soviet policy for a quarter of a century.

On the question of cultural minorities, Stalin was reluctant to accept any degree of real political autonomy for such peoples on the ground that it would run counter to the idea of proletarian unity and would emphasize ethnic nationalism. As a substitute he proposed regional autonomy within the Soviet Union thus hoping to satisfy to some extent the longing for self-determination, but minimizing cultural affinity and stressing class consciousness. On the issue of the peasantry and the problem of land redistribution, Stalin's early theory differed from the later forced collectivization policy which he initiated. Believing as did many Marxists that revolution would have to come in two stages, he argued for peasant seizure of the land and private ownership as a part of the overthrow of czarist autocracy, even though this would mean that temporarily the peasants would be part of the petty bourgeoisie. In time, he reasoned, capitalist agriculture would produce a "rural proletariat" which would then join in the ultimate proletarian revolt.

By far the most significant of Stalin's theoretical efforts was his doctrine of "socialism in one country." In a sense, this concept practically *had* to be concocted. The expected proletarian uprisings in western Europe had not materialized, and if the whole of Marxism-Leninism was not to collapse, the stabilization of socialism in Russia had to be viewed as one step in the march to the millenium. On the other hand, Stalin was enough of an egotist and a zenophobe to believe that socialism could be established in Russia without assistance from the West, and this doctrinal twist could be used against Trotsky whose stand on socialist internationalism made it seem that he depreciated Russian ability to lead the way to communism.

The theory of socialism in one country was coupled with another, that of "capitalist encirclement." This idea was not difficult to develop nor to sell to the public. Since proletarian revolutions had not occurred, obviously capitalism was still firmly rooted, and, by definition, capitalist countries were opposed to socialism. Even more to the point, there had been literal invasions by "capitalist" forces. Therefore, the Soviet Union was pictured as the lone stronghold of socialist-communist ideology surrounded by hostile states bent on destroying it. It followed that there could be no rapid dismantling of the dictatorship of the proletariat; the military apparatus had to be maintained and strengthened; industrialization had to be given priority, and consumer goods had to wait on the satisfaction of defense needs; internal stability and conformity had to be enforced by all the methods of the police state; any questioning of the dictator's will became subversive. That a policy and practice which enshrined the Party leadership in the supposed interest of the state should become a technique in the personal service of *the* leader is not surprising. Even after external threats evaporated, purges, forced labor, informers, and secret police remained as tools to sustain the dominance of Joseph Stalin.

The Molding of the Soviet Economy

By 1927, Russia had recovered relatively well from the ravages of war and revolution. Stalin was well on his way to consolidating his power. The NEP had increased production, and land redistribution had been accomplished. But in Stalin's mind the objectives of the Party remained unfulfilled and the building of socialism in one country was not proceeding at a sufficiently rapid pace. Heavy industry lagged, and the peasants were not being weaned from capitalism to socialism. At this juncture, then, the Party leadership inaugurated the first of a series of Five Year Plans designed to increase the tempo of economic development. At the Fifteenth Party Congress approval was given to a new program of agricultural collectivization and intensified industrialization. Details were supposedly to be worked out by Gosplan (the state central planning agency), but direction of the program remained firmly in the hands of Party leaders—especially Stalin.

The implementation of the plan proved more difficult than was expected. The peasants, committed to individual land holding as they were, resisted collectivization to the point of slaughtering their animals rather than turning them over to the government. As a result, famine was acute in certain areas, and hundreds of thousands of peasants were shipped to Siberia and forced labor camps. For the Soviet leaders this was an unfortunate but inevitable consequence of peasant intransigence. Such bourgeois attitudes in agriculture simply could not be tolerated. Under this ruthless treatment, by 1936 the peasant capitulated, and over 90% of agricultural land had been collectivized, though the prevailing form of collectivization permitted the individual peasant to till a small plot of ground as his own as well as work on the collective farm. Even this grudging concession was subsequently restricted. One might well ask if the price paid in human death, misery, and loss of agricultural production was worth the attainment of this communist ideal of collectivized agriculture.

The collectivization of agriculture was accompanied by an intense drive to upgrade industrialization. Contrary to popular opinion, Russia did not begin this development from scratch; her *rate* of industrial growth was already surpassing that of other more industrialized countries by the time of the revolution, though her total production still remained relatively low. Nevertheless, the task of transforming the Soviet Union into a first rate industrial power was a monumental one. The communists were motivated in this task not only because they felt it necessary to equal the production of their capitalist enemies, but because an unindustrialized Russia was the symbol of the czarist regime, and they proceeded with vigor. The comfort and well being of the individual had to be sacrificed to the goal, and even aspects of ideology which stood in the way had to be circumvented.

The keynote of the industrialization movement was discipline. The free choice of workers was drastically reduced to conform to the plan of industrialization; many peasants were forcibly brought into industrial enterprise; trade unions lost autonomy and became subservient to the state; the right to strike was practically eliminated; the production of consumer goods was held to a minimum in order to concentrate on the building of heavy industry. Monetary and other rewards were given to the most productive workers; the laggards could look forward to forced labor camps. For a movement which promised the emancipation of the worker this regimen was obviously contradictory, but in the end it achieved the goals which it sought even at the expense of the very class which it proposed to benefit.

During this period of feverish development the Soviet society underwent an interesting metamorphosis, the ramifications of which are still to be seen. Instead of creating a classless society of equals from which the elements of capitalism were to be totally obliterated, the Stalinists found themselves resorting to typically capitalist incentives to increase productivity and, in the process, creating classes among which disparities of income and privilege were as prominent as those in the despised free enterprise nations. Not only that, but the Soviet system developed a "bourgeois" morality distinctly reminiscent of Victorian England and a concept of conformity which spread to the arts as well as requiring political orthodoxy.

Out of this impassioned and dictatorial progression, however, the Soviet Union on the eve of World War II had become a power. The non-aggression pact with Nazi Germany in 1939 gave Stalin time to develop his own war machine, and when Hitler attacked Russia in 1941 the Soviet forces were able ultimately to blunt the attack at Stalingrad, though only with the massive assistance of the western democracies and after a distinct propaganda shift in popular appeal from support of communism to patriotic defense of homeland. The end of the global conflict found the Soviet Union in a military and geographic position which permitted it—despite wartime political commitments to the contrary—to establish satellite states in eastern Europe and thus expand its influence and power. As part of the spoils of war the Soviet Union was able to utilize scientific and technological manpower in conjunction with its own scientific apparatus to become a nuclear power in the post-war world. Simultaneously, its research and technical developments made it a leader in space exploration. In short, the Soviet Union emerged from the Second World War as a world power second only to the United States and with a greatly increased potential for spreading its ideology.

This, however, did not signal a new deal for the average Soviet citizen. The ravages of war had to be repaired. The nationalism of the war years had once again to be subjugated to communist domination. Technological advances in nuclear weaponry and space rocketry had to take precedence over consumer production. The exigencies of occupation and control of captive lands postponed other more constructive peacetime pursuits. Until Stalin's death in 1953 the temper of Soviet life remained relatively unchanged from that which had preceded the war. With Stalin's passing a new era in Soviet life began.

Stalin's Successors

The fortunes of those closest to Stalin had varied according to whims of the dictator and the extent to which he felt their presence and influence to represent a threat to his own authority. Immediately prior to Stalin's death in March 1953 it appeared that a new purge was in the making which could have drastically altered the top leadership. Be that as it may, the strong man's demise found a particular arrangement of officials with varying powers and ambitions which led to the leadership developments of the next fifteen years. None of these individuals was clearly in a position immediately to exercise alone the kind of power which Stalin had amassed, so temporarily collective leadership materialized in which first one and then another personality emerged conspicuously.

The first to appear as the new leader of the Soviet Union was Georgi Malenkov—Stalin's heir apparent—who was selected First Secretary of the Party and became Premier (Chairman of the Council of Ministers) of the Soviet Union. Almost immediately a tone of moderation began to instill itself in the regimentation of Soviet society. Labor discipline was relaxed, and there was a partial dismantling of the forced labor camps. Police state techniques and, in particular, the tactics of the secret police were modified. Concern for consumer production began to be expressed. Malenkov seemed to be leading the Russian people into a period of greater freedom and material satisfaction. His leadership, however, was challenged from two principal sources.

The first was the power bid of Lavrenti Beria, chief of the secret police and aspirant to Stalin's total authority. In his position Beria exerted considerable influence in the ruling hierarchy and he set out to create a popular image of himself as being primarily responsible for the relaxation of terror and fear which benefited the Soviet society. Beria's efforts were short-lived, for in June of 1953 he was arrested, tried, and executed as an enemy of the state. Presumably the other members of the collective leadership saw in Beria the personality, ambition, and ruthlessness which could have condemned them to oblivion had he succeeded in rising to the top spot.

The other challenge to Malenkov's position—indicative of the collegiality of leadership—was the demand that he surrender one of the two positions which he occupied. Stalin had used this dual control of Party and government to solidify his position, and Malenkov might do likewise. Though he had risen to prominence within the Party hierarchy in September 1953 Malenkov chose—or was forced to accept—the position of Premier, thus opening the door to a new rival who was finally to replace him and consolidate the duality of leadership in his own hands.

Nikita Khrushchev succeeded to the position of First Secretary when Malenkov surrendered that post. As Stalin had done before him, Khrushchev carefully built support in the Party hierarchy and in the Central Committee, and in January, 1955, he urged a rejection of the budget which emphasized increases in consumer goods at the expense of heavy industry. The Central Committee's agreement led to Malenkov's resignation, but not to his liquidation or even to his full dismissal from the ruling Presidium—in itself a commentary on the new temper of Soviet life. To replace Malenkov Khrushchev influenced the selection of a friend and non-rival Marshal Nikolai Bulganin, and it appeared superficially that power continued to be shared among the leaders. As it developed, however, Khrushchev was merely biding his time.

The picture of the continuing power struggle became clear in mid-1957 when the anti-Khrushchev faction in the eleven member Party Presidium sought to oust the Party leader from his post. Malenkov, the old Bolshevik Vyacheslav Molotov, and Lazar Kaganovich—an early sponsor of Khrushchev—asked and *got* a vote to remove the First Secretary. Khrushchev, however, ignored this loss and took his fight to the Central Committee which reversed the decision and voted confidence in his leadership. Needless to say, the rebels were in turn accused of anti-Party activities and quickly stripped of their position and privilege, though their punishments were again not of the old order, consisting merely of banishment to comparatively insignificant posts in the hinterland. Though this crisis represented a big step in Khrushchev's consolidation of power one or two loose ends remained to be tied. In 1955, the wartime military hero Marshal Georgi Zhukov had been brought back into the political limelight as Minister of Defense, and in 1957 he had been influential in supporting Khrushchev against his critics. However, the Marshal's prominence and popularity were finally seen by Khrushchev as a potential threat to his own position, so, with the usual charges of "obstructionism" and personal enhancement, he was removed from office and sent back to political obscurity. To forestall possible military reaction there followed a moderate purge in the military leadership and the appointment of high officers more oriented to Khrushchev. The final act in the drama was certainly anticlimactic. In March 1958, Bulganin was accused of anti-Party activities, forced to admit his errors, and removed from his position as Premier. Khrushchev immediately assumed this position as government leader while retaining his spot atop the Party hierarchy. The consolidation of power was complete, but the question remained whether Khrushchev was in a position to exercise the unbridled authority of Stalin.

The Khrushchev Leadership. Nikita Khrushchev was born in 1894 in Kalinovka of a peasant family. In his youth he worked in foreign owned mines and factories as a typical proletarian. He did not join the Bolsheviks until 1918 when he began to take part in the civil conflict. In the technical school which he attended at Kharkov he was active in Party activities, and he graduated into organizing functions, soon attracting the sponsorship of no less a person than Kaganovich. After working in the Ukraine for several years he was brought into Moscow where, by the end of the 1930s, he became first a member of the Central Committee and finally a member of the powerful Politbureau. As part of this experience he had been Stalin's director of the purge in the Ukraine, an interesting fact in view of later developments. During the war years he remained primarily in the Ukraine as a Party and governmental functionary, returning to Moscow in 1949 where he was subsequently chosen a secretary of the Central Committee from which position he rose to the dictatorial pinnacle.

Khrushchev's policies reflect the continuing change in both the pattern of Soviet life and the international environment. While Malenkov was removed presumably for urging too strongly consumer production and relaxing too readily the internal control apparatus, this general trend was continued under Khrushchev. As with the prior Soviet leaders, practical events were explained or justified by Khrushchev in ideological terms, and a number of theoretical postulates are of particular interest.

One of the most spectacular pragmatic and ideological shifts occurred in February 1956 when in a prolonged secret speech to the 20th Congress of the Soviet Party Khrushchev initiated what came to be known as the de-Stalinization campaign. De-Stalinization was a program of practical effacement or, at the least, major depreciation of Stalin's position in Soviet history and in the Soviet mind. At the simplest level this meant the removal of pictures and statues, the renaming of public places, and his reinterment in a less hallowed place than Lenin's tomb. Even history was rewritten to eliminate or minimize his stature. At the more sophisticated level, Khrushchev's speech attacked Stalin's "cult of personality"—the personal dictatorial control, the self-aggrandizement, the whimsical nature of his rule, his sadistic vindictiveness, and his generally irrational emotional behavior. The assault on the cult of personality or of the individual was calculated to have—or inadvertently produced—several beneficial results from Khrushchev's point of view. It emphasized the concept of collective leadership thus giving pause to prospective aspirants to Stalin's personal power, while not foreclosing the possibility when any one individual could strengthen his position sufficiently. There was enough intimation of the involvement of others in Stalin's purges to cast suspicion on some probable leaders as unfit, while no mention was made of Khrushchev's own role in the Ukraine. Striking at Stalin was a symbolic rejection by the new leadership of the whole Stalinist regime with its repressions, purges, shortages, and fears; it was the signal for a new and better life in the Soviet Union. No offense was launched against the idea of the dictatorship of the proletariat or Party domination of the state, thus leaving the road open to a perpetuation of dictatorial techniques by a "more benevolent" despot. Externally, the downgrading of Stalin represented a temporary mollification of eastern European leaders who were seeking a redefinition of relations with Moscow and a relaxation of the political and military reins held in the U.S.S.R. De-Stalinization appears to have achieved most of its objectives, though it may have established too forcefully for ambitious leaders the precept of collective leadership.

As regards the communist version of the class struggle, Khrushchev differed from Stalin in asserting that, rather than becoming more acute as socialism prospered, the intensity of conflict would be minimized. Socialism's very strength would be its own sustenance both as a defense against external attack and as a check on internal dissidence. The building of Soviet power and the satisfaction of consumer needs permitted the U.S.S.R. to enter a period of peaceful co-existence and peaceful competition with capitalist states in which socialism would demonstrate its vitality and superiority. Capitalism then would decline because of its own inconsistencies and ineptitude. It could logically be inferred from such a modification of the concepts of the inevitability of conflict and capitalist encirclement that the related practices of dictatorship of the proletariat and police state measures would likewise be reassessed and that relaxation of controls would follow. To a degree, the latter occurred, but Khrushchev worked diligently to maintain the idea of the Party's dominance in the direction of socialist developments and, therefore, his own influence as Party leader. He was careful to build the Party image rather than his own position while, at the same time, strengthening his avenues of control throughout the Party apparatus.

Domestically several prominent changes occurred. One of the most striking was the introduction in 1957 of a program to decentralize economic planning in industry and agriculture. It was hoped that such a maneuver would increase local initiative and responsibility and increase production. Further stimulus to increased productivity was provided by emphasizing "individual economic incentive" (higher pay for better work). In agriculture, which has been consistently an economic headache for the Soviet leaders, various incentives, threats, and directive measures were introduced, including turning over to the collective farms ownership of their own machinery, all with only moderate effect in improved production. Even the development of virgin lands in the Kazakhstan area had only modest success. By 1962 there had occurred a recentralization of economic planning though direction in both industry and agriculture remains more regionalized than under Stalin.

Internationally, Khrushchev's regime was beset primarily by problems generated within its own ideological family rather than by the capitalist world. The growing affluence of the Soviet society, the nationalistic expressions in the satellite states, and the appearance of Red China as a competitor for leadership in the communist camp posed significant ideological questions. Khrushchev conceded that there might be different and equally effective paths to socialism—including a parliamentary one, but he did not relinquish all the old guidelines, and when, as in the case of Hungary, an independence movement was begun which might have surely restricted the application of Moscow's influence it was ruthlessly suppressed. Khrushchev, however, did go so far as to advocate the "law of even development of socialism" implying a responsibility on the part of the Soviet Union to assist economically the less fortunate brethren so as to build a solid front of socialist advancement. Relations with China were still more complex. Not only was Russia unable to satisfy significantly the economic needs of this tremendous population, but it had to cope with the aggressive aspirations of this national giant—some of which impinged on Russia's own sphere of influence, and there was the constant ideological and practical menace of Mao Tse-tung who, in his criticism of the Soviet leaders and policies, sought to establish himself as the preeminent communist ideologist and chief. Khrushchev attempted as best he could to meet the demands and competition of China through moderation and cooperation, but the symptoms of disagreement remained as the Soviet leader continued to maneuver to retain Russia's position of leadership in the eyes of the world's communists.

Khrushchev's seemingly unassailable position was not to remain unchallenged. Almost six years of his more or less undisputed authority had brought with it many problems both domestic and foreign. A number of mistakes had been made, and some embarrassing moments for the Soviet Union had had to be endured. The October 1964 meeting of the Central Committee brought an end to the aging leader's career. The charges brought against him at that time—not surprisingly—added up to an indictment that he was indulging in the very thing for which Stalin had been pilloried, the fostering of a cult of personality, which, in the new era of Soviet life, was not to be countenanced. In part—to the extent that the charge was valid—this appeared to be an accurate assessment of the manifestations of Khrushchev's personality; he was flamboyant, arrogant, and fond of the limelight. In part, however, the image was only the expected reflection of the actions taken by a man who exercised the kind of power which his position conferred. Surely the single-handed rule was not consistent with the post-Stalin idea of collective leadership, especially when it stumbled, bumbled, or failed.

Khrushchev was charged with nepotism—particularly with regard to his son-in-law, Alexei Adzhubei, with unbecoming behavior reflecting discredit on the Soviet Union—as in the case of his shoe-pounding exhibition at the United Nations in 1960, with rejecting sound advice, with bragging and ill-considered utterance, and with other character traits not consonant with the dignity and responsibility of his position. More important, of course, were the indictments on substantive failures. His agricultural policies were attacked even though the inadequacies of Soviet farming could be traced only partially to faulty administrative planning. Industrial shortcomings were laid at his doorstep though the over-all industrial and technological picture in the Soviet Union had been bright. The deteriorating relations with Red China were brought up as an index of his ineptitude in foreign policy, as well as the fluctuating relations with the eastern European satellites. Questions were raised as to the practical results of Russia's foreign aid ventures, and the ignominious diplomatic and propaganda defeat suffered in the Cuban missile crisis of October 1962 (see Chapter 6) was placed squarely on his shoulders. His idea of cutting back Soviet ground forces was maligned. Neither Khrushchev's accomplishments nor his carefully developed Party organizational support could save him. He was removed from his positions (theoretically resigning because of age and health) and stripped of his power. In keeping with the growing political tolerance of the new era his punishment halted there, and he was retired to a comparatively pleasant oblivion.

His successors comprised a new team along the lines originated at the time of Malenkov's ascendancy. Leonid T. Brezhnev became the new First Secretary of the Communist Party, and Aleksei N. Kosygin assumed the post of Premier. Both Brezhnev and Kosygin were protégés of Khrushchev and had risen to power and prominence under his auspices. Only several months before his dismissal Khrushchev had personally selected Brezhnev to be his principal deputy in the Party hierarchy; Kosygin had been Deputy Premier and served as head of government when Khrushchev was off on his many foreign jaunts. They appear to represent the new breed of Soviet politician—suave, sophisticated, tactful, with Brezhnev enjoying a reputation as a bon vivant. Brezhnev is Ukrainian born and an industrial engineer, considered to be a "metal eater," i.e., favoring heavy industry. He was a Khrushchev aide in Stalin's Ukrainian purge and climbed the political ladder with Khrushchev's sponsorship. The affable Kosygin comes from Leningrad and joined the upper echelons of the hierarchy after experience in finance, industry, and economic planning. Unlike Brezhnev he seems more inclined to favor increased production of consumer goods.

The succession of the new leaders naturally aroused a rash of speculation regarding the presumed power struggle which was to occur out of which a new dictator would emerge. Old Bolshevik Anastas Mikoyan was in the background as was Mikhail Suslov who had led the attack on Khrushchev. More important still were the questions raised about prospective changes in Soviet policy. Would relations with the West undergo modification? Would a rapprochement with Red China ensue? Would the Soviet Union adopt a more militant and aggressive attitude? What internal policy changes could be expected?

The doubts and fears proved to be groundless as were any hopes that still further improved relations with the western world were in the offing. Personnel had changed, but policies remained relatively constant. The leadership stabilized, and such changes as were made in Party and government office appeared to be either in the interest of improved administrative efficiency or to correct the unfortunate effects of some of Khrushchev's favoritism. Relations with China remained strained, and the ideological debate continued. Satellite states remained restive, and relations continued in flux. The era of co-existence with capitalist countries continued to be what it was under Khrushchev with, perhaps, a somewhat more moderate tone being adopted by Soviet leaders in foreign policy pronouncements. Internally, the new leadership still struggled with agricultural problems, the issue of productivity incentives, and the increasing demands of the Soviet population for more consumer goods and a better life. The relaxation of controls and restraints initiated by Khrushchev has continued though no new surge of freedom is evident. In short, as of 1969 Brezhnev, Kosygin, and their cohorts have shown themselves to be cautious, competent, effective leaders collectively making and implementing policies which are still "communist" in motive and direction, but communist in the post-Stalin style.

STUDY QUESTIONS AND PROJECT SUGGESTIONS

1. Discuss the nature of the contest for leadership in the Soviet Union following Lenin's death.
2. Outline the major contributions of Stalin to contemporary communist theory.
3. Detail the major phases of socialization of the Russian economy indicating the nature of the obstacles which had to be overcome in the process.
4. Contrast and compare the rise to power of Nikita Khrushchev with that of Stalin.
5. What is meant by "de-Stalinization"?
6. Describe the differences in internal and external policies of the U.S.S.R. under Stalin and Khrushchev.
7. Do the policies of current Soviet leaders suggest a continuation of or a deviation from those inaugurated by Khrushchev? Explain.

CHAPTER 5

THE SOVIET SYSTEM

Any assessment of life in the Soviet Union must begin with the recognition that the *apparent* forces and institutions which shape the Soviet system today are superficial, and that the *real* influence and power lie elsewhere. Insight into the realities of the socio-politico-economic relations in the U.S.S.R. requires a realization that the formal governmental structure and practice is a facade, that political and economic theory is less frequently a guide to action than it is a medium for justifying the pragmatic actions of leaders. That such dichotomy exists between theory and practice, between the seeming and the actual, does not mark the Soviet Union as *sui generis*. Inconsistencies of this nature are to be found in any national system. What is unique in the Soviet case is the continuing insistence, even in this more sophisticated era, that the sham is the genuine. To be sure, modern Soviet leaders are not so naive as to assume that forms, trappings, and phrasings deceive many—including their own citizens, and less emphasis is placed today on maintaining the deception. Further, the maturation of the Soviet society has narrowed the gap between the proclaimed and the real. Nevertheless, discrepancies continue to exist, and to ignore them would lead to false conclusions.

A second pattern which should be remembered consistently is the manner of the Soviet Union's birth, the nature of its development, and the Marxist-Leninist doctrine by which it was motivated. Though theory has never been controlling—nor even consistent, its presence and influence cannot be overlooked. The revolutionary antecedents, the struggle for survival, the distrust of capitalist states, the communist expectations, and the theoretical shifts have all had their share in molding the modern society. To whatever extent Soviet leaders have been personally ambitious, to whatever degree they may have desired to shape their own policies—to write their own theory, it is reasonable to assume that they could not completely escape the thought pattern in which they had been reared, nor could they run the political risk of rejecting totally the precepts of the high priests of communism.

A third point which might be made is the notation that the U.S.S.R. is a nation-state in the three hundred year old tradition of the nation-state system, a power in its own right, and heir to the nationalistic, imperialistic aspirations of Czarist Russia. The nature of communist theory and the pronouncements of Soviet leaders should not blind us to this fact of statehood in a family of states. Particularly in the realm of foreign policy, losing sight of this essential fact can lead us badly astray. The long standing practice in pre-revolutionary Russia of autocratic despotism, of rigid social castes, and of comparative passivity in the masses are part of the historical environment which must be considered in explaining the present, as is the story of Russia's conflict with its neighbors in its rise to power.

Formal Political Structure

The Union of Soviet Socialist Republics is just what its name implies—a federation of semi-autonomous republics not unlike the basic governmental arrangement in the United States. There are currently fifteen of these so-called Union Republics each theoretically having the constitutional right to secede from the Union. Within some of the Union Republics there are autonomous republics, autonomous regions, and national areas—all based on ethnic groupings, and various levels of local government. The relations between the Union and its component parts are outlined in the Constitution of 1936 as it has been periodically amended. This document, known originally as the Stalin Constitution, had been preceded by two others (1918 and 1924), but it is in the latest version of the Soviet fundamental law that the formalities and some of the realities of Soviet social, economic, and political life are to be found.

The federal system is the Soviet answer to solidifying the various ethnic groups of which the country is composed. As individual groups have been absorbed or conquered they have been awarded varying degrees of cultural and political autonomy so as to preserve the feeling of individuality while the process of unification continued unhindered under the aegis of the Communist Party or the force of the Red Army. At the same time, Soviet history indicates a calculated effort to minimize ethnic distinctions and amalgamate the population. Though the Constitution outlines political institutions for both the Union as a whole and the various republics—seemingly assigning spheres of autonomy to the lesser units, a close reading of the document clarifies that supreme authority is vested in the central government. In 1944 the Soviet Union even went so far as to grant to the Union Republics the right to conduct independent foreign relations and to maintain their own armed forces. The intent of these constitutional revisions soon became clear as the U.S.S.R. sought individual representation for each of the Union Republics in the United Nations, succeeding in obtaining seats for the Ukrainian S.S.R. and the Byelorussian S.S.R. No independent foreign policies or armed forces have, of course, been permitted.

The highest organ of state power is designated as the Supreme Soviet of the U.S.S.R. which meets twice a year and consists of two chambers, the Soviet of the Union and the Soviet of Nationalities. Representatives to the former are chosen from electoral districts on the basis of one deputy for every 300,000 persons; representatives to the latter are elected on the basis of 25 deputies from each Union Republic, 11 from each autonomous republic, five from each autonomous region, and one from each national area. The members serve four year terms, and deputies must be at least 23 years old. All citizens over 18 years of age are eligible to vote. This body is supposedly the basic legislative organ of the country and is given the authority to name the Council of Ministers.

The Supreme Soviet chooses a 33-member Presidium whose Chairman is designated the ceremonial head of state. While superficially a collective executive, the Presidium has a vast array of legislative powers including interpretation of laws, issuance of decrees, and annulment of decisions of the Council of Ministers. When the Supreme Soviet is not in session—and it seldom is, the Presidium can appoint or release Ministers on the recommendation of the Chairman of the Council, and it can declare war. The most salient feature of this relationship between the Supreme Soviet and its Presidium is that the seemingly more democratic body—chosen by a nationwide electorate, and that by which legislative power is exercised "exclusively" is in reality dominated by its own inner circle and contents itself in its infrequent meetings with ratification of decrees already proclaimed and actions already taken.

The highest executive and administrative organ of the U.S.S.R. is its Council of Ministers. The Council is accountable to the Supreme Soviet or its Presidium giving an appearance of parliamentary responsibility. The Council usually includes its Chairman (the Premier), the First Deputy Chairman, several Deputy Chairmen, and the heads of the various ministries, commissions, and committees as designated in law. Three classes of ministries of the U.S.S.R. are ordained: (1) All-Union ministries (e.g., foreign trade) which direct their activities from Moscow throughout the U.S.S.R.; (2) Union-Republic ministries (e.g., internal affairs) which administer their activities from Moscow through corresponding ministries in the different Union Republics; and (3) Republican ministries (in the Union Republics) which theoretically administer activities left wholly to the discretion of each Union Republic. The Council directs and coordinates the work of the various ministries, "exercises general guidance in the sphere of relations with foreign states," and directs the organization of the armed forces. The Council is actually controlled by its inner circle normally known as the Presidium of the Council, dominated by the Premier and other leaders. The significant fact about the work of the Council and its leadership group is that they are normally unaccountable to any *governmental* agency, though they remain subservient to *Party* leaders. The basis of the Council's strength—or its impotence as an independent body—is its close relation with the Party leadership, overlapping membership on the Council and in the upper echelons of the Party being common. It should be remembered that both Stalin and Khrushchev held simultaneously the positions of Premier and Party chief.

Political arrangements in the republics and regions parallel those in the Union itself. Soviets, Presidiums, Councils of Ministers, Ministries, and other administrative agencies reflect the image and dovetail the operations of the central governmental mechanism.

Justice is administered in the U.S.S.R. by a whole series of courts ranging from the Supreme Court of the Union down to the People's Courts. The members of the Supreme Court of the U.S.S.R. and all intermediate levels are elected by their respective Soviets. People's Courts are elected by the citizens. Trials are public "unless otherwise provided for by law," and an accused is guaranteed the "right to defence;" judges are held by the Constitution to be "independent." A Procurator General is appointed by the Supreme Soviets to insure strict observance of the law, and he in turn appoints counterparts in the various republics and regions. Reminiscence over some of the purge tactics and farcical public trials over the years may cast some doubt on the adequacy of constitutional provisions for fair trial.

One striking aspect of the Soviet Constitution which is highly exemplary of the conflict between myth and reality is its provisions for the rights of citizens which can be noted in both the first chapter and in the tenth which elaborates at length on the topic. The first interesting feature of the treatment of rights is that they are coupled with a statement of duties. While it is not unreasonable to recognize that citizens do have duties and responsibilities, linking them with rights raises some questions as to whether the duties imply a diminution of the rights. Secondly, the phrasing of some of the rights presents the issue of whether they are in reality rights or responsibilities. Thirdly, can the rights be taken at face value, or must they be measured against the realities of Soviet experience which indicate a contradictory trend? Fourthly, should the whole matter of rights be dismissed simply as a deceiving "front," as Stalin once remarked, an "ideal" toward which the government was working?

In Article 10, the "personal property right of citizens in their incomes and savings from work, in their dwelling-houses and subsidiary husbandries, in articles of domestic economy and use and articles of personal use and convenience, as well as the right of citizens to inherit personal property is protected by law." Of what value is the right measured against the prescription in Article 6 that the land, minerals, waters, forests, mills, factories, mines, transportation facilities, banks, communications, agricultural enterprises, and the "bulk of the dwelling-houses" are "state property"?

Article 118 specifies the "right to work," but Article 12 states that "work in the U.S.S.R. is a duty" according to the "principle 'He who does not work, neither shall he eat.'" Article 130 prescribes the duty to maintain labor discipline. Does this prohibit free choice of job, collective bargaining, the right to strike, to be free from concentration camp labor—all of which might be implied in "right to work"?

Article 119 outlines a right to rest and leisure through stipulation of maximum hours of work, paid vacations, and establishment of vacation resorts. Low monetary returns, increased work quotas, and emphasis on increased productivity are hardly consistent with the proclaimed right. Similarly, the right to maintenance in case of sickness, disability, and old age (Art. 120) has been frequently a myth, although various medical and social services have been provided for citizens.

The right to education appears on the surface to be a clear recognition by Soviet authorities of the importance of this aspect of life, and educational advances have been noteworthy. Practically, however, the promise inherent in the sweeping enunciation in Article 121 has broken down at the upper levels of training. The nature of the system has denied an equal opportunity to all citizens, favoring instead those who could finance their schooling, and political status has too often served as a criterion for admission to collegiate experience.

Articles 122 and 123 state the equality of women with men in all activities and ban discrimination based on race or nationality. These are important features of a system dedicated to the attainment of a classless society. As with other rights, equality of women has been a two-sided coin. Women have had the right to be absorbed in economic and political activity, but they have also had the responsibility of bearing the corresponding burden of manual labor and military service along with men. The provision for equality of races and nationalities must be considered against the background of discrimination against non-Russian national minorities and periodic surges of anti-Semitism.

The guarantee of freedom of conscience and separation of church and state is proclaimed in Article 124. To those reared in a democratic tradition the concept of religious freedom is precious, and the notion of church-state separation is a reasonable means of avoiding religious persecution. Thus, superficially, this provision of the Soviet Constitution would be applauded. Unfortunately, the same clause also guarantees "freedom of anti-religious propaganda," and the position of the Communist

Party has been consistently anti-religious. Those, then, who wished to pursue their traditional religious practices in the U.S.S.R. have found it difficult to do so, and, at times, the obstacles imposed by the government have been insurmountable.

Articles 125 and 126 stipulate those freedoms so dear to democrats and so essential for protection against tyranny: speech, press, assembly, organization, and demonstration. Liberally interpreted and honestly implemented, these rights are the ultimate guarantee of self-government and protection for the dissenter. As utilized by the leaders of the Soviet Union, the rights have been relatively meaningless and have even been perverted into tools of oppression. For one thing, the rights may be exercised only "in conformity with the interests of the working people and in order to strengthen the socialist system." No clearer indication can be found that *critical* commentaries disparaging policies or leaders will not be tolerated. Further, anyone having the temerity to offer criticism might find himself charged as an enemy of the state. Even if such obvious restraint did not exist, since there is but one party and it has a monopoly of the media of communication and a stranglehold on the electoral process, the prospective objector would find it almost impossible to discover a forum for his ideas.

Finally, Soviet citizens are guaranteed inviolability of person, freedom from arrest except through appropriate legal process, privacy of correspondence, and inviolability of homes. It is almost superfluous to note that all of these are completely at odds with the periodic purges, the secret police apparatus, the informer system, the forced labor camps, and the other arbitrary techniques of the police state which have been so common in the U.S.S.R.

Superimposed on the rights, then, are the duties of Soviet citizens. These include observance of the law, maintaining labor discipline, performing public duties honestly, respecting the "rules of socialist intercourse," safeguarding and fortifying socialist property, serving in the armed forces, and defending the country. We might reemphasize that several of these duties are merely the normal expectation of citizenship responsibility in any nation, but we must ask simultaneously to what extent rights might be demanded or exercised without violating labor discipline or the rules of socialist intercourse. When ideological shifts occur with dramatic suddenness and new leaders come to the fore, discretion would seem to indicate that the less individual agitation for rights and privileges the better.

The foregoing commentary is not intended to show that Soviet constitutionalism is a total farce, that there is no coincidence of the theoretical and the actual, or that there has been an unbroken history of continuous violation of constitutional precepts by Soviet leaders from Stalin to the present. Surely the status of the individual citizen's freedom and economic well-being has varied under Stalin, Malenkov, Khrushchev, and Brezhnev and Kosygin. The consolidation of Soviet power and its industrial development have made a constructive contribution to the relaxation of tensions in Soviet life. But it is an inescapable conclusion that the constitutional description of political institutions and the power they exercise as well as the representation of popular rights has been and remains spurious. This being the case, why have the Soviet politicians—the Communist Party commanders—clung so steadfastly to the fiction? What purpose does this myth of constitutionalism serve?

Though the Constitution of the U.S.S.R. does not place any real limitations on governmental authority—or even confer power on the agencies described, though it offers the individual no real protection in his presumed rights and privileges, and though it gives no adequate guide to the loci of political power, its existence does serve several useful purposes from the communist viewpoint. Its most important purpose, especially with regard to the less enlightened and less initiated, is its propaganda value in painting an idealized version of Soviet life. Particularly in the period when the Soviet Union was more of an enigma than it is today, when fewer outsiders were permitted within its borders, when what was known came essentially from a state-controlled press, the image of a federated, parliamentary, constitutional, democratic state was quite impressive. In the second place, the detailed specification of governmental organs is designed to indicate that political authority is not exercised arbitrarily. Certainly, it might be thought, such an institutional panoply by its very existence would delimit dictatorial intent and insure a degree of democratic participation. Third, there is a telling implication internally. The Constitution's emphasis on equality, popular action, and mass participation leads to a mesmerizing self-deception. Under proper propagandistic manipulation, pre-election agitation and massive electoral turnouts serve to suggest to Soviet citizens themselves the unanimity of belief, the rightness of policy, the popularity of leaders, the error of opposition, the sense of belonging, the resistance to foreign antagonists—even when there is only one hand-picked candidate for each position, and opposition to his election is fraught with danger. Should foreign observers be equally deluded by such fraud, there is an extra bonus. Fourth, the exaggerated picture of constitutional stability and economic security sows the seeds of acceptance for communist ideology abroad. Especially when coupled with the unquestionable industrial growth of the Soviet Union and its undoubted technological and scientific strides, the facade of proletarian democracy finds a ready audience among the world's less privileged peoples. Fifth, the extravagance of Soviet constitutionalism is a base of comparison with "other democracies" from which depreciation of deviation from the Soviet norm can be pronounced. Sixth, even the inadequacies of Soviet constitutionalism can be turned to advantage. After all, communists preach the eventual withering away of the state; the dictatorship of the proletariat is a temporary expedient unfortunately saddled with the burden of bourgeois political institutions. Thus contradictions and failures can be traced to the frailties of the system rather than the communist practitioners. Finally, from a more democratic viewpoint, Soviet constitutionalism may have served a more salutary purpose. Soviet leaders may have become victims of their own propaganda. Post-Stalin personnel changes in the upper reaches of leadership and the fate of those deposed suggest a new tone of moderation in political technique. Liquidation has not been the inevitable fate of the losers. Collegial leadership and power shared according to some standard of regulation appears to be the rule rather than the exception. Dictatorial whimsy seems on the wane. While it is still too soon to draw definite conclusions, fifty years of flirtation with constitutionalism may still produce a meaningful union of fact and fiction.

The Communist Party

The clue to understanding the realities of the Soviet system is an appreciation of the position and role of the Communist Party of the Soviet Union (CPSU). In the final analysis, it is the CPSU which wields the real power in Soviet Russia. Even recognizing this, however, is not enough; two further cautions are necessary. First, it is the Leninist version of the nature of the Communist Party which exists. The Party is *not* a broadly based, spontaneous, proletarian grouping as envisaged by some of the early Bolsheviks. It is a tightly knit group of revolutionaries—or their heirs, comparatively few in number, drafting policies and revising theory to fit their needs, and giving leadership to the socialist experiment. Secondly, as is true of Soviet constitutionalism, the apparent in CPSU organization is not the real. The seeming democratic nature of the party system is belied by the reality of the power structure. Power is exercised from the top down, not granted from the bottom up.

The basic unit of the Party hierarchy is the primary organization (formerly known as the "cell"), a grouping of three or more Party members in a factory, farm, educational institution, or elsewhere. This concept of a primary unit is an expression of the Leninist idea of the nature of the Party as a conspiratorial vanguard, highly organized and highly disciplined. The need for such a unit was emphasized by the failure of the 1905 revolutionary effort in which the absence of grass roots organization was clearly seen. As early as 1908, then, the Party organ *Proletarian* called for such an organizing effort, and the cells began to blossom. When their worth was confirmed in the successful Russian revolution, their status was officially incorporated in the Party Statutes at the 8th All-Russia Conference in 1919.

Where such units are sufficiently large, the secretaries devote themselves exclusively to Party work. The primary units have the responsibility for organizational and agitational work, recruitment, political education of members, developing criticism and self-criticism, mobilizing the masses in work and politics, and assisting the higher levels of organization. In other words, it is the function of the primary unit to carry out the normal day to day Party operations according to directives from above. Persons are proposed for membership in the Party at this level, but they must be approved by the next higher echelon and are admitted to membership only after a prolonged candidacy. Once accepted, the member joins a select and elite group in Soviet society (the estimate of total membership as of 1969 being slightly over 13,500,000) enjoying special privileges, but must, at the same time, accept the duties and express the devotion of a dedicated servant to the cause of communism and the Party leaders.

From this base the hierarchical pyramid narrows upward through local, regional, republic, and national levels, each being controlled by a Party bureau and secretary, and each—short of the pinnacle—having control authority over lower levels and responsibilities toward the higher. The total organization supposedly functions on the basis of "democratic centralism" implying both a desire and a right for the lower and intermediate organs to discuss and recommend policies to the highest authorities and election of higher bodies by lower, but a duty to accept and implement unquestioningly the decisions made at the top. The extent to which recommendations and criticisms from below are considered and accepted by the Party leaders is, of course, a moot point, and criticism of Party chiefs simply is not tolerated.

It is, then, the national organization which deserves our main attention as the focal point of decision-making and authority. It is from the wishes of the leading personalities at this level that individuals are advanced or degraded in the ranks, that policy decisions emanate, that the actual revisions occur, that internal and external trends develop. The Party membership as a whole occupies a favored position, but through discipline and manipulation the privileges and prerogatives of elitism broaden as one approaches the zenith of the Party organization.

The supreme organ of the CPSU is theoretically the Party Congress, elected by the lower organs and meeting at least once every four years. There were 18 Congresses up to 1939, but Stalin did not convene the 19th until 1952. Subsequently, Congresses were held in 1956, 1959, 1961, and 1966, but the essence of their subordinate role became more and more apparent. The 2000 or more delegates who attend as well as representatives from communist parties abroad serve as an audience for the pronouncements of CPSU leaders. Some superficial debate and discussion occurs, and, especially in recent years, foreign visitors are accorded the opportunity to make formal speeches and policy statements. In the end, however, the theoretical expositions and policy announcements of the CPSU leaders are unanimously and enthusiastically approved. Though the Congresses may lack independent power, they may well be observed for evidence of new developments in the communist world. It was in the 20th Congress that the de-Stalinization movement and the attack on the cult of personality were inaugurated. In the 23rd in 1966 the failure of the Chinese communists to attend was an enlightening commentary on the status of the Sino-Soviet controversy. At this same gathering, the name of the Party Presidium was changed back to the Stalinist appellation, Politburo, and Brezhnev's title of First Secretary was revised to that of Stalin, General Secretary. What inferences to draw from these nominal switches remain clouded to date.

A more significant body is that which is presumably elected by the Congress, the Central Committee of the Party. The Central

Committee, which since 1952 has had a membership ranging from 125 to 175 with an additional 111 to 156 "candidate members," directs the whole work of the Party during the intervals between the Congresses. The extent to which the Committee is an autonomous body is questionable, the preponderance of evidence indicating that it is more a servant than a master of the bodies which it chooses. However, it should be remembered that the challenge to Khrushchev by the Malenkov-Molotov faction was overcome by action of the entire Committee, and subsequently Khrushchev's ouster was ratified by the same organ. Even if the Central Committee is not the ruling force in the Party it serves as a liaison between the actual leaders and lieutenants down the line, helps to implement Party decisions, and whips up enthusiasm for Party policies. Members of the Central Committee are surely among the Party elite, and many hold high governmental posts as well as Party positions. The Central Committee theoretically elects the members of three other Party organs, in one of which the real site of Party power is located.

The Party Control Committee serves as a sort of watchdog over conformity and orthodoxy throughout the Party. It also functions in the service of the top leaders to assure that policies are being carried out as directed. Adherence to as well as deviation from high level decisions is noted so that reward as well as punishment may follow. Seemingly the Committee has a degree of disciplinary discretion requiring no further confirmation. The Secretariat of the Party, ranging in membership over the years from 5 to 10, directs current work particularly with regard to the selection of personnel at the lower levels concerned with guiding Party fortunes. At one time considered to be a kind of housekeeping and administrative organ, the Secretariat was converted by Stalin into a base from which supreme political power could be consolidated. Since then the position of General Secretary or First Secretary has been synonymous with dictatorial or near dictatorial control of the Party organism and therefore of the Soviet Union. The Secretariat, with its divergent responsibilities concerning internal and external policies in addition to personnel, is not considered to be the center of Party authority, but the membership of its personnel on the remaining central Party organ marks it as an extremely influential agency.

In the most realistic sense, the highest organ of authority— Party or government, political, economic, or social—is the Politburo (more recently designated the Presidium, but renamed as of old in 1966). This body is composed of the dozen top Communist Party leaders, with another half-dozen serving in a candidate or non-voting capacity. Formally, the Politburo members are selected by the Central Committee, but in actuality the membership is determined by cooption from within the Politburo itself. The group is headed by the General Secretary (from Stalin to Brezhnev known as First Secretary) of the Party who may or may not hold a governmental office. Frequently the remaining members represent the friends and supporters of the General Secretary whose nominations are approved by the Central Committee, and admission to or dismissal from the Politburo is a sure index of the contemporary status of personnel in the hierarchy.[1] The Politburo's jurisdiction is boundless, encompassing Party and governmental matters and internal and external policies affecting any sphere of Soviet life. The Politburo meets in secret, and while it may pay some attention to the principle of democratic centralism in its deliberations, its tendency is to be more autocratic, its decisions are final, and implementation of adopted policies must be followed unswervingly.

The position of the General Secretary is singular in that he controls the Secretariat, serves as Chairman of the Politburo and the Central Committee, may—as in the case of Stalin and Khrushchev—serve also as Chairman of the Council of Ministers, presides over Party Congresses, and exercises tremendous influ-

---

[1] This concept and practice of friendship, kinship, or "cronyism" as the basis for the selection of key personnel is not limited to the highest echelons, and suggests—as in all formal organizations—the existence of an informal hierarchy within the conventional configuration in which personal affinity is a stronger bond than doctrinal regularity.

ence on both personnel and policy. The comparatively minor restraints on his personal power existing through the collectivity of leadership is exemplified most clearly in the Stalinist experience. Khrushchev's regime for a while paralleled Stalin's one man rule. Recent developments leave some doubt that the General Secretary's authority will remain as unbridled as formerly, but there is no discounting his position of primacy. Prior to the Sino-Soviet schism this chief of the CPSU was generally recognized as the leader of world communism. Even with the challenge of Mao Tse-tung the military and economic superiority of the Soviet Union gives priority to the General Secretary in international communist affairs. Given the prominence of the position it is no wonder that sweeping power plays emerge periodically to maintain or attain this pinnacle.

The Communist Party dominates every aspect of Soviet life, and the Party leadership represented by the Politburo and the General Secretary manipulate the Party to a large extent in their own interest. Some might quarrel with this analysis of self-centeredness in Party moguls claiming an insufficiency of attention to Marxist dogma, Party interest, or popular welfare as motivational factors. However, the intensity of competition in the succession crises which have been witnessed attests to the importance of personal ambition in gaining and securing positions on the top rungs of the organizational ladder as does the system of periodic purges to check any threat to personal supremacy. And it must be recalled that the economic and social perquisites and the power prerogatives of the highest Party positions can be maintained only through satisfaction of popular needs, maintenance of Party morale and discipline, and substantial adherence to the Marxist-Leninist gospel—or, at least, adequate justification of its modification. Thus self-service requires consideration of the broader arenas of concern.

The Soviet Party-government is not only authoritarian but totalitarian. Its concern embraces every facet of the Soviet society and its demands blanket the economy, social relations, and cultural expression. It brooks no competing power centers nor tolerates dissentient loyalties such as might be developed in religious beliefs, trade unions, professional associations, or other groupings. The primary trait of this totalitarianism is the monopoly of political activity reserved to the Communist Party. No other party or political organization is permitted. For every governmental post from the central government on down only one candidate is placed in nomination, and he must be either a member of the Party or a non-Party nominee approved by the organization. Surprisingly enough, the electorate does enjoy the right of voting against a candidate, but the instances of actual rejection by a majority negative vote are microscopically small and non-existent above the lowest levels of government. In any case, the voters are then presented with another hand-picked candidate. Despite this exclusivity of the Party, each election is attended by an elaborate amount of electioneering and agitation designed to foster popular enthusiasm and to create the impression of almost unanimous support for the regime by massive voter turnouts—all casting assenting votes.

A second major attribute of totalitarianism is the subservience of the governmental apparatus and economic mechanism to the Party. Each agency of government—including the armed forces —and each economic enterprise is supervised by and/or controlled by a corresponding Party agent. It is the latter who is the ultimate director of the supervised activity even though each has its nominal chief and even though the Party agent is technically charged with responsibility for Party affairs as his prime concern. Since the Party representative is judged in large measure by the effective operation of the political or economic institution to which he is attached, his oversight is likely to be oppressively close.

Control of cultural activity is a third manifestation of Soviet totalitarianism. Culture—in the sense of aesthetic expression and artistic creativity in literature, painting, sculpture, and music— is generally considered to be a form of individual productivity only occasionally having political overtones. In the Soviet system such a tolerant attitude toward the conduct of writers and artists has not been prevalent in Party ranks. Works of art—pictures, novels, stories, musical compositions—have been applauded or criticized because they were interpreted as depicting "accurately" proletarian themes or because they were believed to be representative of a bourgeois outlook. Artists have found themselves rewarded for consciously or inadvertently producing creations which were appreciated by Communist leaders, or they have been criticized—or even imprisoned—for works which were construed to be critical of the regime of its policies. Aside from the stifling effect which such interpretation has on creative endeavor, it is a proper gauge of the pervasiveness of Party interest in all endeavors in Soviet society.

Another indicant of the totality of Party control is discovered in the methods which are used to secure desired ends. To begin with, all media of communication are owned, operated, and directed under Party auspices. No independent newspapers, magazines, radio stations, etc., exist to supply truthful and objective reporting of events, instances of inefficiency or corruption in government or economic enterprise, or criticism of policies and leaders. Censorship is rigorous and all-embracing. To support this system of restraint, all modern methods of propaganda are utilized to indoctrinate the population and to convince the people of the virtues of the system. In addition to the communications media, discussion groups, parades, demonstrations, posters, and the whole educational system are used to extol the rectitude of communism and the special integrity of contemporary leaders. Of special note is the attention given to the molding of youth in the communist image. Passing through the "Little Octobrists" and Young Pioneers, adolescents become eligible for the Komsomol (Young Communist League) at age 14. The Komsomol is the basic training ground for prospective Party members and serves to introduce youth to Party activity. Even if Komsomol membership does not culminate in acceptance to the Party, a great deal of inculcation of orthodox beliefs has been accomplished during formative years.

Finally, there remains to notice the most harrowing tools of totalitarianism. Organized violence and terror have been regularly employed from the beginning of the dictatorship of the proletariat to maintain the docility of the masses. The secret police (at various times known as *Cheka*, G.P.U., N.K.V.D., M.V.D., M.G.B., and K.G.B.), operating under broadly drawn legal authority—and frequently simply according to the whim of the Party leader, have arrested, imprisoned, and executed thousands of "enemies of the state" whose only crime may have been to be accused as critics of the regime. Not only have the police tactics removed any real or imagined opponents of Party heads, but the special techniques (night raids and arrests, secret inquisitions, unusual tortures, threats, etc.) of the semi-autonomous agents have so terrorized the populace that a thoroughly intimidated society evolved. A heartening footnote to this sad chapter in Soviet history should be cited. Since the elimination of Lavrenti Beria from the power competition in 1953, there has been a distinct curtailment in the use of secret police tactics in Soviet life.

The Soviet Economy

The complexities and vicissitudes of the Soviet economic system are too multifarious to be detailed here, but there are certain constants worthy of notation, and some generalizations may be ventured. 1] The cornerstone of economic organization and activity is, of course, the Marxist doctrine of public ownership of the means of production. True to the maxim that private property is the bane of society, and presumably aiming for the achievement of the ideal "from each according to his ability, to each according to his needs," the economy of the U.S.S.R. has been contrived so as to minimize or banish private ownership of productive facilities. (Some small amount of private enterprise does exist especially in agriculture.) 2] Similarly, consistent with the claim that capitalism's uncertainties are rooted in chaotic decision-making, economic enterprise has always been subject to centralized planning (this has meant particularly allocation of resources among enterprises). Whether plans were carefully drawn or ill-considered, whether they were discreetly or negligently implemented, the principle of systematic design has been more or less regularly followed. 3] The peasantry— like the industrial proletariat—has always been considered subject to the dogma of scientific socialism. Regardless of peasant attitude or obstinacy, the "rural proletariat" has been destined for incorporation in the total socialist scheme. 4] The nature of the economy has been dictated in large proportion by state objectives as determined by Party bosses. The emphasis on rapid industrialization, the stress on heavy industry early in Soviet history, the relegation of consumer production to a nonessential category, the drive to collectivize agriculture, all reflect the subordination of the economy to the purposes of the state. 5] Variations from the Marxist norm have been instituted with a minimum of qualm. From Lenin's introduction of the NEP to Khrushchev's suggestion of "increased individual economic incentives" Soviet leaders have been wont to deviate from doctrinal paths without scruple when such deviation seemed essential to economic progress. 6] Communist theory, expectation, and inclination have not proved accurate with regard to human nature, historic bent, and personal aspiration in the economic realm. Peasants want land, not collectivization. Consumers want goods, not gigantic industrial enterprise. Workers want better wages and higher living standards, not citations and medals. The carrot works better than the stick in worker motivation. Centralized planning is not a panacea. The political commissar is no substitute for the competent manager. An economy cannot be politically tailored to perfection. 7] Despite the dogmatically initiated and politically inclined economic decisions frequently emanating from the Party leadership, many economic decrees have been prescribed by economic necessity. The decision in recent years to expand the Soviet chemical industry was a direct result of the continuing crisis in agriculture to the solution of which increased and improved fertilization it was believed could make a distinct contribution. 8] Emotional antipathy to communism joined with examples of flagrant economic errors should not obscure the real economic achievements of the Soviet Union any more than a sympathetic empathy with the communist cause should blind us to gross faults in economic theory and practice. 9] There can be no discounting of the positive economic accomplishments of the U.S.S.R. A relatively backward nation has been transformed into an industrial giant. Technical advances and their economic ramifications have been phenomenal. Agriculture—quite possibly the weakest link in the economic chain—has been collectivized as Stalin insisted. Consumer goods have begun to trickle in larger quantities and in better quality to the markets. The socialist system, for all of its frailties, has worked and can improve. Opinions may be held that economic gain may have been superior under another regimen, but there is no gainsaying the workability of the Soviet system in economic terms.

The base of the Soviet economy consists today of a number of quasi-autonomous enterprises having their own financing and their own profit and loss accounts, producing goods according to administrative plan, and being supervised by the Communist Party. With the exception of some recent innovations, the kinds of goods, the costs of materials, the levels of wages, and the prices charged are all determined by fiat from above as are investment programs. Each enterprise is directed by a manager who seeks to fulfill or overfulfill the output quotas dictated by the plan. Profits, represented as a percentage of costs, are built into the plan (on occasion losses as well), but they do not reflect the free play of demand, supply, decreased production costs, and improved productivity. (There are incentives for decreasing costs and improving productivity in that profits resulting from *overplan* production are retained in larger proportion by the enterprise and serve as a fund from which bonuses and other benefits are paid.) Since material costs, wages, and prices are predetermined, profits are likewise foreordained if the plan is fulfilled. Most of the profit is simply transferred to the state budget, the remaining amount being used for capital investment, working capital, and incentive payments. Overplan profits go more to incentives, the building of dwellings, and other consumer uses. As products are sold to wholesalers or retailers they are normally subject to a turnover tax which is the principal source of national revenue.

The Soviet industrial organism has always been beset by problems and many of them remain presently. The question of centralization versus decentralization in planning is still perplexing. Politically motivated economic decisions have caused much dislocation, confusion, and consumer unrest. The problem of incentives and increased productivity against the backdrop of communist theory remains a puzzle. Consistently in planning and production too much emphasis has been placed on quantity, and, specially in recent years, complaints have been increasing about the quality and durability of consumer goods. The Soviets, despite their impressive technical achievements, have not seemed to incorporate the latest technological advances into the productive process. Many hours are lost in shopping due to a still primitive distribution system. Relating supply to demand has been a continuing stumbling block. And in the mid-1960s Premier Kosygin acknowledged that there had been a distinct slowdown in the rate of economic growth.

Under Khrushchev a number of experiments were initiated to try to improve the system. Worker incentives were increased, workers' housing was improved—at least in the cities, the workweek was shortened and vacations lengthened, and greater latitude was allowed in changing jobs. Central planning was modified with the creation of *regional* economic councils (*Sovnarkhozy*) so as to bring decision-making closer to production management. The most spectacular innovation was a venture in greater *plant* autonomy. Two clothing factories were authorized to plan their own production—quantity and type—based on actual orders received from retail outlets, and to revise production based on actual sales, thus introducing the factor of consumer choice in production planning. Under Brezhnev and

Kosygin the decentralization of planning was canceled and centralization reintroduced. At the same time, a long range concept of computerization was initiated with the aim of making readily available great masses of detailed economic information which would allow more effective decisions at the center. The other practices, notably that granting plant autonomy, have been retained or expanded. To what degree factory independence and highly centralized planning will be able to work together remains to be seen. While the consumer has benefited and the role of the professional manager has come to be appreciated in the recent experiments, the Soviet industrial complex is still saddled with numerous problems whose solution must await a more effective rapprochement between political dictation and economic fact.

The blackest spot in the Soviet economic picture has always been agriculture. It should immediately be conceded that many aspects of the agricultural problem are environmental, and that others are perhaps equally inescapable in a total economic system in which priorities must be established. Much of the soil of the U.S.S.R. is not as fertile as that of other major agricultural nations, and climatic conditions are not the best for growth. Women constitute a major proportion of the farm labor force. Farm to market transport facilities and roads are poor. Fertilization facilities were lacking, and irrigation projects are disproportionately expensive with regard to expected yield. However, additional burdens have been placed on the agricultural sector through political action. Agricultural concerns were secondary to a leadership bound on a course of rapid industrialization. The policy of collectivization of agriculture was resisted fanatically by the peasants. Political control of agricultural pursuits was widely resented. Modern farming techniques and equipment were slow in coming to Soviet agriculture. Laboring under these impediments it is not surprising, therefore, to find agricultural development lagging behind that of industry in the U.S.S.R.

Soviet agriculture is organized within two basic structures:

the state farm (*sovkhoz*) and the collective farm (*kolkhoz*). The state farms comprise the smaller proportion of agricultural enterprise, and the workers are essentially state employees. The remainder of agricultural endeavor is undertaken by the collective farms where the workers cooperate in working the land and derive common compensation from their joint labor. In actuality, *kolkhoz* workers are paid in cash and kind by the farm managers so that they too are closer to being salaried employees. The interesting attribute of the *kolkhoz* arrangement is that each peasant family is permitted to have and to work a small plot of ground as their own and to sell its produce on the open market. They are also allotted their own dwellings and may own a cow and fowl. This vestige of free enterprise was something of a compromise with peasant intransigence and has never been fully acceptable to the political leadership. Further, at various times it became apparent that the peasants were shirking their collective responsibilities to work on their respective plots. Despite periodic imposition of various controls on this private sector of the economy, it continues to be a significant contributor of goods on the market and a worry to Party officials. Incentives for collective farms have generally been provided by requiring that a fixed annual quota of produce be delivered to the state at a fixed low price, but authorizing the sale of above quota production on the free market at much higher prices. Unfortunately, when a farm exceeded its quota it found itself burdened with a higher quota the next year.

Khrushchev attempted to meet the agricultural problem in various ways. The virgin lands program in Kazakhstan and Siberia was inaugurated. New plans for developing fertilizer production were announced. Additional social welfare benefits were assigned to collective farm workers. Price increases for selected crops were determined as a spur to increased production. Brezhnev and Kosygin are equally concerned with the situation and appear determined to take the necessary steps to remedy shortcomings. New and logical selective price increases for milk, cattle, and grains were instituted—taking into account area environmental differences, the costs to be borne out of the state budget. Restraints imposed by Khrushchev on the peasants' private plots were lifted to draw into the market the significant produce of which they are capable. Most significantly, collective farms have been granted more autonomy in selecting the products they are best able to provide rather than being required to produce a mixture of goods, some of which they are not able to produce efficiently. New concepts of quotas over a five year period have been adopted apparently guaranteeing to collective farms the opportunity to derive financial benefit from over production without having their quotas raised during this period. Finally, big new investments are to be made in agriculture, and a reappraisal of the entire *kolkhoz* scheme is in the works. For the present, the position of Soviet agriculture remains precarious.

Soviet Life and Culture

On the whole the everyday practices of Soviet society are not unlike those of any other national group. Personal relationships are those to be found among all people with habits of work and leisure intermixed. Education and probable military service are important facets of individual careers. There are many cultural pursuits, and literature, concerts, and ballets are high in Russian esteem. Sports are a major interest to many Soviet citizens. The typical Russian has the same daily concerns as those of any other nationality. Nevertheless, two peculiar aspects of the Soviet society must be emphasized, particularly in view of the pretensions of communist theory. The first is the pervasiveness of Communist Party influence in Soviet life. Not only are the government and the economy subservient to the Party, but the entire nature of the society and the relative position of each individual member are subject to the molding and dictation of the Party elite. Education, recreation, the arts, sports, religion, ethics, and even the family operate within the framework established by the leaders. The second unavoidable observation is the rather rigid class system which exists in the Soviet Union. Contrary to the communist claim of seeking to establish a classless society, the Party has succeeded in building a stratified caste structure permitting little social mobility and insuring distinct and increasing benefits for the higher classes. From the peasantry, through the workers, to the technicians, intelligentsia, and managerial cadres, and finally to the top Party elite, one can discern an influence and living standard differential more acute than that of any democratic-capitalist society which communists so condemn. One intriguing development of the last two decades is the rise to prominence of the technological and managerial aristocracy upon which the modern society depends so heavily, and which may in time challenge the leadership of the Party professionals. The lot of the lowest classes—the peasants and unskilled workers, those who were to be liberated from economic oppression, remains poor, and the glittering promises of communism must appear to them a deceitful hoax.

The formal educational structure of the Soviet Union is a combination of compulsory and permissive branches. It serves to provide the normal training of youth, but it also provides an arena for Marxist-Leninist indoctrination. Grades 1 through 7 are compulsory and state financed. The secondary school level of three years may be vocational, semi-professional, or college preparatory. Admission to this level and the particular training to be pursued is on the basis of academic excellence and political acceptability. At this plateau, and more particularly at the next higher level, sons and daughters of the Party elite receive preference in admission. The highest educational levels are the universities and technical institutes which a carefully selected number of graduates from the secondary program may attend. Graduates of the universities and institutes are, of course, destined for the upper reaches of the economy and government. Adult education courses, correspondence courses, and other supplementary training arrangements round out the formal educational edifice. There is an obvious contradictory element in the selective training of elite groups and the preservation of the proletarian theme of communism. Khrushchev attempted to unify the two by requiring work experience along with schooling for those at the secondary level and by giving preference in university admission to those who had been workers for two years. Factory managers complained of part time and untrained workers, professors complained of decreased academic attainment, students complained of being shunted into insignificant jobs and learning nothing of productive methods, and two-year workers could not compete adequately with recent graduates of secondary institutions in the tough university admission examinations. Khrushchev's successors scrapped the system.

Cultural pursuits have normally flourished in an atmosphere of freedom and individualism. Creativity in music and the arts usually demands the free play of initiative and ingenuity and the inspiration derived from unfettered investigation and expression. But in a totalitarian regime, such endeavors cannot be considered merely as individualistic efforts. Such individualism might take critical form and thus become unacceptable. In the Soviet Union, therefore, music, literature, painting, sculpture, and sports have frequently been considered to be not the artist's unique mode of expression, but activities in the service of the state and the Party. For internal purposes the creative artist must deal with proletarian themes and extol the virtues of the communist system, while in external competition Soviet athletes, singers, and dancers must exhibit the superiority of the socialist society over its decadent counterparts. Again we find a dichotomy between the leadership's desire to regiment the total social structure and to foster the conditions necessary to permit the natural development of artistic talent as a showcase of socialist supremacy.

Under Stalin controls were rigorous and those who did not hew to the Party's prescription of orthodoxy were liable to punishment. Even such a notable personage as the composer Dimitri Shostakovitch was not exempt from Stalin's ire. When the relaxation of tensions in Soviet society began under Khrushchev in the mid-1950s a softening of controls over intellectual and cultural endeavors—formerly exerted in the name of "socialist realism"—likewise occurred. Journalists, poets, and other writers began to feel that their exalted social and economic positions did not depend on a strict conformity to the Party line. Not fearing degradation or imprisonment, literary figures began to dissent, to criticize, to hold up to public view some of the more unsavory aspects of life under the dictatorship of the proletariat. Ilya Ehrenburg published his novel, *The Thaw*, a biting criticism of Stalin's regime and a commentary on life under his successor. Khrushchev himself authorized the publication of a poem by Yevgeney Yevtushenko ("Stalin's Heirs") which attacked the remnants of Stalinism which continued to plague the creative arts. Khrushchev also approved publication of *One Day in the Life of Ivan Denisovich* by Alexander Solzhenitsyn, a graphic description of existence in a Stalinist prison camp. It can be appreciated that since the bulk of the criticism was directed at Stalin and was in line with the de-Stalinization program it was more readily acceptable to the current crop of Soviet chiefs.

Once the blinders are taken off, however, once the air of free criticism has been sniffed, it is not easy to hold the line on what constitutes acceptable criticism. Interpreting limited liberty as critical license proved to be unhealthy for Soviet artists. Only shortly after the publication of his poem, Yevtushenko found himself the subject of criticism and threats for having published an autobiography abroad without prior Party censorship. Similarly, Khrushchev lashed out at the emulators of Solzhenitsyn who, he claimed, were flooding the market with works on the labor camp theme. The then Soviet dictator made it clear to writers that they were stepping dangerously close to the boundary of impermissibility. Perhaps the *cause célèbre* of the resurgence of controls was the case of Boris Pasternak. Capped by his novel *Doctor Zhivago*, Pasternak's work was awarded the Nobel Prize for literature in 1958. *Doctor Zhivago*, however, was critical of the revolution and the ensuing system, and it had been published abroad. As a result Pasternak was hounded and criticized in the press, expelled from the Writer's Union, and told that he could go abroad only if he did not return. He declined the prize.

The new breed of Soviet leadership represented by Brezhnev and Kosygin presumably are realists, freed to some extent from the imperative search for conformity of the Stalin era, and lacking the blustering emotionalism of Khrushchev. They are leaders of a U.S.S.R. which has matured, industrialized, advanced technically, and loosened the reins of the police state. Seemingly, they more than their predecessors can afford to be lenient in the matter of cultural controls. But even at the 23rd Party Congress in 1966 new charges of unacceptable behavior were flung at various writers, and the omens appeared to point to a continuing era of tightened controls in this area. The contemporary Soviet Union has not thrown off all the shackles of the Stalin legacy.

STUDY QUESTIONS AND PROJECT SUGGESTIONS

1. What are the environmental and historic factors which have contributed to the nature of the contemporary Soviet Union?

2. Describe the formal political structure of the U.S.S.R.

3. Write an essay on the theme "The Myth and Reality of Individual Rights in the Soviet Union."

4. What are the external and internal implications of Soviet constitutionalism?

5. Outline the basic structure of the Communist Party of the Soviet Union.

6. Discuss briefly the nature of Soviet totalitarianism.

7. Outline the major characteristics of the Russian economy.

8. Discuss the problem of cultural creativity in a communist society.

CHAPTER 6

COMMUNISM— CHINESE MODEL

Since 1958–59 the world has witnessed the spectacle of a major rift in the apparent solidarity of the two communist giants, the Soviet Union and Red China (People's Republic of China). Speculation as to the exact nature of the schism has been rife in view of the previous cohesion between the two. Was the split the result of conflicting national aspirations of two major powers? Was it a matter of spite growing out of the failure of the Soviet Union to fulfill completely the promises of assistance to Red China especially as regards development of nuclear weaponry? Was it a question of personal ambitions with the Chinese leader Mao Tse-tung attempting to supplant Khrushchev as the legitimate heir to Stalin's ideological leadership? Was it a power play with China seeking to establish itself as the Mecca of Communism around the world? Or was it a sincere and meaningful difference in ideology which could affect the subsequent development of world communism and have repercussions for the non-communist world? Because of the implications for the free world inherent in the continuing disagreement, and because of Red China's significance as an emerging world power, it behooves us to examine the character of Chinese communism, to note similarities and differences vis-à-vis the Russian type, and to venture some conclusions as to the ultimate significance of the current debate.

The Rise to Power

The Chinese Communist Party was formed in Shanghai in July 1921. In a sense, the impetus to the formation of the Party came from the activities and philosophy of Dr. Sun Yat-sen whose plea for a revolutionary nationalist movement to lift China out of its feudal condition and free it from warlord domination had been couched in democratic terms with socialist overtones. At that founding meeting Ch'en Tu-hsiu was chosen as General Secretary, and Mao Tse-tung was one of the delegates. The dual goals of participation in the bourgeois-democratic revolution and the ultimate establishment of the dictatorship of the proletariat were adopted, and a decision was reached that the Party should be organized along Bolshevik lines. The Second National Congress in 1922 pledged the abolition of private property and the gradual attainment of a communist society in China. At the Third Congress in June 1923 it was decided—partly at Stalin's urging—that communists should assist the Kuomintang (National People's Party of Sun Yat-sen and later Chiang Kai-shek) in a revolutionary united front but that the political and organizational independence of the Communist Party should be maintained. It was also at this Congress that Mao was elected to the Party's Central Committee. The Fourth Congress of 1925 discussed the role of the peasant in the revolutionary struggle but took no constructive action in this regard. The Fifth Congress in 1927 criticized the earlier decisions not to fight for the leading role in the revolutionary movement and not to satisfy the peasants' demand for land. Landlord rental property, the delegates concluded, should be confiscated. In the interim between the Fourth and Fifth Congresses Chiang Kai-shek's National Revolutionary Army (including communists) had embarked on an expedition to the North to unify the country and uproot the warlords. Before the objectives were totally attained, however, Chiang turned his attention to suppression of the communists instead, defeated the communist-oriented forces which rebelled in various cities, and emerged as the major Chinese political figure. Stalin, incidentally, did not intervene. Thus ended the first phase of the development of Chinese communism (1921–27), the founding of the Party and the First Revolutionary Civil War.[1]

The second phase—the Second Revolutionary Civil War (1927–37)—compasses a variety of doctrinal and tactical squabbles within the Party, Mao's establishment of the first "revolutionary base" in the countryside in southeast China (later joined by the forces of Chu Teh), the Japanese occupation of Manchuria (1931–32), the further harassment of communist forces by the Nationalist army, the "Long March" which took the Red forces into the northern reaches of China, and the Party's Sixth Congress which was held in Moscow in 1928. It was during this time that Mao rose to the top position (in 1935) among Chinese communists and concocted some of the basic principles of ideology and organization which have come to be known as Maoism. For example, Mao concerned himself extensively with the nature of the Party and the commitment of members, the training of cadres (leaders), "inner-Party rectification" (maintenance of orthodoxy), and the tactics necessary to achieve the Party's goals. The Japanese assault, especially after 1937, gave the Party the opportunity to attract a broader popular following as defenders of the homeland.[2]

The War of Resistance to Japanese Aggression (1937–45) constitutes the third phase in the ascendancy of the Chinese

---

[1] John W. Lewis, ed., *Major Doctrines of Communist China* (New York: W. W. Norton, 1964), pp. 12–13; 20–24.
[2] *Ibid.*, pp. 13–14; 24–28.

communists. It was an intriguing era in which all Chinese sought to repulse the invader, but in which the Nationalist and Red forces continued to fight each other. Two major developments during this period gave a strong impetus to the eventual victory of the communists: 1] Mao's guerrilla tactics were tested and perfected, and 2] the forces of Chiang were badly decimated by the Japanese army. The allied victory over Japan opened the door to the final development of Red China.

The years 1945–49 are designated by Chinese communist historians as the Third Revolutionary Civil War. It was a time in which neither treaty promises of support by the Soviet Union nor massive United States assistance could save Chiang from the ultimate debacle. Contrary to the implications of its international commitment to support the Nationalist regime, the Soviet Union withdrew its forces from Manchuria (sent in the last phase of WW II) in such fashion as to permit Red Chinese access to large stores of captured Japanese military equipment. Mao's forces quickly established themselves in Manchuria. The Kuomintang, meanwhile, seemingly unmindful of growing communist support, refused to adopt any measures which might have attracted peasant support to its side, took no steps to correct the inefficiency and corruption rampant within its ranks, and remained intransigent on any suggestion of cooperation with the communists. Several American overtures to settle differences, notably the mission of General George C. Marshall—later Secretary of State, proved fruitless. Several billion dollars of American aid to the Nationalist cause was equally unavailing. Pushing out from their Manchurian stronghold, the communists nibbled at Chiang's army, isolated the cities, converted the peasantry to their side, and finally, in 1949, drove Chiang and the remnants of his forces off the mainland to the island of Formosa (Taiwan)—all with only moderate assistance from the Soviet Union. Still claiming to be the legal government of China, Chiang and his cohorts formalized the Formosa governmental arrangement and presented the world with the "two-China" problem which persists to the present. On October 1, 1949, the communist leaders proclaimed the existence of the People's Republic of China. The communists had gained their initial objective but were now faced with a new series of problems.

The communists were now on their own with no enemy to serve as scapegoat for failure. The first task, of course, was to consolidate their position. Then they had to eliminate bourgeois elements, effect land reform, rebuild a war-ravaged land, and introduce the socialist system. Many were the victims of this uprooting of the old, though the Red leaders were not so foolish as to eliminate immediately those members of the bourgeoisie whose services they could use. That Red China was becoming a power to be reckoned with was indicated by its intervention in the Korean conflict against United Nations forces in late 1950. In the mid 1950s the base for industrialization began to be laid, China made its voice heard on the international communist stage, and in 1957–58 major ideological and economic reforms were inaugurated, the repercussions of which are still being felt. In terms of its aspirations and its resources, Red Chinese history from that time to the present records achievements and failures. The transformation of the Chinese society into a communist model could not be expected to be an easy task. The change is not yet completed and may never be. An examination of the effort, however, can provide us with certain insights about Chinese communism and give a base for some speculation about the future.

Ideology and Tactics

Is there a uniquely Chinese version of communism? Does it differ radically from the Russian type? Has Marxism-Leninism been perverted, converted to meet new circumstances, abandoned, or merely modified nominally? Given the forementioned flexibility of communist ideology and the doctrinal shifts which occurred under various Soviet leaders it might be easily concluded that it makes little difference in terms of dogma what the Chinese communists say or do. On the other hand, the communist concern with ideology and the constant justification of action in terms of the credo make the Chinese experience of more than passing interest. Whether deviations are a matter of deep-seated principle or serve merely as a basis for leadership competition, their impact cannot be overlooked.

Though much of the "originality" of its ideology and practice can be traced back to Engels, Lenin, and Stalin, there is little question that Chinese communism differs in some respects from that of the senior member of the communist clan. To begin with, Mao, even more than Lenin, saw Marxism merely as a guide to action, not a rigidly confining body of doctrine. Acceptance of the Marxian premises of the class conflict and proletarian uprising would have made it practically impossible for Mao to succeed. Thus necessity became the urge to doctrinal deviation—and brought more clearly into focus the fiction of communism's dogmatic certainty. Yet the deviations themselves continued to be explained as "proper" interpretations of Marxism-Leninism as applied in the peculiar Chinese circumstances. The desire to achieve communism in a shorter span of time has also led to novel experiments which have stretched the bands of flexibility almost to the point where they represent an abandonment of principle. Nevertheless, every effort—no matter how tortuous—is made to describe directional changes as remaining within the bounds of the communist creed.

As regards the formal organization of the Chinese Communist Party—as outlined in the Party Constitution of 1956, there is a great deal of similarity to that in the Soviet Union. The Party is structured as a pyramid rising from the base of rank and file members to the apex of the Standing Committee of the Political Bureau headed by Mao as Party leader. Various committees and congresses exist at all levels supposedly elected from below. Youth groups serve as introductory reservoirs for future Party members. As in the U.S.S.R. the principle of democratic centralism prevails which, in reality, means that lines of authority run from the top down. There is a large coincidence of

Party and government office-holders. Party solidarity is a constant theme of indoctrination, and conflicting interests and the formation of cliques are not tolerated. Much of Party practice does not differ significantly from that of the Russian model, but other techniques and objectives have a special Chinese stamp. As the revolutionary ferment out of which Red China emerged is only two decades in the past, and since most of today's Party members did not participate in the revolution, Chinese Party leadership is much more inclined than the Soviet to foster and perpetuate the revolutionary spirit which they shared and which they find lacking in younger members. Thus, while Mao and his colleagues are not unmindful of the multiplicity of problems involved in transforming their traditional society, a disproportionate amount of time and effort seems to be spent in inculcating the spirit of struggle and tension in Party life—in strengthening a revolutionary fervor in a post-revolutionary environment. This is less a concern with ideology per se than it is with the fostering of the enthusiasm and self-sacrifice engendered by thorough commitment to an ideology.

The special nature of the environment from which the Chinese communists sprang gave to their development a Leninist cast. Almost from its earliest beginnings the Party viewed itself as a professional revolutionary group rather than as a vehicle for the masses. Certainly as it suffered reverses in the mid-1920s it became even more closely knit and highly militant—a posture which characterizes the Party even today when it criticizes the Soviet Union's concept of peaceful coexistence with capitalist powers. Therefore, considerable attention has always been given to the organization of the Party in which the objective of seizing power was always predominant. Party leaders were aware that this was the primary goal—as Lenin had insisted, so such matters as the correct proletarian nature of the Party and other niceties of Marxist doctrine were relegated to a secondary position.

In molding the organization the Chinese communists have concentrated on cadres—the term which they use to describe leaders at various levels in the hierarchy. Particularly since they were attempting to gather an effective revolutionary force from masses of people who were mostly illiterate and certainly ideologically uninitiated, Party leaders had to place great reliance on those who were to serve as their lieutenants. Such persons, then, were carefully selected, rigorously trained, thoroughly indoctrinated, continuously watched and counseled, corrected when necessary, and removed if they persisted in error. As cadres showed loyalty, obedience, and ability they advanced in the ranks; if they failed to live up to expectations they were ultimately dropped.

Together with this emphasis on the superiority of cadres the Chinese Communist Party, much more than the Soviet Party, evolved a distinct "inner-party style." While it is not unusual in communist ranks to indulge in criticism and self-criticism, the lengths to which this has been carried in China are phenomenal. There are constant meetings of Party members—usually in small groups for closer scrutiny in which the process of "thought rectification" occurs. This may well have the effect of imprinting indelibly on members' minds the Party line, and may lead to a ready acceptance of leaders' explanations of tactical deviations, but, by encouraging questions and criticisms, it also gives cadres an opportunity to weed out the less loyal and the less steadfast. Interestingly enough, the process of criticism and self-examination among members does not appear to be designed particularly to eliminate the unfit. Instead, it seems to be a genuine effort to detect error in thought or action and by ideological and moral pressures to bring those who err back to the right path. The inner-party style is not dedicated, however, to any mere rote learning of traditional Marxist clichés or to implanting in members' minds a sense of their own imperfections. This is no simple imitation of Bolshevik practice or enshrining of the Soviet model. Rather, the emphasis in these sessions is on the application of the principles of Marxism-Leninism to Chinese conditions. Such discussions serve the dual purpose of bringing members to grips with the special problems of utilizing communist doctrine in a unique setting and rearing the image of the Party leaders as preeminent communist oracles.

Other characteristics of Chinese communism are also manifestations of the circumstances in which the Party was born and grew. A capacity for temporizing is self-evident. Not only because of their small numbers and political weakness, but because of their impression of the Marxist doctrine of revolutionary progression Chinese communists first joined forces with the Kuomintang so that the bourgeois-democratic revolution could be accomplished prior to the initiation of the socialist revolution. Though, during this period, the communists sought to maintain a separate identity, they did not press for leadership in the revolution. Similarly, it is obvious that Party leaders were possessed of a great deal of perseverance and hardiness. Though battered by Chiang's forces in the 1920s and harassed in the 1930s, communist chiefs and their supporters resolutely undertook the Long March to safer territory, patiently built their organization, and carefully took advantage of every opportunity that the Japanese invasion offered.

Resort to guerrilla warfare was another logical expression of the communist position. Nationalist forces controlled the cities so the Red Chinese took to the countryside; Chiang's troops were mass armies which the communists were too few to confront; partisan tactics of hit and run were called for. The guerrilla technique had several advantages, however, which the communists were quick to apprehend. Being in the rural areas the Reds were in the best position to attract the peasants whose dissatisfaction with land tenure and landlords could be turned into a potent revolutionary force. Communist presence in the hinterland was a constant reminder that the Kuomintang armies were unable to exert total control over China; an image of communist invincibility could thus be created. Operating in small groups, striking and retreating, avoiding head-on battle with superior forces, the Red Chinese were able to inflict casualties on their enemies at relatively small costs to themselves. Thus the spirit and tactics of partisanship—spawned of compulsion—

became an ingrained aspect of procedure which persists in communist thought even though it is no longer requisite on the mainland. The concept does have continuing significance, of course, for the Chinese-inspired revolutionary movements in other countries.

Communist relations with the peasants is one of the singular aspects of Maoism. Again, an inescapable reality became in time an article of faith. Marxist—and even Leninist—theory envisioned revolution as stemming from proletarian uprising. The industrial workers under communist leadership were to sweep the capitalists from the scene. In China, however, the industrial proletariat was so minute as to be incapable of forming even a nucleus for upheaval. Chinese communists then had little alternative but to turn to the peasant masses for support. The long-standing desire for land reform could replace proletariat economic dissatisfaction as the revolutionary motive. This is not to say that industrial workers were ignored or that the communists did not play on their unrest in traditional fashion, but the masses in China were of a different order. Much as Lenin thought about the factory workers, however, Mao believed that peasants did not possess an innate revolutionary zeal which would lead to the overthrow of the bourgeois state and the installation of the socialist system. It was necessary in Mao's opinion for a revolutionary ideology to be consciously introduced by an outside intelligentsia—this time from the cities. The Party then becomes—as in the Soviet Union—the unquestionable source of definition of proper revolutionary spirit and behavior.

Several corollaries follow. If the Party is the sole interpreter of the objective realities which must be dealt with, the lone arbiter of socialist morality and tactics, it becomes practically infallible, since even past mistakes, when attributed to specific individuals and when "corrected," are part of the constantly evolving pattern of development by which the collective Party leadership in its omniscience is creating the proper socialist society. Any objection to prevailing policy—even one which ultimately fails

—becomes, by definition, heretical. Since the Party is constructed on authoritarian principles, its role as the source of ideological accuracy naturally enhances the position of the leader. To be sure, democratic centralism implies a collectivity of decision-making, but, as we have seen, collegiality of leadership has been a front for dictatorship. In Mao's case the reality of power has been buttressed by the building of an image to justify his omnipotence. He is pictured as the wise father, the dedicated scholar, the practical peasant, the practicing athlete, and the humble servant of his people shunning the adulation of his public. And to the extent that he has served as an effective leader for the communist cause, the image is not difficult for the Chinese people to accept. Finally, if the Party defines what is right ideologically and practically, any tactic ordered is ethically justifiable. The history of the Chinese Communist Party is replete with examples of typical police state tactics. Campaigns of terrorism, forced resettlement programs, involuntary labor camps, heavy doses of propaganda, and periodic purges and individual liquidations have been common since the establishment of the People's Republic. Somewhat surprisingly, however, Party leaders have not been unequivocally devoted to the elimination of class enemies. They have exerted a great deal of energy in attempting to convert bourgeois elements in the society to communism—and with moderate success. Not wishing to lose the talents of various entrepreneurs, but not being able to accept their "exploiting" position, Chinese communists embarked on a scheme of indoctrination which made converts —perhaps because the alternative to conversion was not particularly attractive.

Other aspects of Chinese communism illustrate similarities and differences vis-à-vis the Soviet system. One notable distinction in the Chinese model has been the emphasis placed on linking communism with Chinese nationalism (though in World War II the Russian leaders found it practical—if not essential—to make a patriotic appeal to the people to stem the Nazi tide). In the beginning the Red Chinese did not picture themselves so much the vanguard of a new economic system as they did the representatives of those who wished to overthrow the warlord system and unite China as a national entity. Subsequently they declared themselves in opposition to the Chiang regime as unable to create a unified China or to satisfy the economic and social aspirations of the bulk of the people. In more recent times it became evident that Chinese objectives have been less communistic than they have traditionally nationalistic in that they wished to recreate the domain and the influence of the ancient Chinese empire or at least achieve the status of major power in the modern world. In two additional respects the Chinese and Russian versions of communism are similar. Chinese communism like its Russian counterpart is totalitarian. Not only does it hold the reins of political and economic power, but it demands complete subservience of all societal relations. Intellectuals and artists must reflect in their work the communist ideal or risk suppression or punishment. Family life, traditionally so significant to the Chinese, has been subjected to the disruption occasioned by Party experiment. Work experience is held to be imperative for a true appreciation of communist values. Mao, like Khrushchev, has spoken often of the importance of physical toil. While neither completely disparaged intellectual endeavor, both believed that manual labor was an essential ingredient in the development of a good communist. Only by experiencing the workers' lot, said Mao, can the individual begin to understand nature and man's relationship to his natural surroundings.

Once in power the Chinese Communist Party had to translate theory and slogans into a practical socialist society. Agricultural production was (and remains) inadequate to feed China's millions, and land reform—though badly needed—offered no ready solution to the problem of providing more food. The industrial plant was primitive, but the Chinese communists were as determined as their Soviet neighbors to create in China a modern industrialized society. All of the propagandistic and coercive maneuvers of the Party were applied to enlist popular cooperation in developing the socialist economy, and shortly a series of five-year-plans was inaugurated. The Chinese were assisted in their economic endeavors when they negotiated in 1950 a mutual assistance pact with the Soviet Union. The pact proclaimed the common revolutionary heritage of the two nations and established a military alliance of frightening proportions for the free world. But most important from the Chinese viewpoint were the provisions relating to economic assistance, loans, and the supplying of technical advisers. This was not a one-sided proposition since the Soviet Union stood to benefit on the world scene from the rapid development of a major partner in the communist camp. Nevertheless, the Soviet masters must have had some reservations about an arrangement with a regime which had reached power with a minimum of Russian assistance and by means unorthodox in Soviet eyes. There may have been further doubts about aiding the development of a major nation with geographic and other ambitions in the Soviet Union's back yard. Be that as it may, with Soviet help the Chinese communists made initial strides in the building of their model. Little by little progress was made toward planned goals, but, as in Russia, the price paid by the people was high. Many disputes obviously existed regarding plans and techniques, but despite uncertainty and opposition China was slowly socialized. The degree to which insecurity and dissatisfaction existed, even within communist ranks, as the march to socialism proceeded was stunningly exhibited in 1956 and 1957 by which time considerable economic progress had been made.

Announced as a program for ideological development, a new plan of self-examination was encouraged with the theme "let a hundred flowers blossom, a hundred schools of thought contend." The scheme was consistent with the long-standing principle of criticism and self-criticism, but it seemed to have a different significance. Was it designed to stir the flagging enthusiasm of the people? Was it prompted as a method for "letting off steam" to blunt a rising sense of dissatisfaction with the regime? Was it an indication that Party leaders believed themselves so solidly entrenched that they could afford the luxury of ideological debate? Or was it a subtle way of uncovering the real dissidents who remained undetected so long as the demand for orthodoxy required their silence? Subsequent pronouncements by the leadership appeared to emphasize the idea of rebuilding ideological fervor, and the flowers of criticism blossomed, but the final act in the drama spotlighted the danger of open dissent. In 1957—about a year after the inauguration of the program—the government suddenly turned on its detractors. There followed a purge of the intellectuals which left little doubt that the definition of orthodoxy remained a monopoly of the Party. Many teachers were removed from their posts; former leaders of "intellectual rectitude" were condemned and demoted; new guidelines were set down limiting the nature of acceptable criticism; Mao emerged as the sole purveyor of the proper communist gospel. The whole episode reaffirmed the nature of the Communist Party leadership, but also brought to light the large amount of disagreement over policy and practice.

The next momentous development was enunciated in 1958, by which time the first indications of the Sino-Soviet rift had been seen. This was the so-called "Great Leap Forward," a program of economic and social reorientation of gigantic proportions in which expanded industrialization was the prime target. Apparently conceived as the Chinese desire to accomplish in a decade that which it had taken the Soviet Union over thirty years to achieve and, at the same time, to demonstrate the innate superiority of the Chinese system, the plan was a blueprint for "leaping over objective conditions" to the higher stage of communism without waiting for the full development of socialism. (The Soviet Party leaders had always contended that the ideal of the communist society could not be reached until the socialist system had come to full fruition.) The core of the Great Leap was to be the establishment of "people's communes" —involuntary village style cooperatives in which up to 5000 families would be joined together for productive endeavor. The communes were to be, however, not merely the sites of all-out economic effort from which private ownership was banned but the arenas for novel social experiments. The economic aspects of the arrangement consisted primarily of collectivized agriculture and "cottage industries"—what have been referred to as "backyard steel mills." Lacking adequate capital to broaden the base of industrial production through the creation of major manufacturing enterprises, as much as they desired to do so, the Chinese hoped to up total production from the contributions of many small plants. Socially, the commune system dealt a harsh blow to the traditional concept of the peasant household. Barracks living replaced the individual family unit; women were to be utilized as laborers, and nurseries were created for the care of the young; public mess halls were to be used for common dining. In addition to their normal work load, members of the communes also had the responsibility for becoming part of a peasant militia as a complement to the regular armed forces. The extent to which the communist ideal was to be stressed in the communes was exemplified by the fact that there were to be no money wages paid and the principle of "from each according to his ability, to each according to his needs" was to be implemented. The high hopes which the Chinese Communist Party held for this ambitious plan were not to be fulfilled despite initial enthusiasm and some moderate successes.

The Soviet leaders who observed this development pointed out disparagingly—though accurately—that communism of this sort could only have its base in an economy of abundance not one of scarcity. They noted further that their own experiences with communes had convinced them that the level of production in Soviet society was inadequate to support the ideal— clearly implying that the Chinese economy which lagged far behind that of the U.S.S.R. was much less able to conduct the experiment successfully. Fear and compulsion can, of course, command adherence to pattern despite its proven inadequacies, and the Chinese leaders have not officially renounced either the principles or the practices of the Great Leap Forward. In reality it has undergone significant modification. The production expectations were never reached, and the discontent of the people with the social distortions caused distinct renovations. Agricultural production was seriously hampered by drought and other natural disasters leading to famine conditions in many parts of the country. In an effort to overcome failures and to bolster the sagging economy, Party bosses have more recently decided on a program of mass transportation of agricultural workers to industrial sites when planting and harvesting seasons do not require their presence. To what extent this utilization of non-specialized labor in industrial work will contribute to total production remains to be assessed fully.

The most striking internal development in Communist China since the Great Leap is perhaps the most confusing and the least explicable in the history of the People's Republic. In 1966 the Great Proletarian Cultural Revolution was broadcast—the ramifications of which have not been completely probed in early 1969. The Cultural Revolution appears to have had its origin in the Socialist Education Movement instigated in 1963. Like the "hundred flowers" experience this latter move showed the continuing concern of the leadership with proper ideological indoctrination. But like the earlier program it was destined to produce unexpected results. A supposed economic motivation behind the Revolution was the previously noted scheme of mass movement of workers from farm to factory and back, but there were persistent hints that political and ideological motives were more prominent than economic, and the intensity of the upheaval which followed was as frightening as it was obscure in intent. As a matter of fact, at this writing, it is questionable whether Red Chinese leaders unleashed in the Cultural Revolution a force which they can again control and manipulate.

By late 1965 evidences of political shuffling and a major purge became apparent though only minimum publicity was given to the changes. By mid-1966 the force of the eruption was unmistakable. In June of that year the Red Guards were created under the sponsorship of Madame Mao-Chiang Ch'ing. The guiding spirit of the Guards, however, was one soon to be elevated to public prominence—Lin Piao. The Red Guards consisted of boys and girls in their teens or early twenties, attired in military type uniforms with distinctive arm bands, entrusted with preserving the spirit of the communist revolution and enshrining Mao as its leader. When properly instructed and loosed on the population, the Red Guards embarked on a frenzied attack on all things Western and an orgy of violence directed against anyone or anything not consistent with "Mao-think." Street names were arbitrarily changed, clerics were abused, demonstrations were held, intellectuals—as well as workers and peasants—were denounced and physically mistreated, schools were emptied, the Guards became practically a law unto themselves, and their famous wall posters became the leading source of ideological orthodoxy. The picayunishness of many of their attacks and the capriciousness of many of their concerns were indicative of the high emotionalism which had been stirred and the minimum of limitation which had been placed on their behavior.

It is not surprising in this atmosphere that Western analysts had difficulty in discerning the real meaning of the Cultural Revolution. It is equally unsurprising that the frequently meaningless spectacle elicited the practically unanimous condemnation of the other members of the communist camp. Had the Chinese leaders lost control or was this all a conscious device to attain a particular objective? Did the movement have its origin in a power plan against Mao or was Mao resigning his leadership, with the struggle manifesting the competition for his mantle? Was Mao himself using the Cultural Revolution as a cover for a drastic new purge? Was it merely an additional tactic for invigorating youth along communist lines? What relation did it all have to Sino-Soviet relations? It is doubtful that we can be certain as to the motives behind or the results of this amazing occurrence. Certain speculations can be advanced, however, on the basis of available evidence. One fact emerging from the period of the Revolution is the demotion of Liu Shao-ch'i. Having long served as President of the People's

Republic Liu was always thought to be the heir apparent to Mao. The leadership hierarchy announced in 1966 dropped Liu at least to seventh place and raised General Lin Piao to the number two spot. By late 1968 Liu had been read completely out of the Party and deprived of all power. Whether Liu—almost as aged as Mao—was thought to have outlived his usefulness, or whether Mao detected in Liu a threat to his position has not been clarified. It is clear that Lin Piao is apparently devoted to Mao and that even as a military leader he espouses the doctrine of putting politics in the most prominent place—the philosophy that ideological knowledge is the key to success in practical endeavor. He is also an apostle of self-criticism, a devotee of further class eradication (officially even of officer ranks in the army), and a supporter of the practice of informing on those with bourgeois tendencies. It could well be that Mao saw in Lin a clearer reflection of his own thoughts than he did in Liu. That the excesses of the Cultural Revolution were contrived rather than accidental likewise seems logical. Little attempt was made to clamp down on the rampaging youth. There is no doubt that students and others were stimulated to a higher reverence for Mao. There is no question that Mao is still in control. Thus the whole move bears the imprint of Mao's decision as a means to self-enhancement and renewed revolutionary vigor.

At the Ninth Congress of the Chinese Communist Party in April 1969 Mao's continuing leadership was emphatically affirmed, and Lin's elevation to the second position as Mao's successor was confirmed. Premier Chou En-lai was designated as third in the hierarchy. Liu's name, as well as those of other former prominent Party members, was not even listed among the 176 members chosen to the Congress presidium. Mao and Lin both gave important speeches praising the Cultural Revolution, and Mao's thought was equated with Marxism-Leninism The Congress also adopted a "new" constitution and selected a new central committee reflecting the rise or decline of individuals in Mao's esteem.

And yet the full and exact meaning of the whole political circus remains clouded. With some difficulty the ardor of the Red Guards has been dampened and the students have been ordered back to school. The army has been authorized to restore order where strife and chaos still prevailed. Personnel changes in the Party's upper echelons have been accomplished. From a more cynical viewpoint, the attention of the people has been distracted from economic and social failures. The Chinese revolutionary spirit has been demonstrated for Soviet viewers. But whether imbuing youth with the rebellious zeal shown in the Cultural Revolution will foster repercussions unforeseen by their tutors remains to be seen.

The Sino-Soviet Schism

Red China's foreign policy, like that of all other nations, is a reflection of its own assessment of its interests and a product of its peculiar historical heritage. In foreign affairs each nation must arrive at a definition of its national interests, weigh them in terms of the international environment in which they are to be pursued, and determine strategies and tactics which will best forward those interests within the limitations imposed by the international milieu. In the case of the Chinese Reds the overriding factors in policy determination would seem to be the nature of the communist ideology which supposedly guides their actions, the revolutionary motif which marked their rise to power, and their relations with the other states in the communist world. (Presumably they would be opposed to all capitalist powers, join with other communist states in confronting the capitalist-imperialists, and seek to foment communist upheavals throughout the world.) Certainly these factors are weighty in Red China's deliberations on foreign policy matters, but they cannot be accepted as the total determinants of her external policy. Chinese communists are the descendants of many generations of other Chinese whose socio-politico-economic outlook was quite different and whose attitude toward the world was shaped by long historical experience. The current generations may be communist, but they are still Chinese, and it would be misleading to attempt to analyze contemporary policy exclusively in terms of communist orientation.

Red China is heir to the tradition of ancient Chinese empires and imperial dynasties which persisted through the 19th century. Chinese communists are the legatees of a cultured and sophisticated society which considered all of those outside its vast domain as barbarians, and to the arrogance and haughtiness of Chinese aristocracy. They have inherited the memory of large slices of territory hacked away by other powers (including Russia) for over a century. They can recall very vividly the trade concessions and spheres of influence granted to Europeans and Americans by China at the point of a gun, the forced acceptance of the right of extraterritoriality for foreign nationals accused of crimes, the repeated military incursions from abroad during the 19th and 20th centuries. The Russo-Japanese war of this century involved territory claimed by China (Manchuria); Korea fell to Japanese control early in the century; German concessions in China were turned over to the Japanese after World War I; later there came the actual invasion of China by Japan; after World War II various awards of territory and influence were made to the Soviet Union at China's expense. It is certainly no wonder that contemporary Chinese are well aware of the nature of imperialism and the fact that industrial weakness was a major cause of China's troubles. It is impossible, therefore, to dissociate Chinese communists from this legacy. Both Chiang and Mao have made reference to irredentist territories; even without the impetus of this claim, it would be ridiculous to discount the natural territorial ambitions of a rising national power. Chinese xenophobia is a logical outgrowth of centuries of experience. That China might now wish to carve out its own spheres of influence is quite understandable in the light of its past.

It is essential to keep this historical perspective in mind when trying to analyze Red China's foreign policy. This is not to discount the impact of the communist philosophy as motivation nor to discard the goal of world communist domination as a hope, but it is to recognize—as was noted previously about the Soviet Union—that China is a national state, reared in the traditions of a nation-state system, equipped with the experiences, fears, and aspirations of other nations, and urged to customary national objectives. It is to remember that while the Soviet Union is a communist affiliate and a recent source of military and economic assistance, it is also a nibbler at Chinese territory for over two centuries, it is a powerful neighbor, it is a state whose leadership failed to grant all the aid desired by Chinese communists, and it is a contender for territory and influence in the same geographic sphere. The importance of this recognition for the free world lies in the proper assessment of Chinese (and Russian) motivations and actions—as well as Sino-Soviet relations, and effecting the proper response on the international scene. Concepts of communist theory and ill-considered emotional reaction to the "communist menace" should not blind policy makers to the national interests involved.

The revolutionary effort which produced the People's Republic, though it had large popular support, was not acclaimed in democratic circles—in part, of course, because of its communist coloration. The United States, which had offered massive financial support to the Nationalist regime, refused to recognize the new government (continuing the legal fiction that Chiang's government spoke for the mainland), and a number of other states joined suit—though many others then and since have extended recognition. Despite the obvious *de facto* existence of the communist regime American action was prompted by Red China's belligerent attitude and its seeming unwillingness to respect its international obligations as a sovereign state—though it could well be argued that the American decision was made in no small measure with an eye on the domestic political scene. The American position was justified, however, by communist treatment of U.S. consular officials and confiscation of

American property. On the same grounds, America opposed Red China's entrance into the United Nations, and in early 1969 neither United States recognition nor U.N. membership has been accorded the People's Republic. To what extent this nominal exclusion from the international society has contributed to China's continued belligerency and vituperative foreign policy pronouncements remains debatable.

For whatever reasons, during the first dozen years of its existence the Chinese People's Republic was anything but peace loving and non-aggressive. By 1960 Red China had absorbed Tibet and become deeply involved in the Korean conflict against U.N. forces—ostensibly through the use of "volunteers." In Indo-China in 1952–53 she was supporting the communist forces of Ho Chi Minh in their efforts to oust the French and take over all of Vietnam. In 1954 she exerted influence in the Geneva Agreements which partitioned Vietnam and sought to extend her spiritual sway throughout southeast Asia, posing as the model for all Far East communists. By 1955 she threatened an invasion of Formosa which was stymied primarily by a U.S. congressional resolution authorizing the interposition of the U.S. Seventh Fleet between Red China and its target. In 1958 the offshore islands of Quemoy and Matsu still held by the Nationalists came under sporadic bombardment as though preparatory to an invasion attempt, but in time the harassment ceased. And in 1962 there was a serious border clash with India which fortunately did not grow to major proportions, though the issue of potential conflict remained unresolved. Currently there is evidence to suggest Chinese involvement on behalf of North Vietnam in its fight with South Vietnamese and American forces, but it appears that the North Vietnamese are not simply the puppets of Red China. All of these actions have been accompanied by periodic enunciations of animosity toward the West, expositions of the theme of continuing communist revolution, feverish building of an industrial plant which could support aggressive action, and an intense drive to acquire nuclear weapons which has finally been achieved. It would not be illogical to conclude from these events and other actions of Red China in various parts of the world that she was committed to a course of expansion which must ultimately destroy world peace. It might seem that from ideologic or nationalist motives she could not be deterred from aggressive designs. But it must be remembered that, for the most part, Red China has drawn back from actions which might have precipitated the cataclysm of world war (an attitude matched by the U.S. as in the Korean conflict and by the Soviet Union in the Cuban missile crisis of 1962). She has been bumptious in adolescent fashion, but has shrewdly backed away from irreversible confrontation, with Korea as the notable exception. There has been a high degree of immaturity in her activities as she sought general recognition of the power position she has assigned herself, in which muscle flexing is a cover for lack of concrete achievement. Whether the external irresponsibility of immaturity can be displaced by internal developments (somewhat along the lines of Soviet experience), and whether Chinese leaders will be mollified by a sense of achievement for their people and an appreciation of their already significant *de facto* power position is still questionable and hinges largely on the Chinese communist ability to solve internal economic dilemmas.

During most of its early life the People's Republic of China acted in concert with the Soviet Union, depending heavily on its economic assistance, and accepting its leadership in the communist camp. The Sino-Soviet bloc appeared a monolith of philosophical unity and physical strength determined to spread the communist system around the world. A common foreign policy strategy seemed to underlie the individual actions of the two partners, and Marxist-Leninist doctrine looked like the guiding force. Even apparently antagonistic actions taken by either member of the axis were interpreted as deceptions designed to ensnare an unwary free society. But beginning in the mid-1960s clues began to be discovered which suggested that the superficial unity and the ready acceptance of Soviet leadership by the Chinese was more ephemeral than actual. The first evidence was not at all conclusive, and where it might be construed to indicate a break in unity, caution dictated an initial interpretation that this was a further attempt to delude a hopeful West. Though such an analysis is still not completely outmoded, the sequel to early Sino-Soviet disagreement argues strenuously for a reinterpretation of Russo-Chinese relations. Bonds of alliance remain strong, but deep-seated differences have produced marked cleavages in previously unified ranks. What are the origins and nature of the rift, and what are its implications for the Western world?

The first basis of disagreement arose in 1955 out of Khrushchev's attempt to reach a rapprochement with Tito's Yugoslavia which had been read out of the Marxist-Leninist circle by Stalin in 1948. In a sense this was a prelude to the de-Stalinization episode of the 20th Congress of the CPSU as it signified a rejection of one aspect of Stalin's policies. While not immediately apparent, Soviet relations with Tito were to become one item of interest to the Chinese, as they had opened the whole question of intra-bloc relations. It was in 1956, however, that the issues leading to disagreement were multiplied. Not only was the de-Stalinization campaign inaugurated, but the Soviet Union was faced with the monumental problems presented by its Polish and Hungarian satellites. De-Stalinization may have been directed against the cult of the individual or Stalin's abuse of power, but it inadvertently brought into question the whole theme of communist unity under Soviet hegemony (which theme was already being discussed against the background of the Yugoslav behavior) and the contribution made by the machinery of the dictatorship of the proletariat to Stalinist errors. Many, including the Chinese, believed that the anti-Stalinist campaign had obscured the positive aspects of Stalin's reign, cast doubt on the doctrine of proletarian dictatorship, and shaken the basis of worldwide communist unity. In the summer of 1956 the Poznan riots in Poland prefaced demands by the Polish leader Wladyslaw Gomulka for a redefinition of Russo-Polish relations in which the Poles would have a greater autonomy in their internal affairs. With Chinese backing Poland secured its objectives. Then in October 1956 the Soviet Union was faced with a still more significant issue—the revolt in Hungary. Should Soviet leaders compromise on the questions involved or should they crush the rebellion by force? Would the uprising—induced in part by U.S. propaganda—be supported by American arms? Perhaps recognizing Western involvement in the then existing Middle East crisis over the Suez Canal and counting on American reluctance to intervene, the Soviets resorted to forceful suppression of the revolt. In each of these instances—the Yugoslav détente, the de-Stalinization venture, the Polish affair, and the Hungarian crisis—the Chinese communists made themselves heard—not necessarily in an antagonistic vein, but in a voice which suggested new authority. Even while pleading for communist unity and ostensibly upholding Soviet leadership the Red Chinese implied that they held the formula for doctrinal rectitude. Chinese criticism of Yugoslavia led to a new excommunication in 1958 (but Tito was accepted back into the fold two years later); the Chinese stand restored to some degree the stature of Stalinism; Poland's internal autonomy was achieved with China's support; the decision to crush the Hungarian uprising was based in part on China's advice. Thus, while no split was evident this early, it was true that issues on which differing opinions were held were intruding on Sino-Soviet solidarity, and it became more and more apparent that Mao sought a stronger role in the partnership.

From 1957 on the disagreements grew although there were one or two instances when quarrels were temporarily patched up. In that year the Soviet Union's advances in rocketry and its successful launching of the first space vehicle prompted the Chinese to urge upon the U.S.S.R. a more vigorous antagonism toward the West. Khrushchev, however, did not wish to sacrifice his building of a détente with the West by assisting the Chinese in their aggressive adventures in the Far East. China was briefly satisfied with a promise of Soviet assistance in the development of its own nuclear weapons. Simultaneously the Chinese were proclaiming the superiority of their commune system as the model for achieving the highest stage of communism while Soviet leaders criticized both the conception and the inadequacies of the communes. The comparative failure of the experiment did nothing to ameliorate Sino-Soviet relations. Over the next two years intermittent sniping continued, and there were growing intimations that Soviet aid to Red China would be diminished and that Russia would demand from its partner renewed subservience. By 1959 a critical stage had been reached. Khrushchev reneged on his promise of aid in the development of atomic bombs, and in 1959–60 drastically curtailed economic assistance to the People's Republic and recalled Soviet technicians stationed there. This brazen attempt to force compliance with Soviet wishes was unsuccessful and widened the breach between the two. Mao responded by initiating a border incident with India, renewing Chinese demands for Taiwan, and condemning Khrushchev's talks with President Eisenhower at Camp David. Meanwhile charges and countercharges of dogmatism, sectarianism, adventurism, revisionism, left and right extremism, and Trotskyitism began to flow with greater rapidity. In June 1960 at the communist meeting in Bucharest Albania openly sided with the Chinese Communist Party thereby adding ideological support to the Chinese position. In November the Moscow conference, the realities of which were first blurred because of its secrecy, found delegates vitriolic in their mutual condemnations. The resulting pronouncement, however, stipulated a new phase of pacification within communist ranks in which ideological compromise had been the order of the day. The truce was not to last.

The 22nd Congress of the CPSU in 1961 was the occasion for new fireworks. Chou En-lai openly chastised Soviet leaders for their attacks on Albania, visited Stalin's grave, and departed. The dispute was further exacerbated the following year by the Chinese attack on India—against Soviet wishes, and by the Cuban missile crisis. The Indian skirmish was brief, but adequate to indicate Chinese ambitions, strength, and independence. The Cuban affair was a much more dangerous adventure with more significant repercussions. As part of its effort to extend its influence in the western hemisphere the Soviet Union had agreed to emplace intermediate range ballistic missiles in Cuba. Such missiles would have posed a distinct nuclear threat to much of the United States. President John F. Kennedy, when thoroughly apprised of the Soviet action, decided on the firmest of stands, and cautioned that any launching of missiles from Cuban sites to points anywhere in the hemisphere would be interpreted as Soviet aggression (see Chapter 8). The adamance of the American position convinced Khrushchev, and the missiles were withdrawn. The whole episode—initially approved by the Chinese—gave Peking another opportunity to accuse the Soviet Union of adventurism and to criticize the ignominious capitulation which caused communism such a loss of face.

Bitter exchanges followed into 1963, and the Chinese issued their "Proposal Concerning the General Line of the International Communist Movement," a lengthy document stating and justifying their ideological position. Sino-Soviet border disputes came out, and some Chinese diplomats were expelled from Moscow. Farther afield new efforts appeared on the part of the Chinese to splinter or subvert Soviet-dominated communist organizations in Asia and Africa and to replace them with Chinese-oriented organs. The highlight of the year in terms of the festering antagonism was probably the signing of the Nuclear Test Ban Treaty. Red China saw this as an attempt to shut it off from developing a nuclear capability and roundly condemned its erstwhile partner. From that point forward the gloves were off, and denunciations of either side by the other were much more scathing and personal than previously. Ideological differences, personal enmities, border disputes, economic dissatisfactions, atomic strategy, and the proper nature of the national liberation movements in Asia, Africa, and Latin America all emerged with greater clarity as issues involved in the rift. The most recent episode of antagonism occurred in March 1969 when border tensions in the far northeast erupted into a military clash between Chinese and Russian troops at Damansky island in the Ussuri river subsequently spreading to other border points. The results were inconclusive, but significant casualties were incurred on both sides which did nothing to abate the continuing antipathy. At this writing the strife and tension of the schism remains though a formal break in relations has thus far been avoided. The impact on the solidity of the world communist camp has, of course, been great.

Various interpretations may be made of the origins and nature of the Sino-Soviet split, and each has a kind of compelling logic. 1] The dispute may be viewed as having its roots in sincere ideological differences. One observer[3] has characterized the dogmatic issues as follows: a] the inevitability of war, with the Russians contending that changed circumstances have made this Leninist doctrine outmoded, and the Chinese contending that imperialism must ultimately be confronted by force; b] the efficacy of local wars, with the Soviets holding that today's power potentials make such "brush fire" conflicts too dangerous, while Red China argues that such affairs must and can be pursued without the danger of escalation into world war; c] the achievement of socialism through peaceful means, the Soviet Union insisting that the world environment now permits the peaceful road to socialism, and the Chinese being equally insistent that capitalist strength still requires the application of violence for its defeat; d] the desirability of peaceful coexistence, the Russians advocating this course from their position of relative power and growing affluence and wishing to demonstrate the superiority of the socialist economic system, and the Chinese leaders being willing to accept peaceful coexistence—if at all—only as a temporary expedient to lull the capitalist world while communist strength grows; e] the communist position relative to bourgeois liberation movements, the Soviets

---

[3] Edward Crankshaw, *The Observer* (February 12, 1961).

adopting an affirmative stand on the grounds that anything which tends to weaken the imperialist camp ultimately redounds to the benefit of the communist world, the Chinese expressing the view that this support actually undermines genuine (communist) revolutionary activity and postpones unnecessarily the attainment of the real objective—the creation of a socialist regime; and *f*] the proper Marxist interpretation of the contemporary scene, the Chinese suggesting that it is an era of wars and revolutions, the Russians viewing it as an epoch in which imperialism is disintegrating, the transition to socialism is accelerating, and the development of a world socialist system imminent. That these differences stem from the respective stages of development of the two communist giants is unmistakable. But whether the distinctions drawn are motivations to dispute or results of disagreement is not so clear. They could just as well be justifications for real animosity as they could be bases for hostility.

Surely other "ideologic" dissimilarities can be catalogued. The position of the peasantry in revolutionary upheaval is one. Did the core of communist rebellion have to be the industrial proletariat as Marx postulated, or could the peasantry serve in the same capacity as Mao demonstrated? Given what we know of Lenin's use of the peasants in his time, the question seems to be pedantic, but it has arisen prominently in the Sino-Soviet polemics. Was the attack on the cult of the individual a correct interpretation of Marxism-Leninism? Could the supposed excesses of a megalomaniac be separated from the institutions within which he acted, institutions which were essential elements for the building of the socialist society? Could the builder of socialism in one country be so reviled without casting doubt on the validity of the premises on which he acted? Mao—though no lover of Stalin—could respect his stature in the communist hierarchy and could follow his example in his own tactics. Was de-Stalinization then an attack on Mao as well? There were also differences over the right relations among "fraternal" communist parties. Was the Soviet Union right in tolerating Tito's desires for autonomy? The Chinese thought not. Should a redefinition of Russo-Polish relations be permitted? The Chinese believed that this was desirable. Should the Hungarian uprising be crushed by force or should issues be negotiated? The Chinese advised the application of force. Should Russian hegemony be the unquestioned order in communist ranks, or should there be the development of a community voice? While superficially supporting the former, Red China seems to be more dedicated to the latter.

2] The Sino-Soviet break may not be ideologic at all, but simply the expression of conflicting nationalisms. We have seen that both the Soviet Union and the People's Republic are typical nation-states regardless of their philosophical antecedents. They are motivated by the same considerations as non-communist states and possess ambitions having little to do with Marxist-Leninist doctrine. Assuring national security, enhancing economic position, expanding territorial domain, exerting external influence, and achieving historical prominence are aims which can and do exist independently of communist dogma. In the case of Sino-Soviet relations, these ambitions conflict at many points. A gain by one partner constitutes in the end a loss for the other. So long as the dominance of the Soviet Union was clearly recognized and Red China was content to accept the junior role in the partnership, the U.S.S.R. could afford to assist China and contribute to the building of its strength, because a unified communist front faced the free world with a much greater threat. But when Red China reached a stage of power development which allowed her to demand a greater voice in communist councils and permitted her to pursue her own ambitions, the Russians had to think twice about the stakes involved and decide whether a portrayal of communist solidarity took precedence over their own national interests. The evolution of the Sino-Soviet dispute argues strongly that national interest has won out over ideological unity.

3] It is conceivable that while ideology and national interests are both significantly present as issues in the debate, the basic motive may be more personal—a contest between Mao Tse-tung and the Soviet leaders for recognition as the legitimate head of world communism. There is, of course, tremendous prestige attached to such recognition, and the prestige can be translated into power. As a Marxist of long standing and the leader of his own successful communist revolt, Mao naturally saw himself as the heir to Stalin's position. Khrushchev's credentials, thought Mao, were not as good as his own, and Brezhnev's less so. When Khrushchev's policies seemed to Mao not only bad Marxism-Leninism but designed to stymie China's rise in communist decision-making, he was all the more convinced of the correctness of his position and determined to exert himself in accordance with his stature. There is in Mao's appraisal and action much more than a petty search for adulation. Vanity may well be involved, but the competition incorporates more than this personal satisfaction.

4] A final analysis involves a particularization of the broader theme of conflicting nationalisms. Red China did not begin its existence on a very sound economic base. It was a backward agricultural society plagued with food shortages, its industrial plant was primitive, and it had to contend with the ravages of World War II and its own civil conflict. As a communist state it expected assistance from the senior member of the camp, and its expectations were initially fulfilled in the 1950 pact. But the Red Chinese were in a hurry, they wished to attain an equality with the Soviet Union in a minimum of time; they were not ready to accept indefinitely a minor position in the alliance. They were especially anxious to achieve membership in the exclusive nuclear club—to exert the influence which the possession of atomic armaments insured. As the Soviet leaders watched the growing strength of the People's Republic and sensed the danger to their own position, they developed a greater reluctance to contribute to the evolution of a monster which could eventually threaten them. In China's eyes, then, the discontinuance of economic assistance, the withdrawal of technicians, and the refusal to assist in the creation of a nuclear capacity constituted a violation of a solemn commitment, a betrayal of communist unity, and a personal affront. It raised for the Red Chinese the spectre of a Russo-American agreement aimed at the isolation of the People's Republic and its economic strangulation.

There is no question that, whatever the reasons, Sino-Soviet relations have deteriorated badly over the last decade. Suspicions that the disagreements were a smoke screen to hide a continuing solidarity, a lure to delude an unsuspecting free world have now been laid. Conflicts between the two, having been subjected to rigorous analysis, have proved to be real and frequently intense. This fact should not be cause for unrestrained joy in the non-communist world; it should not obscure another fact of equal importance. While we have insisted that communist affiliation should not be assumed to override pressures of national concern or personal animosity, it would be equally foolhardy to ignore the actuality of doctrinal affinity or the reality of the community of interests shared by the U.S.S.R. and Red China. The developing nations in Asia, Africa, and Latin America offer a fertile field for communist agitators; a unified effort is preferable to a competitive one. Communist leaders are not so foolish as to sacrifice a joint gain to satisfy personal pique. When the stakes are sufficiently large, it can still be expected that the communist world will act in concert. The rift has brought realignments of loyalties, and differences may be exploited by the West to its advantage, but common national or ideological interests continue to hold the world communist movement at least loosely together.

STUDY QUESTIONS AND PROJECT SUGGESTIONS

1. Outline the historical developments which culminated in the rise to political power of the Chinese communists.
2. Detail the ideological differences between the Russian and Chinese versions of communism.

3. What is the nature and meaning of the "Great Proletarian Cultural Revolution"?

4. A. What are the reasons underlying the current Sino-Soviet rift?

   B. On what bases may a rapprochement be effected?

5. To what extent is Red China's foreign policy dictated by traditional imperialist aspirations as contrasted with communist ideology?

6. A. Analyze the reasons for U.S. refusal to recognize Red China.

   B. Is it in American interest to continue to withhold recognition of the communist regime?

CHAPTER 7

COMMUNIST
INTERNATIONALISM

Communist theory has been international from its inception. As envisioned by Karl Marx communism was a class doctrine which overrode national loyalties and flowed across geographic boundaries. It was and is the ultimate objective of communism to create those conditions in which the national state—having outlived its usefulness—will disintegrate. Nevertheless, the national entity has been a constant context for communist action. Marx—although internationalist in outlook—believed that the first communist uprising would occur in Germany and then infect neighboring states. Stalin built socialism in one country. Mao worked within the framework of the Chinese state. Other communist parties though nominally subservient to Moscow have tended to retain their own national idiosyncrasies. This interaction of nationalism and internationalism is an intriguing feature of communist history and gives perceptions which throw additional light on the realities of the communist world. To what extent has the communist tenet of internationalism and class unity submerged centuries old national leanings? To what degree have communist leaders placed dedication to dogma above national responsibilities? Have doctrinal debates and maneuvers reflected serious thought regarding doctrinal interpretations or have they represented efforts to rationalize nationalistic decisions on dogmatic grounds? Does the international class concept assure a solidity of purpose, a unity of thought, and concert of action for communists everywhere? The answers to such questions are enlightening, but to arrive at them a brief examination of the internationalist history of communism is required. One important point to be kept in mind as we proceed is that communist internationalism has taken distinctly different forms at different times. We will pursue the implications of this variety of international arrangements.

The Internationals

The first formal international communist organization was the Communist League of 1848 formed in London by English, French, and Belgian communists out of which came the *Communist Manifesto*. This body was important as a manifestation of communism's international character, and its program—the *Manifesto*—remains the communist bible. However, the League was banned in France and Germany, and Marx and other leaders disagreed on tactics. The upshot was that the headquarters was transferred from London to Cologne where Marx had supporters, and within two years, for all practical purposes, the Communist League became moribund, and communist activities continued along national lines.

It was roughly fifteen years later that the second major step in international organizing occurred. London was again the scene of a meeting in 1864 among representatives of French, German, British, Italian, Swiss, and Polish workers to discuss the practice of importing cheap foreign labor. The meeting produced the International Federation of Working Men subsequently to be known as the First International. Marx became a member of its fifty-five member General Council. At the International's second congress at Geneva in 1865 it adopted a set of statutes drafted by Marx which mirrored the revolutionary outlook and the call for class solidarity of the *Manifesto*. For several years thereafter the International held annual congresses at which theory and strategy were discussed, but neither Marx nor Engels attended which seems to attest their dissatisfaction with the International as a suitable instrumentality for communist purposes though they could accept the organization as a symbol of the unity of the working classes. The major difficulty facing the International (and one which has persisted to the present) was the fact that despite the protestations of unity, the opinions of members were shaped basically by their respective national heritages and their unique political and economic problems. British trade unionism and limited economic objectives, for example, did not accord with German radicalism or French anarchism. Such differences did not, however, prevent positive achievement. Even Marx's enthusiasm was kindled to some degree by occasional actions of the International which went beyond the symbolic. Within six years it boasted a dues-paying membership of 800,000 and affiliation with other labor groups having a total strength of approximately 5,000,000—a notable demonstration of proletarian unity. It had secured a wage increase for some Paris workers and financial support for strikers in France and Belgium.[1] Ironically the First International was to be destroyed by the very revolutionary action which Marx found to be missing from the organization's activities.

The Paris Commune of 1871 did more than anything else to bring about the collapse of the First International. The Commune was a revolt of the French workers who seized control of Paris after the German victory in the Franco-Prussian War. Surprisingly, Marx the revolutionary had actually cautioned against this particular uprising and turned to its support only when it was a *fait accompli*. The revolt which lasted for a little

[1] R. N. Carew Hunt, *The Theory and Practice of Communism* (New York: Macmillan, 1954), p. 103.

over two months was attended by large scale violence both on the part of the rebels and the government forces which restored order. Some 20,000 persons were estimated to have been killed during the period. Though ruthlessness was by no means one-sided, it was the workers who were the main recipients of public wrath. Popular antagonism made itself felt not only against the Commune, but against the International as well since a number of its leaders had had prominent roles in the uprising. The account of the Commune by Marx in his *Civil War in France* removed any public doubt of its connection with the International. All the adverse publicity lost for the International much of its former support, and in its weakened state it could not withstand a final crisis.

This crisis came in the form of a confrontation between Marx and Michael Bakunin who had disagreed for years. Marx and Bakunin shared the revolutionary viewpoint but differed violently as to the sequel to revolutionary action. Bakunin—who by all accounts was a man of tremendous talent—was an anarchist and an atheist as well as a revolutionary. He was no more willing to accept a dictatorship of the proletariat than he was any other form of tyranny, and his concept of voluntary association could not fit the Marxist blueprint for the establishment of the socialist system. Marx's Germanic sense of system was naturally repelled by Bakunin's chaotic anarchism. While he was a member of the International Bakunin was engaged in other organizational activities, particularly in Italy and Spain, designed to improve his position in the International, a stature which he attained judging by his dominance of the 1869 congress which Marx did not attend. By 1872 the growing competition between the two leaders came to a head. At the congress in the Hague, Marx, supported by Engels, succeeded in having Bakunin excluded from the International. To escape any vestiges of Bakunin's influence Marx had the headquarters of the International transferred to New York. The anarchist was effectively shut out, but the International, deprived of its European context, withered on the vine. It was officially dissolved in 1876.

In summation, it can be noted that the First International was a curious mixture of evolutionary and revolutionary ideas and groups. Its theoretical motif included revolutionary Marxism, the gradualism of British trade unionism, and the anarchism of Proudhon and Bakunin. It was beset from the beginning by national differences and the conflict of personal ambitions. Its revolutionary tone was not matched by its readiness for revolt. Its achievements were primarily symbolic and moderate in nature. Perhaps its prime contribution to international communism was the attention it called to mistakes to be avoided in the future and the difficulty of molding an international class-conscious movement out of groupings with particularistic backgrounds and aims.

The demise of the First International did not prompt Marx to undertake the creation of another. He believed that the residual spirit of the defunct organization made a greater contribution to the communist cause than would a new body whose deliberations might unmask differences detrimental to the general movement. He was especially distrustful of moderate socialists whose piecemeal achievements might undermine revolutionary fervor. Thus the foundation of the Second International after Marx's death was only partially the work of Marxists. Socialist parties had grown in strength in England and on the continent, and their desires for amalgamation were a contribution to the creation of this successor in 1889. This time the locale was Paris where the Marxists and non-Marxists meeting in separate congresses agreed to combine. Though adopting the Marxian principles of class struggle, proletarian unity of action, and elimination of private property, the Second International's composition was such as to insure a more moderate tone than the Marxists would have desired.[2]

Delegates to the Second International were chosen by their respective affiliated groups and reflected in their deliberations

---

[2] *Ibid.*, pp. 113–114.

the opinions of such groups—many of which were distinctly non-revolutionary. Little attempt was made to enforce a conformity on associated bodies, with the exception that anarchists were early excluded. In fact, given the nature of capitalism during the existence of the Second International, the leaders found themselves seeking additional privileges for the working classes *within* the framework of the capitalist system rather than spearheading attacks on that system and calling for its replacement. Though there were always Marxist elements in the Second International it was the moderates who dominated. In France prominent socialists even held office in bourgeois governments, and in Germany Eduard Bernstein concocted the philosophy known as revisionism. Bernstein pointed out that the Marxian prognosis of the evolution of capitalism had failed to materialize, that Marx's materialism conflicted with the ideals of socialism which required an ethical system, and that enfranchisement of the workers required of them not only a class loyalty but a national loyalty as well. Bernstein's position, then, was a much more evolutionary one in which enlightened trade unionism was a prominent feature. The increasingly significant point of debate within the Second International became—in the twentieth century—the question of internationalism versus nationalism. As the war clouds gathered over Europe it became apparent that socialist internationalism was splintering; national loyalties were winning out over class consciousness. Finally, in 1914 the German Social Democratic Party supported the Kaiser's request for war appropriations, and the death knell of the Second International had been sounded. When socialists went willingly into their various national armies socialist internationalism was temporarily lost. World War I, of course, overshadowed any interest in an international socialist movement, and at its close a new type of international came into being. Technically, however, the Second International was not officially dissolved until 1923.

The most important of the internationals was the Third or

Communist International (Comintern).[3] Lenin had long been dissatisfied with the casual organization and lack of discipline of the Second International. He wished to forge a new international organ which would parallel on the world scene the tightly knit, disciplined organization of the CPSU. He also wanted the international to have a true revolutionary vigor and to accept the leadership of the Soviet Union in the fight to establish worldwide communism. The war years postponed any immediate action, but when the Russian revolution succeeded Lenin did not wait until his own regime was stabilized before proceeding with his international plans. In March, 1919, representatives of various communist groups assembled in Moscow where the Comintern was launched. Trotsky's Manifesto of the Communist International made it clear that violent action and military victory were inherent in plans for overthrowing bourgeois governments, that moderates in the socialist movement were not to be trusted, and that the example of the Soviet Union was to be emulated by communists everywhere. Any idea among the members that they were to have an equal voice in the deliberations and decisions of the Comintern was soon dispelled by the early adoption of a representational formula which favored the larger national parties and by the presence of Zinoviev as Chairman of the organization for the first seven years of its existence.

While communists from time to time were urged to participate in united front agreements to unseat right-wing governments, the essential fact of uniqueness of organization and action by communists and opposition to evolutionary socialists was clarified at the Second Comintern Congress in 1920 in Lenin's twenty-one conditions to which all communist parties should subscribe. All propaganda and agitation must be genuinely communist in char-

[3] After the formation of the Comintern, those groups which did not wish to associate with it but which had withdrawn from the disabled Second formed the "Two-and-a-half" (Vienna) International. Attempts to merge this with the Third failed, and the Vienna group disbanded in 1923. A new organ, the Labour and Socialist International, took its place and led a desultory existence until 1945.

acter; all organizations wishing to join the International must remove reformists and centrists from positions of authority; illegal organizations must be formed and no trust placed in bourgeois legality; special attention must be given to agitation in the army and in the countryside (leaving no doubt as to the importance Lenin attached to the military and the peasantry); concepts of social-patriotism must be destroyed and reformist policy disavowed; all parties wishing to associate with the Comintern must incessantly oppose imperialist policies and demand freedom for existing colonies; trade unions and other workers' organizations must be special targets for systematic and persistent communist activity; all affiliated parties must accept within their own organizations the principle of democratic centralism (which, Lenin proceeded to explain, emphasizes highly centralized organization, iron discipline, and a party center equipped with the most comprehensive powers); care must be taken to cleanse periodically petty bourgeois elements which may have infiltrated the organization; all parties must support any Soviet republic in its struggle with counter-revolutionary forces; all decisions of the Comintern and its Executive Committee (dominated by the Soviet Union) are binding on all member parties; every party joining the International must insure—as a matter of principle—that the name of the party include the title "Communist"; any member party failing to conform to these conditions will be expelled from the Comintern. In short, these conditions indicated the dichotomy between socialists and communists, insisted on rigid discipline and centralized authority in party organization, and trumpeted the unrelenting determination to overturn bourgeois states by overt revolutionary action. These conditions, however, were not to be strictly enforced since the circumstances which might have permitted their fulfillment did not exist. The world simply was not ripe for that kind of revolution.

Lenin and Stalin, of course, dominated the Executive Committee of the Comintern, but many other prominent European communist leaders were members and presumably played some role in deliberations of the body. Maurice Thorèz of France, Palmiro Togliatti of Italy, Walter Ulbricht and Wilhelm Pieck of Germany, George Dimitrov of Bulgaria, Wladyslaw Gomulka of Poland, and (Josip Broz) Tito of Yugoslavia were all participants at various times.[4] Though these men were of different nationalities, their selection as Committee members suggests their initial subservience to Moscow. (Subsequently, a number of them—including Togliatti, Gomulka, and Tito—expressed ideas and took actions which signaled their dissidence within the world communist movement.) Normally the Chairmanship of the Committee was held by a Russian—notably Zinoviev and Stalin, but occasionally the position was entrusted to a non-Russian such as Dimitrov in 1934 to create the impression that the Comintern was truly international in character and not totally subject to the wishes of the Soviet Union. That Dimitrov or anyone else was in no position to oppose the Soviet leaders on policy matters is palpable. The extent of control by the U.S.S.R. is further evidenced by the history of the Comintern congresses. Early in the game a nominal amount of debate was permitted among the delegates supposedly as a basis for Executive Committee decisions. But very quickly the congresses, called irregularly, became showcases where the delegates (like those to the congresses of the CPSU) listened to speeches by outstanding leaders and approved enthusiastically reports of the Executive Committee. When Stalin assumed the helm not even the façade of discussion was preserved, and for the last fifteen years of its life the Comintern was practically ignored by the Soviet leader (the Sixth Congress was held in 1928, the Seventh and last in 1935, and the organization was dissolved in 1943 by Stalin's fiat).[5]

Aside from its general propaganda value, the creation of the image of world communist solidarity, and the service which it rendered as an organizational arm of Soviet policy, the Comin-

[4] Andrew Gyorgy, *Communism in Perspective* (Boston: Allyn and Bacon, 1964), p. 192.
[5] *Ibid.*

tern fostered certain policies and actions which are demonstrative of communist intent and tactical flexibility. Almost simultaneously with the inception of the Comintern a revolt in Hungary succeeded in placing the notorious Bela Kun in power and inaugurated a reign of terror undertaken in the name of the dictatorship of the proletariat. Outside intervention suppressed the short-lived regime, but Kun escaped to Moscow.[6] The significance of the episode rests in its exemplification of the revolutionary fervor of the Comintern and the communist expectation that a wave of revolutions would sweep Europe in the wake of the success of the Russian revolt. But its failure also testifies to the reality of the international environment which was more than ready to cope with isolated attempts to mimic the Soviet experience.

Of far greater importance in the long run were two policies espoused by the Comintern in the 1920s and 1930s. The first of these is what has come to be known as a "peace offensive." At least by the time of the Sixth Congress in 1928 the Comintern had begun to concern itself with the propaganda advantage to be gained by designating itself as an organ committed to world peace. By the time of the Seventh Congress in 1935 Togliatti had prepared a report recommending that a major peace campaign be undertaken under the auspices of the Comintern.[7] The psychological benefit of such a stand is obvious. If one can be identified as an apostle of peace, and one's enemies tagged as imperialist warmongers, the masses of the people will certainly rally to your banner. What is surprising, however, is the comparative long-term success which the communists have had with this device. To be sure, the peace offensive of the 1930s was undertaken too late to have any effect on the advent of World War II. Forces were already in motion which were destined to plunge the world into that cataclysm. But the policy has been pursued in the post-war world and it has managed to deceive millions hoping for peace despite the oft-repeated communist

[6] *Ibid.*, p. 193.
[7] *Ibid.*, pp. 198–99.

insistence on world revolution and the multiple evidence of communist-inspired "brush fire" wars. An additional import of this policy is to be found in the discovery of the tactical pliability which it illustrates. After having declared war on the bourgeois state, after exhorting the worker to embark on a fight to the finish, after insisting on the inevitability of conflict and rejecting totally the democratic process, after sounding the call to arms, the Comintern then blithely (and hypocritically) picks up the olive branch and adopts the dove of peace as its symbol. That such inconsistency can go unnoticed and converts to the communist camp be made on such ground is startling and more than a little alarming.

The second policy is a similar manifestation of the tactical shifts of which the communists are capable when appraising the milieu in which they must operate. Lenin's twenty-one conditions had dogmatically disclaimed any virtue of cooperating with moderate socialist elements. More than this they implied a positive danger to the communist cause in such association. Communist activity was to be separate and distinct. Then in the 1930s came the "popular front" policy of the Comintern. This program was an active seeking of political allies in order to stem the growing attraction and power of fascism. Not only were socialists courted (as ideological brethren), but other political groupings which could add strength to an anti-fascist crusade in any country. The tactic had several potential advantages. It could result in the coalition becoming the political majority thus affording the communists an opportunity to participate in policy formulation. It gave the communists an aura of respectability. It suggested communist concern with the problems of the population generally not just the working classes. It permitted the opportunity for communists to infiltrate non-revolutionary bodies. None of these potentials was appreciably realized, and fascism triumphed momentarily, but the policy zig-zag should be a consistent reminder that ideological principle is no sure guide to communist tactics which are extremely opportunistic.

The encroaching realities of power politics finally brought an end to the Comintern. Throughout most of the 1930s communists in general and the Soviet Union in particular levied a constant attack on fascism and its aggressive tendencies as exemplified by the leadership of Benito Mussolini and Adolf Hitler. Neither this attack nor the search for compromise tried by the western democracies deterred Hitler from his imperialist course. Faced with Hitler's intransigence, Russia's comparative military unpreparedness, and the possible threat to its own security the Soviet Union did an about-face which left the communist world dizzy and confused. In 1939 Stalin signed a non-aggression pact with Nazi Germany. Overnight mortal enemies became comrades. Communist propaganda was all askew and communist leaders befuddled as to the proper course to follow. When Hitler—now protected to the east—launched his assaults to dominate Europe, Stalin not only acquiesced but shared in the Polish spoils. With England and France drawn into the war and receiving American military equipment Moscow's orders to indigenous communists were to interfere with effective opposition. Comintern leaders who were too stunned by the shift or who opposed the policy change were ruthlessly purged from their positions and/or eliminated. France fell in 1940, and as the German air force rained merciless blows on Britain it appeared that her collapse was imminent. Now secure in the west, Hitler turned and attacked his erstwhile Russian comrade in 1941. This presented a further shock to communist propagandists who had abruptly to return to the old anti-fascist line. (It rather shook the democratic capitalists of the West as well who had to decide whether to make common cause with former communist enemies or risk facing alone a Hitlerian Germany in full control of Europe.) But the issue was more than a contest of ideology and propaganda for the U.S.S.R.; it was a life and death struggle. The West did, of course, come to the aid of the Soviet Union, and while the Germans intruded deeply into Russian territory, their advance was finally blunted at Stalingrad. The United States, in the meanwhile, had been attacked by Japan in December, 1941, and the Berlin-Rome-Tokyo axis established to conquer the world. Against the facists were ranged the Western democracies and the U.S.S.R. The course and outcome of World War II are too well known to be repeated here, but its progress contributed to the Comintern's demise. As noted, Stalin had already relegated the Comintern to a secondary role in the world communist movement; now he was persuaded to discard it altogether. Being aware of the pre-war antagonism of the U.S. toward communism and being so dependent on American aid for survival, as a placating gesture Stalin ordered the dissolution of the Comintern in May, 1943.

In retrospect it may be seen that the Comintern was not much more successful than its predecessors. It did not succeed in fostering the communist revolutions for which it stood. It did not even succeed in implanting the revolutionary zeal it desired. It could not eliminate the moderates in the movement. Its anti-fascist, pacifist crusade was either too late or too inadequate. It did, however, illustrate a new trend in communist international-ism. No longer was there to be a loose union of socialist sym-pathizers periodically discussing esoteric ideological points and issuing theoretical statements. No longer was there to be demo-cratic debate. The new model emphasized centralized organiza-tion, unflinching commitment, and unswerving dedication to revolutionary action. Above all it emphasized Soviet leadership of the movement, a fact which accounts in large measure for the post-World War II course of communist internationalism.

For four years after the Comintern's dissolution no new in-ternational body replaced it, though much was happening on the communist international scene. The Soviet aim of world communism was certainly not abandoned, as the West learned soon after the war's end, nor was the role of Russian leadership modified. As a strategic maneuver, however, during the latter stages of World War II and immediately thereafter the image of a worldwide communist unity was shelved in favor of giving to each Communist Party a distinctly national flavor. This re-moved from such parties the stigma of alien interference in national affairs and permitted national communist leaders who achieved patriotic stature during the war to take advantage of this prestige for communist purposes. Many French communists, for example, were prominent in the underground resistance during the German occupation and in the liberation, and their activities paid enormous political dividends in post-war France. On this foundation and with the assistance of some native leaders who spent the war years in the Soviet Union, a new type of communist internationalism flourished in the two years following the cessation of hostilities. Like so many plans, however, this one which stressed the national character of communist movements was to present later difficulties for the Soviet Union.

In September 1947 another agency of communist internationalism was created—the Communist Information Bureau (Cominform). The decision to form the agency appears to have been triggered by the announcement of two American policies in 1947—the Truman Doctrine and the Marshall Plan. The former, which gave military and economic assistance to Greece and Turkey, was a proposal to aid nations threatened with internal or external communist subversion or aggression. The latter was originally a plan of economic assistance to rebuild the war-ravaged countries of Europe, but which, when the communists refused to participate, became an anti-communist weapon as it stabilized the economies of Western Europe. Believing that these American initiatives required some counter move Stalin assembled representatives of France, Italy, Yugoslavia, Poland, Hungary, Rumania, Bulgaria, and Czechoslovakia in Warsaw and there organized the Cominform. Selecting Belgrade as its headquarters the Cominform leaders announced that the new organ would coordinate the Party activities of its members and confront American imperialism.

Less than a year after its inception the harmony of the Cominform was rudely jolted as Tito of Yugoslavia came under fire from the Kremlin. Tito's ascendancy in Yugoslavia had been achieved at the end of World War II primarily without Soviet assistance and by partisan tactics not approved by Stalin. Thus, from the beginning, Tito's position in the communist world had been a semi-independent one which rejected full subservience to the U.S.S.R. Subsequently, Tito attempted to exert his influence and extend his prestige throughout the Balkans. This was an obvious threat to Stalin's insistence on the leadership of the Soviet Union in communist affairs, so, when Tito showed no sign of regeneracy, Yugoslavia was expelled from the Cominform in 1948. (Tito has been variously in and out of favor ever since.) Charged with disloyalty, heresy, and sympathy for the West, Tito was a target of Cominform ire for the next seven years, and the organization's headquarters was moved to Bucharest. Tito's stand, it should be noted, was to have serious repercussions for international communism during the 1950s. With only eight remaining members the Cominform limped along until 1956 issuing publications, denouncing and pressuring Tito—with little success, and serving as a source for the Party line. When, under Khrushchev, the Soviet Union sought a rapprochement with Tito and was confronted with the idea of polycentric communism, the Cominform had reached the end of its limited usefulness and was dissolved. It had never displayed any special vitality, and the Tito-Stalin split had undermined its sense of unity from the beginning.

Since 1958 there has appeared a new look in communist internationalism. The so-called "Prague International" was created on a loosely organized basis, its prime activity being the publication of the magazine *Problems of Peace and Socialism*. It was designed as a journal for coordinating world communist policy and one in which Marxist-Leninist issues could be freely discussed. However, the absence of Yugoslavia from the beginning, the Sino-Soviet split, and the withdrawal of Red China and Albania have seriously weakened the organization's search for communist universality, and the magazine's contents have frequently been pejorative. The comparative organizational laxity seems to be in keeping with the contemporary theme of intra-bloc relations which depreciates centralized power over the whole communist camp and elevates bilateral and multilateral conferences as the best means of coordinating policy. Two other organs are of some significance in the sphere of international communism—the Council of Economic Mutual Assistance (1949) and the Warsaw Pact (1955). The first was designed to correlate the economic activities of communist countries, but it has not had notable success. The second was a plan to unify the countries of Eastern Europe militarily as a response to the Western North Atlantic Treaty Organization. Never a truly viable military alliance, in recent years this arrangement has served as a forum for political as well as military pronouncements.

Retrospectively, communist internationalism can be seen as having followed a tortuous path. The attempt to organize and implement the Marxist concept of class unity across national boundaries, to structure world revolution, has not had much success. Despite all claims to the monolithic nature of communist doctrine, ideological differences have haunted the internationals. Personal animosities have threatened unity, and nationalistic emotions have overridden class consciousness. Domination by the Soviet Union has been chafing to fellow members in international bodies, and the ambitions of national leaders were not consistent with meek submission to Moscow. And the rise of Red China as a major competing power center has pretty well shattered any Soviet dream of reestablishing the monolith under Russian hegemony. The likelihood of meaningful organizational reconsolidation is small in spite of the residue of common interest which is shared by communists everywhere.

The Communist Party in France and Italy

The internationalist and nationalist aspects of communism are amply illustrated by the experiences of the French and Italian Communist Parties. Operating within the confines of societies generally dedicated to the capitalist economic system and circumscribed by national political and social traditions, these

Parties have been hard put to walk the orthodox Marxist line
while trying to secure the political power which would permit
the inauguration of scientific socialism.

The French Communist Party originated in 1920 when the
more radical members separated from the Unified Socialists.
This new body at once declared its subordination to the Third
International and subscribed to the "twenty-one conditions" proposed by Lenin as guidelines for Party action. But while the
Party copied the organizational format of the CPSU and strove
for policy conformity with Moscow, it always remained a captive
of its environment. In typical communist fashion the French
Party urged social ownership of the means of production, the
creation of a distinctly working class party, proletarian internationalism, the necessity for a dictatorship of the proletariat in
establishing socialist democracy, and the abolition of all colonial
oppression. However, from its inception the Party felt con-
strained to create an image of legality, respectability, and parliamentary persuasion, and over the years it sought to create a
united front with the Socialist Party—a front which it hoped to
dominate. Its program has advocated such moderate reforms as
higher wages, a 40-hour week, tax reform, a *gradual* socialist
transformation of agriculture, an *electoral* domination of the
National Assembly, civil service reform, separation of church and
state (rather than an outright condemnation of religion), and
selective (rather than total) nationalization of economic enterprise. In foreign policy matters, of course, the Party generally
echoed the position of the Soviet Union—anti-imperialism, anti-
fascism, and, more recently, anti-NATO and anti-American.

Though communism's revolutionary stance is thoroughly in
accord with the French revolutionary tradition of 1789, the
Party nevertheless must function in an atmosphere strongly
dedicated to democratic processes and must deal with a citizenry
divided by deep commitments to a variety of conflicting ideals
and organizations. Monarchy, democracy, individualism, collec-
tivism, anarchism, the Catholic Church, anti-clericalism, trade
unionism, and other ideas and institutions all have devoted

followers. Thus, in the pursuit of power the French Communist Party must tailor its appeals to attract a following from disparate sources.

The high point of the communist political advance came in 1946 when the Party received 29% of the vote in legislative elections and captured 166 parliamentary seats. This success apparently stemmed from the fact that the wartime alliance with the Soviet Union had given the Party a new stature in French eyes. In addition, the role of Party members in the resistance movement during the German occupation seemed to mark them as national patriots, and electoral support came easily. However, the rapid post-war economic recovery, the aggressive actions of the U.S.S.R., the opposition of the non-communist parties, and the enactment of a complex new electoral law designed to diminish communist voting strength quickly deteriorated the strategic position. The reappearance of Charles de Gaulle on the political scene reduced the communists practically to political impotency.

Despite the long radical strain in French tradition the policy impact of the French Communist Party has been minimal. It has served as a focal point for the expression of discontent with the leadership of other parties or with existing policies, but it has not been an effective instigator of public policy. Its prime organizational venture has been the domination of the major trade union, the *Confédération Générale du Travail* (CGT), and its voting support has come primarily from the ranks of the workers. But even here the Party has not been able to call the tune for labor whenever it chose. Additional electoral backing has come periodically from small farmers, merchants, civil servants, and intellectuals. Such backing, however, should not be construed as literal acceptance of communist dogma or leadership. For these individuals a communist vote is merely a way of objecting to some aspect of the politico-economic-social scene, and the appearance of a more attractive alternative immediately dissipates this communist strength. Therefore, while it must be acknowledged that the French Communist Party is a distinct part of the pattern of French politics, it cannot presently be described as a potent force in those politics. To the extent that it has exercised an influence it has been disruptive rather than constructive.

The Italian Communist Party was formed in 1921 and, like its French counterpart, originated with dissident Socialists who desired affiliation with the Third International and who adopted the basic Russian Party format and the principle of democratic centralism. As in the French experience, its primary achievements were in the industrial areas, and it suffered the additional burden of struggling for simple existence under Mussolini's fascist regime. The Italian communists were also heavily engaged in partisan activity during World War II and emerged at the war's end with a new stature. But Allied occupation policy militated against any coup, and the communists were forced into a policy of democratic collaboration.

The coalition concept did not discourage the communists who hoped to direct the arrangement and to initiate policies in line with Marxist doctrine. As a matter of fact, in the ensuing antifascist regimen a number of policies were adopted which seemed to fit the communist scheme including taxes on capital assets, confiscation of private property, and some nationalization of industrial enterprise. Simultaneously the Party sought an amalgamation of workers, peasants, and salaried employees into a single confederation as an organizational base permeated with Marxist thought. However, unlike their French brethren, the Italian communists were in for rude jolts which were administered by the electorate in the elections of 1946 and 1948. In each case the Catholic-oriented parties triumphed, and the communists found themselves on the outside and in uneasy alliance with the Socialist Party. The position of the Roman Catholic Church in Italy and its anti-communist stand need hardly be emphasized as a major factor in the Italian national environment acting adversely on the communist cause.

A more telling blow fell in 1956 with the de-Stalinization program inaugurated in the Soviet Union which placed the

Italian leadership in an embarrassing position, and it was compounded by Russian intervention in the subsequent Hungarian uprising which, when defended by the Communist Party, led to an estrangement from the Socialists. Despite these incidents the Party was far from moribund and continues to exercise considerable influence among the working classes.

The French and Italian Communist Parties exemplify the difficulties of operating as a minority group in an essentially hostile milieu. Particularly in the Italian case, Allied occupation of a conquered enemy was not likely to advance communist aspirations regardless of the position of the U.S.S.R. as comrade-in-arms. In both instances the bellicosity of the Soviet Union deprived the national communists of an exalted status derived from wartime experiences. In both countries there was sufficient socialist experience as to make Marxist doctrine moderately acceptable. But in both there were contrary trends and mores which made the atmosphere less than congenial for the spread of communism as an idea or a political force. It would be incorrect to say that neither Party—especially the French—has had any effect on the course of the nation's political life, but neither group has had the impact which the amount of publicity regarding its efforts would seem to suggest. In part the difficulties of these Parties have been the result of Moscow's insistence that communists everywhere follow the pattern of the Russian prototype and reflect the thinking in the Kremlin. Thus, national communist leaders have found themselves trapped in the conflict between communist internationalism and national idiosyncrasies which had to be taken into account in political manipulation. Nonetheless, the Communist Parties of France and Italy remain relatively virile and are the outstanding outposts of communism in the non-communist world.

Satellitism and Polycentrism

The end of the Second World War brought with it a hope for a lasting peace. The aggressors had been conquered, the

United Nations had been created as an international organization symbolizing world unity, agreements had been reached among the major allies regarding post-war plans for the vanquished, and, at Yalta, the U.S.S.R. had pledged the establishment of democratic governments in Eastern Europe. The United States in particular was so war-weary and so optimistic that it began an immediate dismantling of the mighty war machine it had created. The high hope for permanent tranquility was not to be realized. Almost immediately the aggressive and obstreperous intent of the Soviet Union became apparent, and the still intact military might at Stalin's command was transformed into an ominous threat. Not only was Russia's lack of cooperation within the U.N. an index of Moscow's continuing commitment to the doctrine of communist expansion, but developments in Eastern Europe clearly evinced Soviet territorial aspirations. In appraising the unfolding of events in Eastern Europe from 1944 we should recollect that communist doctrine was not the sole motivating force. Keeping in mind traditional Russian nationalistic objectives helps to explain the sequence of developments.

By the end of 1944 the Red Army had begun its push through the Balkans as German forces retreated. Eastern Poland and Rumania were first occupied, and subsequently Bulgaria, Hungary, Yugoslavia, Albania, Czechoslovakia, and East Germany were overrun by Soviet troops. This physical presence of the Soviet military was to be a significant factor in the political moves which followed. By the time of the Potsdam Conference in the summer of 1945 which outlined the terms under which Germany would be occupied Soviet determination to create in Eastern Europe a cluster of satellite states subservient to its wishes was unmistakable and the process of subjugation was well under way. The pattern of takeover in each country was basically the same though there were individual differences, and in each instance Stalin attempted to portray the seizure of the governmental apparatus as a popularly supported democratic measure.

The foundation on which each satellite was built was the threat of naked force—the presence of Soviet troops. Though every effort was made to avoid the application of military might the ubiquity of Russian forces was a constant reminder of the lack of political alternatives. Indigenous forces were purged and revamped so that Russian officers or local officers loyal to Moscow appeared in leadership positions. Military leaders exercised important political influence, and when necessity demanded it, military action supplemented political maneuvering.

In the political realm several techniques served. To begin with, local communist groups were revitalized and strengthened and other leaders bolstered by Soviet support. In some instances former leaders who had received sanctuary and further indoctrination in Moscow during the war were reintroduced to their countries to lead the drives for political power. Under the guise of de-Nazification, various programs were instigated to weaken or eliminate any political party or group which opposed the communists. In those areas where communist support was strong, maximum reliance was placed on legal procedure and the electoral process—as in Czechoslovakia in 1946; in other places, intimidation, harassment, fraud, and overt intervention assured the desired results—as in Poland in 1947.[8] A common technique was the fostering of and participation in popular front (coalition) governments, such as the Fatherland Front in Bulgaria and the National Liberation Front in Albania—both in 1944. Superficially such bodies suggested a cooperation among the various groups aspiring to political power, but in reality they were temporary expedients to give the communists time to undercut the opposition, woo the public, and assume full control of the government. Operations on the formal political front were accompanied by feverish work in trade unions, youth groups, and other organizations to develop as wide a base of public support as possible. In general the anti-fascist sentiment which pervaded the population and/or the fact that a number of local

[8] Robert Bass, *Eastern Europe* (New York: Foreign Policy Assoc., 1964; Headline Series, #168), pp. 10–11.

leaders could be identified as Nazi sympathizers or collaborators and thus subject to legitimate removal made the communist task easier. In most instances every step taken to insure the ultimate ascendancy of the Communist Party in each of the satellites was so handled by the Soviet propagandists as to appear a logical step in the national interest and in creating a "democratic" regime. To the West, however, it was all too clear that Soviet redemption of their Yalta pledge involved a redefinition of "democratic" to "anti-fascist" and a further delineation of anti-fascism to mean essentially communist.

Political moves in all cases were bolstered by economic and cultural pressures. Economically the moves were tied to the war and to "reforms" which were part of anti-fascism. In those states which had been linked to Nazi Germany heavy reparations were demanded, and whole factories were dismantled and shipped to the Soviet Union. Heavy demands were also made on natural resources such as petroleum, bauxite, and uranium. In other states the strength of the political "right" was weakened through the confiscation and breaking up of large estates in the name of land reform, which, in some instances, was overdue. Economic agreements were subsequently negotiated which gave the Soviet Union an influential voice in satellite affairs. On the cultural side the communists directed their particular attention to education and religion. The schools were a fertile ground for indoctrination, and Soviet experts did their best to transform satellite systems to conform to the Russian pattern. The study of the Russian language and literature became compulsory subjects.[9] The organized churches—particularly the Roman Catholic Church—were correctly recognized as being implacable enemies of communism. Not only did the religious views conflict diametrically with communistic atheism, but the churches were a bastion of conservatism, and their large land holdings and educational facilities were a tempting prize for the communists. Therefore, it is not surprising that undermining church

[9] Gyorgy, *op. cit.*, p. 67.

influence became a major aim in the transformation of the satellites. Lands were confiscated, schools and churches were closed, clerics were silenced, and in Hungary, Yugoslavia, and Poland leading prelates (Cardinals Mindszenty, Stepinac, and Wyszynsky) were brought to trial on trumped up charges and convicted as enemies of the state. Too late the Soviet Union learned that the religious convictions of the people were too deep to be carelessly extirpated, and the persecution of religious leaders proved to be a propaganda boomerang which incensed not only the indigenous population but the world at large. Thereafter, the communists tread more carefully on this dangerous ground.

A further insight into communist intent and tactics in developing the satellite system may be gained by examining in greater detail the experiences of Poland and Czechoslovakia. The Polish case involved the essential elements of the Stalinist theory of "revolution from above": military occupation, elimination or severe weakening of all opposition, establishment of a puppet government subservient to Moscow's will, periodic purges even within communist ranks, and religious persecution.[10] The first chapter of the story was written in 1939–40 when, following the Nazi victory in Poland, the eastern part of the country was occupied by the Russians. Over the next two years it is estimated that some 1,500,000 were deported to labor camps in the Soviet Union. Perhaps more significant in a power sense was the disappearance of approximately 15,000 Polish army officers who were supposedly interned. Despite Soviet denial of any complicity in the event, the discovery by the Germans in 1943 of a mass grave in the Katyn forest gave strong evidence of genocide at the hands of the U.S.S.R. The fate of the remaining officers was never revealed, but speculation attached to the idea of a similar execution. In 1941 and after, other indications appeared that leaders in the Polish resistance movement were more likely to be eliminated when discovered than welcomed

[10] For an elaboration of the Polish story, see Stefan T. Possony, *A Century of Conflict* (Chicago: Henry Regnery, 1953), pp. 270–275.

as brothers-in-arms by Soviet forces. A still more dastardly event transpired in mid-1944 when, having directly instigated an uprising by Polish patriots in Warsaw against the German forces and strongly implying imminent Russian support, the Soviets stood idly by and permitted the slaughter of the insurgent Poles. Thus when the Red Army finally occupied Poland the centers of potential opposition were thoroughly decimated. In the wake of the occupation Polish military forces were sovietized and pseudo-Poles assigned to the most sensitive leadership positions.

On the political front—the groundwork having been laid—in late 1944 the Polish Committee on National Liberation (Lublin Committee) declared itself to be the new government of Poland. This group of communists and communist supporters was a creature of Moscow which gave it formal recognition. The West, however, continued to recognize the Polish government-in-exile and urged that, according to the spirit of the Yalta agreements, all parties should be represented in the determination of a new government for Poland. Temporarily non-communist elements were given a voice in the provisional government, but the Lublin group had established itself in the saddle and was not to be dislodged. From this position of superiority the Kremlin-oriented puppets began to prepare for "free elections" in Poland. The opposition parties were constantly harassed and terrorized, their organs of opinion censored, and their leaders arrested. Within two years the communist leaders felt sufficiently secure, and in January 1947 general elections produced an overwhelming majority for the communist forces. Poland had become a satellite of the U.S.S.R. However, matters were not permitted to rest there. Until 1956 when a redefinition of Russo-Polish relations was obtained, the Soviet Union directed periodic housecleanings within the Polish hierarchy to insure devotion and command obedience; Stalin certainly was not tolerant of "independent" communists. Simultaneously the previously mentioned anti-religious crusade was launched to aid in the "communization" of the Polish people. The success of this effort is highly questionable, and the best estimate is that the program backfired. Nonetheless, it is a criterion of the thoroughness which characterized the communist attempt to blanket the society with its ideology as a basis for exercising practical political leadership.

The Czechoslovakian experience was somewhat different.[11] Red troops occupied much of the country in 1944–45, but the forces of the West were also present. The latter, however, did not push on to Prague, and after the war the United States decided to remove all of its troops from the area. This encouraged the communists while doing little to stimulate the democrats. A provisional coalition government was established in 1945 under President Eduard Benes in which the communists were able to secure the key ministries of interior and information. The normal anti-fascist campaign began and rightist political elements were purged. In May of the next year the communists, having a sizeable popular following, polled 38% of the vote in the parliamentary elections and in conjunction with the Social Democrats were able to effect a working majority. The communist leader, Klement Gottwald, became Prime Minister, and half the cabinet positions went to the communists. With the communist influence fairly well entrenched, the police force becoming more oriented to the communist viewpoint, and the democratic forces splintered, the Red Army gradually withdrew. By the end of 1947, however, Czechoslovakia's democratic heritage began to reassert itself, the moderate parties were revitalized, and new leaders emerged who were not so willing to accommodate Soviet aims. Recognizing the dangers immanent in these developments the communists decided on sterner measures. The Interior Minister, Vaclav Nosek, set about converting the security police into an active organ of the Communist Party. This prompted the non-communist ministers to pass a resolution of objection which was ignored both by the Interior Minister and the Prime Minister. In protest twelve non-communist ministers—but no Social Democrats—resigned. Superficially seeking the basis for a new coalition, Gottwald announced that he could not work with any

[11] *Ibid.*, pp. 292–295.

of those who had resigned, and the foundation for the bloodless coup which followed was established. Street demonstrations by communists were staged, and the trade unions engaged in a protest strike against the moderates. Opposition leaders were intimidated, their offices searched, and some were arrested. Communist activists gained ascendancy in factories, communications facilities, and government offices. At this juncture (possibly finding no viable alternative) the Social Democrats asserted their willingness to form a new government with the Communist Party. The new ministerial list was published in February, 1948, and a new constitution was submitted in May to President Benes who refused to approve it and later resigned. Nevertheless, a communist-dominated legislature was chosen and Gottwald became the new President. In sum, the satellitization of Czechoslovakia while assisted by the usual techniques of infiltration, pressure, and terror was unique in the apparently genuine nature of the coalition government which existed temporarily, the inability of the democratic forces to unify and mount an effective offensive against the communists, the misuse of parliamentary tactics by the moderates who saw their resignation as a rallying point for opposition, the continuing aloofness of the West which might have made greater use of its cultural ties with the people, and the minimum use of Soviet military force as a factor in the final outcome. As a postscript it might be noted that this episode is an eloquent commentary on the extent to which the communists had made inroads in the Czechoslovakian society and on the readiness of the Party leaders to resort to more effective means to secure their objectives if reliance on democratic process fails to achieve the desired results.

In similar fashion the governments of Albania, Bulgaria, Hungary, Rumania, and Yugoslavia were—between 1944 and 1948—transformed into puppet regimes under the direction of the U.S.S.R. A large segment of the Russian territorial aspirations had been gained by indirection. A flimsy façade of democratic choice had been erected to disguise the blatant neo-imperialism of the Soviet Union. In 1949, East Germany was added to the list of satellites, and Russia had created an impressive territorial and ideological bulwark between itself and its so-called capitalist enemies. An iron curtain had been closed against the West. (In passing we should accentuate the fact that in 1940 the U.S.S.R. had absorbed the Baltic states of Latvia, Lithuania, and Estonia into the union as autonomous republics, thereby inaugurating the program of geographic expansion which broadened in the post-World War II era.) Treating the satellite system collectively, what ensued following the communist acquisition of power was the expected. Externally the satellites echoed the voice and desire of the Soviet Union; there was a communist bloc which expressed a unified objective and tone in international relations. New industrialization programs were launched without too much thought to coordinating the raw material flow and the market potentials among the satellites. As critical cogs in this industrial machine labor unions became agents of the government for implementation of production schemes and lost their positions as voices of the workingmen. Financing of this massive effort was secured through the imposition of heavier taxes which impoverished the bourgeoisie, and the deemphasis of consumer production led to drastically lowered living standards for most of the populations. Agriculture likewise was collectivized primarily to assure state control of all segments of economic activity but also as a punitive measure directed at those opposing the communist ideology. As in the Soviet Union itself, this forced collectivization stirred a hornet's nest of peasant resistance, and in numerous instances such intransigence coupled with "political" farm management led to serious curtailment of agricultural output. Nor were the other aspects of life in the satellites left untouched by the Russian desire to sovietize the captive states. Teachers, professional people, and technicians began to be judged not by their specialized competence but by their political orthodoxy. Any demonstrated affinity for the ideas and values of the West was grounds for suspicion and possible reprisal. Advancement in the educational system was less a function of intellectual attainment and academic excellence than it was a function of demonstrated doctrinal regularity and willing subservience to the communist regime. Attacks against religion and a considerable amount of anti-Semitism flourished. In summary, the experience in the satellite states added up to the imposition of the Soviet culture pattern on a basically non-cooperating people, with all the resulting faults, the inconsistencies, and the antagonisms which the U.S.S.R. had undergone in its earlier days.

Polycentrism. Despite all the effort and determination of the Russian masters to enslave the satellites, they were not destined to achieve total success. The first inkling of the prospective failure came in 1948 with Yugoslavian opposition. As mentioned earlier, the nature of Yugoslavia's communism and the temperament of Tito had brought a confrontation with Moscow resulting in a temporary rupture in Soviet-Yugoslavian relations. The incident did not lead to any immediate widespread fracture in the satellite system, but it offered a hint of things to come. Tito had shown that it was possible for "national communism" to exist. He had broken with Moscow while still retaining his personal leadership position and continuing to be a communist in a communized society. Even the stigma of condemnation from the leader of world communism brought no collapse. The mystical concept of Russia's unquestioned leadership in the communist bloc had been seriously shaken. Later developments were to enlarge this rent in the fabric of Soviet hegemony.

In each of the subject states there continued to exist during the period of Soviet domination two elements which, in the long run, promised change. One was the sense of national identity which refused to be submerged in communist universality; the other was the personal aspiration of each local communist leader. Each wished to be a pocket-Stalin in his own right, but for a time the best insurance—though not perfect—for remaining in power was to kowtow to the Kremlin. Stalin's death in

1953 seemed to be a signal for modification in existing relations.[12]

The first intimations of discontent were seen in workers riots in Czechoslovakia and the East Berlin uprising of June, 1953. Both were suppressed, but the underlying unrest of the people was not dissipated. The elevation of Malenkov to the pinnacle of Soviet leadership and the policy modifications he announced for the U.S.S.R. had important ramifications for the satellites. In these areas as well as at home there was a relaxation of police state tactics, and a greater concern was shown for the production of consumer goods. The errors of forced collectivization were acknowledged, and a new emphasis placed on agricultural production. The loosening of the reins of control did not augur a complete shift in policy or process, but it inaugurated a political climate in which a new spirit of criticism was to express itself and in which a growing sense of popular freedom would make extremely difficult the reimposition of Stalinist restraints.

The succession of Khrushchev as head of the CPSU brought a momentary halt to the change in economic policies in Eastern Europe, but, in general, the aura of moderation prevailed. The Austrian peace treaty was signed, and Soviet troops withdrew. A reconciliation with Tito was undertaken which appeared to approve the theme that different roads to socialism could be followed. Greater attention was given to the economic needs of the satellites, and their assistance was encouraged in mounting a common effort to woo the emerging nations of the world. Terror as a tactic remained definitely in the background, and there was a reaffirmation of adherence to the principle of socialist legality. Of these developments the rapprochement with Yugoslavia seems, in retrospect, to have had the most important long-term effect. Slavish imitation of the Soviet model was no longer considered to be the only—or the best—road to communism for all countries. Tito's emulators who, in some instances,

[12] A brief summary of developments in the satellite system can be found in Bass, *op. cit.*, pp. 17–29.

had been executed as traitors, began to be considered as patriots whose reputations deserved posthumous rehabilitation. Long-time Tito critics were confused and undecided about the future as their traditional guideline appeared to have disintegrated. Criticisms of leaders, especially in Hungary, became more flagrant as uncertainty mounted in the minds of the satellite Stalinists.

Then in 1956 came the 20th Congress of the CPSU and the initiation of the de-Stalinization campaign. The impact was tremendous for Soviet-satellite relations. For the non-communist it served as a basis for questioning not only everything Stalinist about the regime under which he lived, but the very system of communism which could spawn such a creature. Intellectuals who were chafing under the restraints of socialist realism were confirmed in their alienation and, at the same time, prompted to launch a vigorous new criticism. For the communists themselves, many witnessed a public discrediting of the very process by which they had achieved and maintained power. They saw themselves indicted as conspirators in the elimination of aspiring colleagues, and foresaw themselves as victims in an ideological shift not of their own making. The ground on which they stood had suddenly become quicksand which might easily swallow them. Khrushchev's attempt to separate the sin of the cult of personality from the communist system itself was not very effective, and the more basic issue of the rectitude of communist dogma as interpreted by Russian leaders was the one which occupied satellite attention.

Between February and June, 1956, an increasing disquietude was observable in Eastern Europe. Writers in Hungary were excessively vocal in their criticism of Party boss Matyas Rakosi and demanded the return of the nationalist Imre Nagy. In Poland, Gomulka was released from confinement practically with an apology for his imprisonment. In Bulgaria, the Premier resigned. Writers in Czechoslovakia likewise protested against communist leadership and the silencing of talent. In Budapest, the tone of criticism against Soviet domination was more and more radical. Then in June a doctrinal bombshell was dropped in the laps of the leaders of the U.S.S.R. In an interview published on June 16 the Italian communist leader Palmiro Togliatti discussed the de-Stalinization issue and its implications for the world communist movement. He emphasized first that attributing to Stalin personally all the ills and shortcomings of the Soviet society was no more accurate than attributing all the positive accomplishments of Russian communism to the super-human qualities of one individual. In either case, Togliatti said, the "criterion of judgment intrinsic in Marxism" is violated. The true problem, he continued, was how the Soviet society reached a point in which forms alien to democracy and socialist legality had evolved. He then went on to criticize the bureaucracy of the U.S.S.R. Acknowledging that in the beginning a maximum of centralized power was required to crush counter-revolution, he condemned the development of a Stalin-directed apparatus which was uncritical of unfortunate internal developments. He felt the Party to be responsible for the establishment of a hierarchy which so divorced itself from the democratic creativity of the masses. He saw in the exaggerated praise of even minimal achievements in industry and agriculture a self-deception which blinded the Party to realistic faults and failings. He believed that there had been a tremendous deceit in ascribing the ills of the Soviet system to the capitalist enemies which encircled the U.S.S.R., and he indicted the Party for its substantiation of this hypocrisy. Having thus founded the bases of objection, Togliatti proceeded to postulate a philosophic and political renovation of the inner workings of the communist movement. He stated that the front of socialist construction had so broadened that "the Soviet model cannot and must not any longer be obligatory. In every country governed by the Communists, the objective and subjective conditions, traditions, the organizational forms of the movement can and must assert their influence in different ways." Noting that the socialist movement was at different stages in different parts of the world he argued that the "whole system becomes polycentric, and even in the Communist movement itself we cannot speak of a single guide but rather of a progress which is achieved by following paths which are often different." [13] The reality of national communism as exemplified by Yugoslavia had now been phrased ideologically as the doctrine of polycentrism, and the translation of the concept to hard political fact was not long in coming.

On June 28 a workers' strike in Poznan, Poland, began. Though the strike was directly related to living standards, its political overtones were quite clear as observed by many Westerners attending a trade fair there. The strike turned into a bloody riot. The meaning of the Poznan demonstration was not lost on Polish Party leaders, and a decision was reached to grant concessions to the nationalists in the Party. Charges against Gomulka and his colleagues were formally cancelled, and by October Gomulka—the advocate of a Polish road to socialism—had been chosen First Secretary. At this juncture a Soviet delegation arrived to try to halt the nationalist upsurge, apparently going so far as to imply military intervention, but to no avail. The Poles were adamant, and the Russians capitulated. A new era in Soviet-Polish relations was thus begun in which Poland gained the right to make many of its own internal decisions and to effect internal reform. In this novel state of affairs dealings between Poland and the U.S.S.R. became much more an exchange between sovereign entities, and the Poles were even able to extract additional economic assistance from their former masters. Poland had not fully escaped domination, nor had it thrown off the communist cloak, but it had achieved a degree of independence and embarked on a course of national communism as Tito had done eight years earlier.

Developments in Hungary were not so pleasant. Criticism of the communist regime—which was itself split—had mounted to such a pitch that by mid-1956 Rakosi resigned as Party chief. The head of the secret police apparatus was likewise removed.

---

[13] "Nine Questions on Stalinism," *Nuovi Argumenti,* June 16, 1956. Quoted in Robert Daniels, ed., *A Documentary History of Communism* (New York: Random House, 1960), Vol. II, pp. 234–235.

Rakosi was succeeded by Erno Gero whose past record suggested that the situation was not much more likely to be improved than under his predecessor. Matters came to a head on October 23 with a demonstration of students in Budapest demanding the installation of Nagy as head of government, a stronger voice for workers in industry, greater freedom for the peasants, and a revision of the relations between Hungary and the Soviet Union. The government was not prone to grant the requests and fighting broke out. The affair turned into a national insurrection which pitted students, workers, farmers, and some Hungarian soldiers against the secret police and contingents of the Soviet armed forces. As the world watched, it appeared momentarily as though the Hungarians would succeed in their quest. Nagy was reappointed Premier and established a coalition government in which the major political groups were represented. Russian forces withdrew from Budapest. As the fighting subsided Nagy proclaimed his intention to continue multi-party government and proposed that Hungary withdraw from the Warsaw Pact with a U.S. guarantee of its neutrality. New freedoms were instituted for the press and the trade unions. At the same time, the U.S.S.R. announced its continuing friendship with all socialist states and its willingness to cooperate in reconsidering the political, economic, and military relations with the satellites. Several days after its withdrawal the Red Army reentered Budapest, deposed Nagy, and by naked force broke the back of the rebellion and established a new government under the more pliable Janos Kadar. Thousands of Hungarians were killed or imprisoned in the process, and 200,000 more escaped to the West. Nagy was ultimately executed.

Three principal factors stand out in accounting for this debacle. First, the nature of the local communist leadership was such as to encourage the build-up to the insurrection. The Stalinist wing of the Party, while in control, was a minority whose excesses riled the populace and whose intransigence in the face of complaint encouraged a popular uprising. Second, and probably most important, was the importance of the threat to the Soviet Union. Within the Hungarian Communist Party at all levels there was a strong nationalist strain. Intellectuals, students, trade unionists, and segments of the military along with political leaders like Nagy were opposed to the domination of the U.S.S.R. through its Hungarian puppets. Thus when the revolt occurred and Nagy reappeared as leader, the Soviets were faced not simply with a redefinition of relations with a satellite in which the Communist Party remained firmly in control, but with a state which seemed to be on the verge of leaving the Eastern European bloc completely. This was indeed too great an affront to Soviet hegemony; if successful, it was too tempting an example which might inspire emulation by the remaining satellites, especially after Poland's earlier experience. The U.S.S.R. had to risk the use of force to keep Hungary within its orbit, otherwise the whole empire might fall apart. Third, the attitude of the West, and particularly of the United States, allowed the suppression of Hungary with less risk than the Soviet Union feared. As a matter of fact it can be argued that America made an inadvertent contribution to the revolt when official pronouncements in the 1950s shifted in emphasis from "containment" of communism to "liberation" of communist-dominated captive peoples. Looking back it is abundantly clear that such talk was primarily for internal political purpose and never represented official policy, but it may well have encouraged unrest with the expectation that an indigenous uprising woud precipitate American assistance. Unfortunately, in the crisis the United States remained militarily aloof, an attitude probably occasioned by an unfavorable world opinion generated by its association with the British and French who together with the Israelis had intervened in Egypt over the Suez Canal issue a few days before the Hungarian incident. This failure of response left the field totally to the U.S.S.R.

The Fractured Monolith

The quelling of the Hungarian upheaval combined with Western inaction seriously undermined the hope and determination of Eastern Europe's anti-communists and appeared to usher in a new period of Soviet control. Albania, Bulgaria, Czechoslovakia, and Rumania had not been shaken by Tito's maneuvers or the de-Stalinization issue and remained steadfastly within the Russian orbit. Hungary had been subjugated anew by force. A tentative détente with Tito was secured by Khrushchev, and Gomulka's Poland, after initial gains in autonomy, began to find itself once more subject to Russian pressures for conformity. A new Soviet effort (1957–60) to give constructive assistance to the sagging economies of the satellites and to coordinate their production and distribution systems made the acceptance of Soviet leadership less galling. As early as November 1957 a joint declaration of Communist Parties established stringently narrowed limits within which national differences among communists could be expressed and specifically reaffirmed the leadership of the U.S.S.R. in the socialist camp. It looked as though the iron curtain had clanged down again and national communism relegated to the position of meaningless myth.

Such, however, was not to be the case. The economic resurgence which had been stimulated in the satellites by the infusion of Soviet aid began to run down, and old dissatisfactions reappeared. National interests reasserted themselves when individual members of the bloc felt that they were being asked to make economic sacrifices in the interest of the whole. The united effort on the part of the bloc to extend its influence into Asia, Africa, the Middle East, and Latin America reawakened old desires on the part of individual members to enhance their economic positions by developing peculiarly advantageous arrangements which might not be wholly consistent with the politico-economic offensive which the bloc was waging. The rise of Red China as a power center competing with Moscow (previously described) capped the process of decentralization. Whatever reluctance the satellite states may have had to confront Moscow alone was now diluted by the recognition of a new "ally" which would welcome them in restating their own status in the world communist movement. Albania opted for the most extreme course and openly sided with the Chinese communists. For the others, the spectre of Red China provided an opportunity to demand of the U.S.S.R. a greater latitude as the price of loyalty. As the center of communist authority diffused and a bi-polarity developed, the old patterns of control changed. By virtue of geographical proximity the emerging communist systems of North Korea and North Vietnam were likely to come under the primary influence of Red China. When the Soviet Union's venture in Cuba failed (see Chapter 8), a disillusioned Fidel Castro felt impelled to accept Communist China's overtures. As Mao grew in stature as a competitor to Soviet leaders, communist parties around the world grasped the chance to play off the major partners against each other and thereby gain for themselves a degree of autonomy consistent with the hopes of their individual leaders. Togliatti's conception of polycentrism became less a theoretical exercise and more a reality.

To read into the foregoing analysis a dissolution of the world communist movement or the collapse of communism as a system, a faith, or a conspiracy would be overly optimistic. Both the theory and the practice of communism have proved too hardy for such wishful thinking on the part of anti-communists. Even the Sino-Soviet schism should be interpreted realistically as an intramural struggle for power readily discardable in the face of a mutual threat. Whatever confidence might be drawn from this internal communist rupture should be tempered with the realization that there remain two *power* centers from which the tentacles of communism extend. Nevertheless, it would be equally ridiculous to view the communist world as though it continued to exist in the same way as it did from the end of World War II until Stalin's death. The relationships between the U.S.S.R. and the satellites have changed. Red China and its disagreements with the Soviet Union are facts. Communist parties around the globe no longer look exclusively to Moscow for guidance and leadership. National interests can and do override doctrinal commitments. As recently as February, 1968, when the Consultative Conference of Communist Parties met in Budapest to outline a scheme of reunification, the concept of polycentrism seemed to outweigh the theme of proletarian internationalism, and new stirrings were noticeable in Poland and Czechoslovakia. The Chinese, Yugoslavian, Albanian, North Korean, and Japanese communists did not attend the meeting, and while Moscow continued to proclaim the doctrine of proletarian internationalism and preach cohesion, condemning any heretical, schismatic, or apostate position, their absence plus a reticent support from the old guard confirms the irremediable change in the once formidable communist monolith.

The August 1968 military suffocation of the program of new freedom inaugurated in Czechoslovakia reminds us, however, that the Soviet Union is still reluctant to tolerate serious deviations by its satellites from the communist guidelines laid down in Moscow, even when it runs the risk of severe condemnation by world opinion for its actions. The drama began in October 1967 with a Prague student upheaval protesting limitations on individual freedom. In December, Leonid Brezhnev visited Czechoslovakia in an attempt to retain the existing Party leadership and to muffle dissent. His purpose was not accomplished, and in January 1968 Alexander Dubcek was chosen as the new Secretary of the Communist Party. During March and April Dubcek unveiled a new program of freedom for the Czechs which shook traditional communist leaders by the extent to which it permitted free expression and criticism. With a display of seeming equanimity Soviet Premier Kosygin came to Czechoslovakia in May to conclude arrangements for Warsaw Pact military maneuvers in the country—to which the Czechs agreed. However, at the conclusion of the war games in July, Soviet troops failed to withdraw on schedule and fears were raised regarding Russian intentions. At the end of the month calm settled again when a conference of communist leaders in Cierna arranged for the removal of forces and seemed to have signalled acceptance by the group of the Czech program. And on August 3 still another meeting at Bratislava declared the unity of communist nations suggesting that Party leaders were willing to overlook internal Czech liberalism in return for Dubcek's pledge of loyalty to the international movement. What was not generally known at the time was that East Germany's Walter Ulbricht was particularly concerned with the developments and had suggested to the leaders of the U.S.S.R. that the virus of Czech liberty might be highly contagious.

Apparently the Soviet communists were of the same mind, because the façade of agreement was shattered on August 20 when military units of the Soviet Union, Poland, Hungary, Bulgaria, and East Germany suddenly invaded Czechoslovakia—supposedly at the request of "communist loyalists" who saw a threat to communist solidarity in the new regime. Though some blood was shed in the intensity of Czech revulsion to the occurrence, pleas for patience from the leadership to the people averted a greater slaughter. Party boss Dubcek and President Ludvik Svoboda were spirited to Moscow for deliberations and returned with some small hope of retaining aspects of the new freedom in return for permission for Warsaw Pact troops to remain on Czech soil for an indefinite period. The general tenor of future developments became apparent as Soviet *military* leaders arrived in Prague for additional discussions. Despite the pressures, however, liberal Czech communist leaders stood their ground and did their best to defend the looser controls. They were, of course, in an impossible position, and little by little most of the ground was lost. For propaganda purposes Dubcek was kept on as Party chief, but in May 1969 even this ruse was abandoned and he was replaced by Gustav Husak who pledged to restore order and discipline.

The sequence of events clearly indicates the lengths to which the U.S.S.R. is willing to go at this juncture to maintain its control over its empire. It also emphasizes that there remain a number of old line communists who see their careers best served by sycophancy to Moscow. A realistic political autonomy is not yet a discretion allowable to satellite leaders. But the events likewise show the amount of satellite chafing at the Russian bit, the desire for the reinstitution of old freedoms, the urge for a practical sovereignty, and, above all, the lack of unity in a supposedly solid communist camp—a fact which the mid-1969 summit meeting of communist parties in Moscow could not have underscored more heavily with its internecine bickerings.

STUDY QUESTIONS AND PROJECT SUGGESTIONS

1. A. Detail the history of the communist "Internationals" from 1848 to 1956.
   B. Why were the international communist organs no more successful than they were?
2. Discuss the techniques by which the U.S.S.R. established its satellite system in Eastern Europe following World War II.
3. Write an essay on the theme "Titoism and the Kremlin."
4. Explain the concept of communist "polycentrism."
5. Discuss thoroughly the significance of the 1956 Hungarian uprising and its suppression by the Soviet Union.
6. What inferences may be drawn from Russo-Czechoslovakian relations in 1968–69?
7. Is the Stalinist communist monolith truly fractured?

CHAPTER 8

COLD WAR AND
COEXISTENCE

The creation of the satellite system by the Soviet Union, the rise of Communist China to a position of authority in the world socialist movement, and the subsequent rift in communist ranks all occurred within the broader context of what is generally called the "cold war." This is the overall descriptive term for the antagonistic relations between the communist and non-communist states instigated by the aggressive actions of the U.S.S.R. immediately following World War II and played out against the background of mutual nuclear capabilities which made overt conflict practically unthinkable. The phrase encompasses attitudes and beliefs as well as strategies and actions which exemplify the mutual distrust of the two camps, and a brief examination of the cold war as such is worthwhile first as a phenomenon of post-war international relations and second as a point of departure in assessing the changing nature of contemporary communist techniques of penetration. The specific events of the cold war are too well known to require more than a summary sketch here, and more attention will be given to the

relationship between this series of events and the metamorphosis which has occurred in world communism.

The opening skirmish in the East-West conflict was, of course,
the undisguised Soviet determination to subjugate the Balkan
states contrary to the pledge which it had given at Yalta. The
Western allies were immediately alerted to the danger but still
hopeful that their worst fears would not be realized. Within
two years after the cessation of hostilities the U.S.S.R. had
structured its satellite system, and the bi-polar nature of the
then existing power system was made clear. Then when the
communists sought to subvert the Greek and Turkish governments, the United States responded in 1947 with the Truman
Doctrine. President Harry Truman requested and received from
the Congress appropriations to assist the two beleaguered states
which had asked for aid. The funds were made available within
the context of the Doctrine which pledged U.S. assistance to
any free people under pressure from an armed internal minority
or outside sources. The Truman Doctrine was thus the first
pronouncement in the evolution of the policy which was called
"containment of communism." In that same year the Marshall
Plan was announced as a program of American monetary support for the rebuilding of the war-torn European economies,
and, when the Soviet Union would not permit the satellites to
participate, the Plan became an economic buttress against the
spread of communism into the West.

In 1948 the communists engineered the Czech coup and tried
to isolate Berlin—located in the Russian zone of occupation—by
closing the roads leading from the Western occupation zones.
The United States countered with the famous "airlift" which
kept the city supplied with essential materials for almost a year
when the Soviets reopened the road. The Americans and their
allies strengthened their positions in 1949 with the announcement of a new program of technical assistance for developing
countries around the globe and the establishment of the North
Atlantic Treaty Organization. The NATO pact was a landmark
agreement for the United States which had not been party to a

formal alliance since 1800. The NATO partners[1] agreed that an attack on any of them would be considered an attack on all, and pledged themselves to assist such victim of aggression by any means including armed force. It had been made clear to the Soviet Union that any intention of piecemeal aggression would be met by a united defense. In the same year the West German Republic was proclaimed indicating the determination of the free world to resist a further territorial encroachment by the U.S.S.R. In the meantime the drama of China had drawn to a close.

The mid-century brought the North Korean invasion of South Korea and the American and United Nations response. The event was shocking not simply because of the bald aggression but because it suggested a communist conspiracy probing around the world to extend its power wherever weakness was suspected. Late in the year the Chinese "volunteers" intervened and the battle seesawed until the 1953 truce which found the demarcation line between the two Koreas approximately the same as it had been prior to the invasion. The communists meanwhile had been acting to extend their influence elsewhere, notably in Latin America and Indo-China. In 1954 matters came to a head in Guatemala with the overthrow of the communist-oriented regime by Guatemalan exiles (assisted by the U.S.), and in Indo-China where the French were ousted and the Geneva Conference partitioned Vietnam into two parts. The year also saw the United States enter into new defense agreements, especially the Southeast Asia Treaty Organization (SEATO).[2] This Asian counterpart of NATO joined Great Britain, France, Australia, New Zealand, the Philippines, Paki-

---

[1] England, France, Canada, Italy, Belgium, the Netherlands, Luxembourg, Norway, Denmark, Iceland, Portugal, and the United States were the original signatories. Greece, Turkey, and West Germany joined later.

[2] Bilateral agreements were signed with South Korea and Japan in 1954 and the Formosa government in 1955. In 1952 the U.S. had negotiated the ANZUS pact with Australia and New Zealand, and a bilateral defense treaty with the Philippines.

stan, and Thailand with the U.S. in a mutually protective alliance (though the commitment by the participants to the use of armed force is less demanding in case of attack).

This brief outline of the major events of the cold war during the decade following the termination of the Second World War is sufficient to show us the various facets of this unique conflict. The end of hostilities had been so welcomed that most of the world's peoples heaved a collective sigh of relief and prepared to enjoy the benefits of peace. There was a general relaxation and the expectation of a new era of world cooperation which would produce mutual benefits. It was in this atmosphere that Stalin decided to pursue his objectives, coldly taking advantage of the world's war weariness and banking on the assumption that the United States would not use its monopolistic position in atomic weapons to deter his adventure. With his initial maneuvers successful, and with the Russian development of its own nuclear weapon capability, Stalin pushed communist aggressiveness wherever there was a likely gain. As Mao established himself in China there could be observed a new Sino-Soviet offensive which further threatened all free people who wished to avoid either subjugation or further hostilities. Only reluctantly did the West take up the challenge. Especially in the United States it was difficult to generate enthusiasm for remilitarization following the massive demobilization of the late 1940s. But as the threat was unmistakable there was no alternative. Eschewing the counter threat of nuclear attack with its attendant destructiveness, the U.S. and, in time, its allies sought peaceful means to stymie the menace. The first course was economic. The Greek and Turkish assistance and the Marshall Plan were designed to help peoples to help themselves against aggression. The latter particularly was intended to create a bulwark against communism's ideological attractiveness (and subsequent political subversion) by rebuilding Western European economies to a state of stability in which consumer satisfaction would blunt any communist appeal. (It should be acknowledged that while the Marshall Plan was tinged with altruism it likewise served the self-interest of the United States not only as a barricade against communism but as a contribution to America's own economic vitality.) The economic offensive was soon supplemented by an even more humanitarian gesture in the form of the "Point Four" program of technical assistance. Again the emphasis was on assisting people in self-development through the sharing of techniques and processes. During this early phase of reaction only minimum attention was placed on military preparedness, and much reliance was placed on acting through the organs of the United Nations.

The second five years of the post-war decade saw the shift to politico-military tactics. In a sense NATO was part of the gigantic international poker game begun after World War II. Just as the Soviets had had to gamble that America would not use its atomic superiority as a deterrent to Russia's Eastern European expansionism, so the West had to assume that the U.S.S.R. would recognize that the NATO commitment meant general war should any attempt be made to pick off the weakest of the members. While it cannot be said that NATO was the absolute shield against further aggression, it must be admitted that its presence was coincident with a halt in the Soviet move to the west. The multiple defensive agreements which followed can be traced to NATO experience. The Berlin airlift was an early indication that resort to military measures had not been ruled out by the Western Allies, but the real test came in Korea. From the communist viewpoint the crucial question was whether the United States and its defense associates would resist blunt aggression. The answer was given in 1950. Had the invasion gone unchallenged on the battlefield the communists would have been encouraged to further adventures and the tactic of using indigenous forces—of planning wars of "national liberation"—would have proved itself. The reaction of the U.S. to Korea was not only clear evidence that force would be met with force, but that it would occur insofar as possible under the aegis of the United Nations. It was further evinced that the free world preferred peace—or at worst limited war—when the

U.S. decided not to use atomic weapons or broaden the sphere of hostilities to Chinese soil.

In summary then it can be said that the essence of the early period was the impatient aggression of the communist camp and the unavoidable response of the free nations. Hopes for peace and tranquility were replaced by distrust and finally by a sense of impending disaster which called for action. While hoping to achieve containment by moderation, the West was eventually forced to demonstrate its willingness and its ability to utilize military might in the face of the growing menace.

The death of Stalin ushered in a new era in intra-communist and world relations. First under Malenkov and then under Khrushchev the intensity of Soviet foreign policy began to mellow. There was no overnight thaw in the cold war, and the expansionist motif did not vanish from the actions of the U.S.S.R. However, a subtle change could be sensed in both the activities and the pronouncements of the Kremlin. Much of the bombastic propagandizing remained, but it was tempered by a new tone of conciliation. Whether it was prompted primarily by a desire to digest and stabilize its gains, by its concern with developments in Red China, or by the determined defense of the West, Russian foreign policy was somewhat transformed. Instead of proclaiming the inevitability of war between the capitalist and communist camps, Soviet propagandists and Party leaders now began to speak of a new phase of competitive coexistence. As Khrushchev noted, the socialist societies were now so advanced that they could outshine the capitalists states in their own primacy—economy productivity. This concept brought a shift in emphasis in techniques of proselyting and penetration. These were not new weapons in the Soviet arsenal, nor were the old methods of combat discarded, but there was a distinct shift from one to the other.

From 1955 to 1965 many vestiges of the original cold war remained, and thrust and counter thrust exhibited themselves periodically. In 1957, for example, in the midst of developing troubles in the Middle East, America proclaimed the Eisenhower Doctrine which promised assistance—including military —to any nation in the area subject to armed aggression from any state under communist control, and in 1958 American troops landed in Lebanon (by request) to quell disturbances. In 1960 Cuban-American relations began to be disturbed over Castro's communist policies, and diplomatic relations were severed the following year. That year was one of momentous events including Russia's orbiting of the first manned space vehicle and detonation of a 50 megaton bomb—both having significant propaganda value. However, the Berlin wall was also constructed, an open confession that citizens of East Berlin could only be retained by force. For the U.S. the low point was reached with the disastrous "Bay of Pigs" invasion of Cuba. Cuban exiles were anxious to reenter the homeland and unseat Castro and had prevailed on the United States to assist them. Not wishing to become thoroughly involved, America provided only the training and equipment, and lacking air cover the exile forces were overwhelmed. But the really big crisis occurred in 1962. The Soviet Union, anxious to extend its influence in the Western Hemisphere, had secretly begun to establish intermediate range nuclear missile sites in Cuba. When this was confirmed, a confrontation of tremendous import followed. President Kennedy, before a nationwide television audience, announced the development and detailed the threat which it entailed not only for the United States but the entire hemisphere. He then initiated a naval blockade of Cuba to prevent the entry of additional missiles and equipment en route, called for the immediate withdrawal of weapons already arrived, and flatly proclaimed that the launching of any missile from Cuba at any target in the hemisphere would be deemed to have come from the U.S.S.R. and would call forth immediate U.S. retaliation on *Moscow*. Had Khrushchev been intransigent, America would in all probability have invaded Cuba to remove the threat forcibly, and a nuclear exchange could have ensued. The firmness of the American stand weighed against the modest gain which the Cuban adventure represented apparently convinced the Soviet Union that discretion was called for, and the missile bases were dismantled.

The next several years saw a growing entente between the U.S.S.R. and the West. Speculation suggests that this stemmed from Russia's unsettled relations with its satellites, the burgeoning influence of Red China, and the Soviet Union's recognition that its own society—reaching a stage of economic adequacy—stood to benefit from a continuation of peace. It has even been suggested that the Red Chinese challenge convinced the Soviet Union that it could not afford the intense antagonism of the West to which it might have to turn for assistance in blunting Chinese aggression. In this atmosphere, therefore, two modest steps were taken in 1963 to moderate the possibility of nuclear war and to minimize tensions in American-Soviet relations. The first was the signing of the Nuclear Test Ban Treaty limiting the kinds of nuclear tests which could be conducted by the signatories. (The failure of France and Red China to subscribe to the agreement seriously impaired its effectiveness.) The second was the installation of the so-called "hot line" telephone connection between Washington and Moscow providing instantaneous communication which can prevent war by error or miscalculation. Old distrusts remained, but the pressures of the contemporary world had worked a revision on long-standing enmities.

Since 1965 the most pressing problem has been the American military involvement in Vietnam. Begun as a military advisory endeavor at the request of the South Vietnamese government (and under the terms of the SEATO agreement) the American commitment has expanded to a major role in the hostilities involving over 500,000 men. The questionable virtue of the American position, combined with the complex nature of the Vietnamese problem, has occasioned strong opposition to the role from Americans themselves. The war dragged on with little observable concrete progress while casualties mounted and thousands of civilians were killed. Resistance to conscription has been supplemented by outspoken criticism from prominent politicians, educators, clergymen, and others. On the other hand, those who support American policy see it as a continuation of the containment policy and/or a manifestation of America's pledge to keep free people free. There is much difficulty in ascertaining the true circumstances surrounding the conflict. The Vietnamese under Ho Chi Minh drove out the French and were partitioned by the Geneva Conference with the intention that the country should be reunified by general elections later. These elections were never held at the insistence of the South Vietnamese (with American support) on the ground that in the communist North free elections were impossible. From that time forward the situation deteriorated, with Ho becoming more impatient for unification and insisting that the leaders of the South were not popular representatives. A dissident group in the South—the Viet Cong—was fostered by the North, and ultimately fighting broke out finally involving both the Americans and North Vietnamese regulars. Against this background many questions could be posed. How sincere is the desire for unification on either side? Can truly free elections be held throughout the country? To what extent, if any, is the North Vietnamese effort directed by the Soviet Union or Red China? Would Ho Chi Minh as the Vietnamese leader be an "independent" communist? (Ho's death in September, 1969, leaves the same question regarding his successor.) Would the withdrawal of American forces be interpreted as a sign of weakness and an open invitation to further aggression by the communists? Does the stability and territorial integrity of the rest of Southeast Asia require an American presence? Does the continuation of hostilities inflict more suffering on the people of both sides than a "communist victory" would entail? Would an American "retreat" be considered an abandonment of a commitment to the South Vietnamese government? These and other issues have made a settlement of the conflict extremely complex, and fighting has been prolonged into 1969. Current diplomatic and military maneuvers give some hope for peace negotiations which may bring tranquility to that troubled land.

The importance of Vietnam for this study is the light it throws on the cold war in its most recent phase. It is apparent that, beginning with the fight against the French, the Vietnam effort would be classed—particularly by the Red Chinese—as a "war of national liberation." This does not mean simply an undertaking by indigenous people to free themselves from foreign domination. Rather, in the communist lexicon, it represents a popular rebellion against bourgeois domination in which local forces alone are utilized though moral and material support may be forthcoming from one or both major communist partners. It is in short the "export of revolution." Whatever interests and intents motivate the North Vietnamese and the Viet Cong, the broader communist camp views the struggle as one which would spread communist influence further, even if the Vietnamese communists were not puppets of a major communist state. The United States likewise chose to view the aggression from the North as a phase of the world communist movement. Its containment policy dictated a response. But an interesting sidelight of the whole picture is the manner in which the goliaths of East and West behaved over the years of fighting. Red China, of course, has been a major supplier of the North Vietnamese, but it has refrained from sending "volunteers" or other forces to join the fray. The Soviet Union has also supplied war material and has periodically loosed propaganda blasts at the United States, but it has shown no indication to exacerbate the situation or broaden the field of conflict. The United States for its part, while applying considerable military prowess, has demonstrated a selective restraint in its bombing activities and has continually sought an honorable way out of the fighting. In short, the comparative restraints of both sides are intimations of a continuation of the spirit of amelioration initiated a half-dozen years earlier which changed the complexion of the cold war. The contest has evolved into one in which military power is still the final resort, but in which other practices are utilized to a far greater extent to achieve desired objectives.

Contemporary Communist Techniques
of Penetration

The subtlety of the transformation of the cold war should not lead to the misconstruction that there has really been no change at all. To reemphasize, the initial communist tactics of primary reliance on military force and violent subjugation or elimination of competitors have not been completely abandoned. Nor do contemporary techniques represent the institution of totally novel methods; they have been present to a greater or lesser degree throughout the history of the communist movement. It is the accentuation of the latter over the former which has provided the new context of competition, and it is in the atmosphere of coexistence that the containment policy of the free world requires reexamination. Surely the Sino-Soviet rift has demolished the myth that there is an indestructible communist unity whose centralized policy decisions lie behind disturbances anywhere in the world. However, since either major communist partner is known to have an interest in using any national upheaval for its own benefit, it behooves us to understand the manner in which communist tactics may contribute to the generation of national discontent or seek to exploit legitimate grievances for the communist cause.

One development was the reactivation of "front" organizations. We have previously noted the utilization or support of political fronts by the communists as a means of insinuating themselves into the governmental hierarchy or as temporizing devices to permit a build up of communist strength. The new fronts were somewhat different in character and were used for different purposes. They were designated as international bodies and encompassed a wide variety of social groups—trade unions, students, teachers, journalists, communications specialists, and professional people. Each particular front appeared to take its policy cue from the "super front," the World Peace Council which came to the fore in 1949–50.[3] Several characteristics of these fronts as distinguished from the earlier models are worthy of notice. Of prime importance was the fact that they were not designed as semi-official mouthpieces of the Communist Party. To the contrary, they functioned with only a minimum of notable communist affiliation—and that in the background. The effort was to convince the participants that they functioned as independent agents for whatever cause the front organ served. Secondly, the fronts were devoted to the support of broad, nebulous, but genuine ideals. Such items as peace, solidarity, anti-colonialism, or national independence were the concerns of these organizations. It was, therefore, not difficult to enlist support for conferences, petitions, or demonstrations dedicated to the furtherance of such ideals. Nor was it difficult for members to see in their efforts a good unrelated to the ideological affinities of the sponsoring front. Thirdly, the geographical emphasis of the fronts shifted from Europe to the Middle East, Asia, and Africa. These were the areas of the world in ferment. It was here that anti-colonialism and independence were the most significant items; it was here that valid national aspirations might be linked to communist dogma. The high emotionalism, the lack of political experience, the longing for modernization could all be exploited for the communist camp. It was here that Soviet (and later Chinese) specialists could ingratiate themselves with evolving local governments and contribute to the image of the communist camp as the "peoples'" friend. In other words, the communists were becoming more sophisticated. No longer were fronts to be the more or less obvious propaganda outlets of former years. No longer were they to serve as agencies of unity and discipline for Communist Party members. Instead they were to foster allegiance for programs of peace and independence unrelated to Marxist doctrine, but usable by the communists because of the degree of emotional-

---

[3] Robert H. Bass, *Problems of Communism*, Vol. IX, #5. (Sept.–Oct. 1960), cited in D. E. Pentony, ed., *Red World in Tumult* (San Francisco: Chandler, 1962), p. 201.

ism they generated or for the political and economic turmoil they could produce.

The utility of the fronts has been limited. They were only auxiliary weapons to begin with, and they have achieved only moderate success. For one thing, Asians have been reluctant to accept the Soviet Union's self-designation as an "Asian" nation. For another, the advent of Red China's international ventures and its advocacy of its own brand of Marxism-Leninism has raised serious problems of dogma for the fronts. In some cases the front organizations have been too anxious to fit national developments within a warped international context which betrayed underlying communist motives. But the most telling blow to the aims of the fronts has been the rapidly developing political awareness of the newly emerging states. While naive and ingenuous at birth and welcoming any offer of assistance to economic stability, leaders of peoples of the new nations have learned quickly that they could become unwittingly enmeshed politically by engagements which seemed free of snares. They now question more maturely that which they previously accepted with little or no reservation.

One particular political front of a unique nature is worth mentioning because of the insight it provides regarding current penetration techniques and the risks which they entail insofar as achievements are concerned. In 1946, at a meeting in Bamako, Mali, there was formed the *Rassemblement Démocratique Africain* (RDA). The RDA brought together in a loose interterritorial grouping a number of territorial political parties in French West Africa, with Felix Houphouet-Boigny of the Ivory Coast a major figure in the movement. The RDA retained close ties with the French Communist Party, and Moscow—though it had not initiated the scheme—encouraged the relationship which it saw as an avenue of influence in Africa. The novelty of the situation was, of course, that the French CP was the ideological and organizational link rather than the CPSU. For a number of years RDA members mouthed Marxist slogans and continental communists supported the African demands for independence. Superficially it appeared as though the communists had secured the desired foothold in Africa. As the independence movements gained momentum, however, and it became evident that communist affiliations were more of a hindrance than a help to local political success a number of the individual parties broke their communist ties and worked within their respective African contexts to throw off the colonial yoke. Since achieving independence the leaders of only one or two West African states continue to pay lip service to Marxism, and a development-minded Houphouet-Boigny has encouraged free enterprise as the best road to prosperity for his country. In the final analysis communism's support of African anti-colonial sentiment in the RDA did not make steadfast converts to Marxism.

Besides the fronts the communists have used a whole arsenal of tactics in their drive to influence or subvert governments in the contemporary world. These tactics are essentially peaceful and, in some instances, distinctly beneficial to the target countries, but these facts do not alter the purposes for which they are used. Before proceeding we should acknowledge that many of these same techniques have been utilized by the United States or the West generally; in fact it was the free world which pioneered with some of these devices. It is also true that some of the problems which beset the communist bloc in its maneuvers likewise troubled the Americans and their allies. The distinctive difference between the two camps, however, has been the underlying motives for the strategy employed. While the West has not been loath to accept the degree of influence in other states which some tactics might engender, its basic strategy has been to contribute to the creation of viable political and economic entities—to establish truly independent states in an open world society. The communists on the other hand have sought to tie newly emerging or developing states to the communist bloc and thus limit their spheres of independent action.

It is not at all surprising that communist efforts have been concentrated in specific geographic areas—Latin America, the

Middle East, and Africa. It is in these areas hypothetically that the greatest potentiality for Marxist gain exists. It was here that political ferment was prevalent; it is here that economic insecurity and economic aspirations offer fertile ground for communist exploitation. Where the spirit of independence was high and the old colonialism breaking down, communists, by adopting an anti-colonial stance, sought to make common cause with the newly emerging states and to discredit the old colonial powers and—by implication—the United States whose allies they were. Even where independence had long been a reality the Soviet bloc sought to take advantage of social unrest, political instability, or the "revolution of rising expectations." Racial and religious animosities, national antagonisms, conflicting personal ambitions, and any internal dissidence were all grist for the communist mills. Even where no specific concrete advantage could be registered, the creation or perpetuation of socio-politico-economic turmoil was assessed by the communists as representing a gain which could ultimately work to their benefit.

But the whole exercise of infiltrating other societies was not for the Soviet neo-imperialists simply the process of fishing in troubled waters. Their motives and their objectives were frequently more specific. In addition to the overall aim of injecting communist influence or seeking a foothold for subversion, communists generally pursued the more focused goal of weaning pro-Western nations to a position of neutrality or non-alignment or attracting those states already non-aligned to a pro-communist position. Still more specifically, in Latin America the Soviet camp wished to secure universal diplomatic recognition as the basis for establishing embassies in every Latin American country which could serve as observation and listening posts and as headquarters for espionage and other penetration techniques. Failing this, the Soviets hoped to reduce the support which the United States normally received in the United Nations from its hemispheric neighbors. When Red China got into the game and attempted to intrude its influence beyond contiguous territories, still other precise goals of the new style communist aggression became apparent. For the Chinese communists Africa represented a continent of vast resources to be tapped for Red China's benefit; it offered a tremendous territorial arena whose relatively sparse population suggested a prospective site for the absorption of part of China's millions of people; the new African states might be convinced to lend their support to communist China's admission to the United Nations; and African nations—especially on a racial basis to which the Chinese appealed strongly—might be attracted to Mao's side in the conflict with Russian leaders. For the Russians, the under-developed nations of both hemispheres appeared to offer attractive long-range economic partnerships aside from any political results which could be achieved.

Probably the most impressive of the programs undertaken by the Soviets—or the Sino-Soviet bloc—in pursuit of their objectives was the economic offensive. Having seen the impact of American economic assistance in Western Europe and elsewhere, as soon as they were able the Soviets embarked on similar programs in those areas deemed most suitable. The economic offensive consisted basically of offers of long-term loans at low interest rates for various projects which would presumably contribute to the economic development of recipient states. In some few instances outright gifts were made to needy regimes, and in others economic assistance took the form of "mutually beneficial" trade agreements. One commentator estimated that in the decade up to 1964 Soviet *offers* of economic aid amounted to $4 billion (excluding Cuba)—compared to $39 billion offered and *delivered* by the free world.[4] Economic assistance programs were, of course, supplemented by offers of technological instruction which could demonstrate practically the high level of achievement of Soviet technicians while helping the technically less advanced nations in their own development.

The motivations behind the economic offensive were patent, and dulled the attractiveness of what might have been con-

[4] Victor Lasky, *The Ugly Russian* (New York: Pocket Books, 1966), p. 21.

sidered otherwise a meritorious endeavor. One objective was to impress recipients with the fact that the Soviet Union had achieved a state of economic abundance which permitted it to rival the U.S. in its largesse. A second was to emphasize the undoubtedly rapid scientific and technical advance of the U.S.S.R. A third was to convince the newly emerging states of the sincere interest which the Russians had in their development. A fourth was to seek advantageous trade relations providing new markets for some Soviet products and new sources of supply for goods in demand in the U.S.S.R. A fifth was to flood a country with Soviet technicians whose functions might not be wholly confined to their fields of technical competence. A sixth was to tie the economies of aid recipients to that of the Soviet Union for purposes of maintenance, repairs, and spare parts for machinery supplied by Russia. A seventh was to manipulate currency exchange in trade dealings so as to supply the U.S.S.R. with hard currencies. And an eighth—and least publicized—aim was to establish through economic assistance an entree for political infiltration and subversion.

The success of the economic offensive has been limited. There is no question that the U.S.S.R. has completed some dramatic and monumental projects which were not only important contributions to the well-being of the states concerned but which constituted significant propaganda victories for the Soviets. The Aswan dam in Egypt and the Bhilai steel mill in India are of this category. Lesser—though still important—projects and accomplishments have been numerous. But the overall record is—from the communist viewpoint—more gloomy. The Soviets have been frequently unimaginative, clumsy, careless in planning and implementation, overbearing, or downright crude in their ventures, and the end result has been a much lighter impact than that for which they hoped. For example, the Russians have often gone in for showy, impressive, or luxury construction projects like hotels or sports stadiums rather than investments in a country's basic requirements such as agriculture or education. Even when completed, such projects did not long impress populations which quickly recognized that their essential economic needs had not been assuaged one iota. Too often offers of aid—gleaming in their promise—have been too slowly, inadequately, or never fulfilled. In many instances the quality of goods delivered fell far short of expectations or assumptions. Failure to take into account environmental conditions in the receiving states has sometimes resulted in rapid deterioration of aid goods or total unsuitability. Spare parts are often unavailable. Irregular and sometimes unannounced and surprising shipping schedules have resulted in the complete loss of tons of materials when they could not be practically utilized at that specific point in an economic project. Or expected goods may arrive far later than the promised delivery date. On a number of occasions Soviet insistence on completing a project by a proposed deadline has led to insufficient concern with safety precautions and the resulting deaths of many local workers. Errors in cost estimation for projects have angered governments and peoples who accepted Soviet offers as have demands that all technical personnel be Russian and that all materials to be used be purchased from the U.S.S.R. or its satellites.[5]

To be sure, much of the debacle of the Soviet bloc's economic aid programs is not of its own making, nor should the total offensive be considered a fiasco; successes have far outnumbered failures. In some cases, blunders have resulted from shortcomings on the part of the beneficiaries. Matching funds for projects have not materialized; local labor forces have been inadequately trained; concern for maintenance to be supplied by the receiving nation has been minimal or non-existent; new governments have shown a distinct lack of enthusiasm for "non-prestige" projects; leaders have been reluctant to tax their populations for necessary development of an initial project. Thus much of the blame for gross faults in the Soviet assistance scheme—as in the American—must be attributed in part to the recipients themselves.

[5] The failures of the Sino-Soviet economic offensive are elaborated—perhaps out of proportion—in Lasky, *The Ugly Russian*.

The communist attempt to use economic tactics for political purpose has not been limited to negotiating loans, gifts, trade agreements, and the provision of scientific and technical personnel. In some instances the U.S.S.R. has bought goods which it certainly did not need in order to show its good will to a state in which it was interested. In other instances it has offered higher than normal prices as an inducement to economic relations. Still other techniques have had a tinge of force or fraud about them. For example, the Soviets have been known to threaten to dump on the world market large amounts of resources they possess—such as petroleum—in order to lower world prices and thus affect adversely the economy of some state which depends on a stable price for the commodity in question. Its price for restraint in such matter has been the acceptance of an economic agreement with the U.S.S.R. on more or less its own terms. Another practice which has not endeared the Russians to the developing nations relates to the acquisition of dollars through devious means. Some resources have been especially good dollar earners for those countries which sold them to America. On occasion the Soviets, according to trade arrangements, have bought large quantities of such resource or product—perhaps offering more than the regular price—ostensibly for shipment to the U.S.S.R. with the understanding that such goods could not be resold outside of the purchasing country. Nevertheless, once the product was loaded and shipped, vessels were diverted to Western ports where the shipments could be disposed of for hard cash.[6]

As part of the aid game, but more reminiscent of the earlier cold war practice, military aid—either in terms of arms or advice and training—has been a part of Soviet strategy. Special recipients of communist bloc weapons and military advisers have been countries of the Middle East and Africa, and Cuba in the western hemisphere. Red China, of course, was and is a major supplier of armaments in North Korea and North Viet-

[6] Lasky, *op. cit.*, p. 41.

nam. Such war materiel can serve as the wherewithal to create internal disturbances which the communists can turn to their own advantage. At the very least, providing weapons can fan the flames of old animosities, continuing tensions from which the communists can benefit and earning a degree of influence for the suppliers in the recipient nations.

In conjunction with military assistance the communists—especially the Chinese—have embarked upon a particularly insidious program of exploiting racial differences in the newly emerging states and elsewhere. While most of the world is working consciously to minimize racial distinctions and create mutual understanding, the communists have played on the emotions generated by the period of "white colonialism" and have sought to insinuate themselves into the good graces of new regimes by posing as common "colored brethren" united in the fight against white overlordship. Though not very successful, this tactic indicates the many-faceted approach of the communists in pursuit of their objectives.

Another strategy in the era of coexistence, particularly directed at Africa, has been the attraction of students from newly independent states to universities in Moscow and Eastern European academic centers. To a rising generation of newly independent youth anxious for the education which would assure their own status and contribute to the development of their countries Moscow's offers were indeed alluring. Not only were all-expense scholarships given, but the meteoric scientific advances of the U.S.S.R. served to entice those who sought similar dramatic developments in their own countries. As in the matter of trade, however, the effectiveness of the educational program fell short of Soviet hopes. Again this may not have been entirely the fault of the Russians, but a certain degree of ineptness made its contribution. Africans found themselves in an alien environment with somewhat strange food and a frigid climate which contrasted markedly with that of their homelands. The glamour of Soviet science was sometimes overshadowed by the drabness of Soviet life and the absence of many of the expected amenities. Although the Russians tried to picture themselves as racially aligned with Africa, a definitely racist attitude was exhibited toward the Africans by many Russian students, and they were ignored, ostracized, maligned, and in a few instances assaulted. When Moscow established Patrice Lumumba (originally Friendship) University as a special center for African students, there could be little doubt of the racial bias. More galling to the Africans was the massive indoctrination in Marxism-Leninism which they received. Though many had leftist leanings, these heavy doses—cutting into the time devoted to their professional studies—became unacceptable. The Africans also learned that they were being exploited by Moscow for propaganda purposes.

Cultural exchange and tourism have played major roles in the Kremlin's new strategy. Cultural exchange has, since the end of World War II, become an important technique for both the East and West as a means of influencing opinion. Each has sought to propagandize its viewpoint and the excellence of its type of society among the nations of the world. While both the United States and the Soviet Union have tried to sell an idealized picture of their respective cultures, the U.S. has relied more heavily on truth and accuracy, risking the disclosure of the imperfect aspects of American society in the interest of giving the lie to the misconceptions implanted by communist propagandists. The U.S.S.R., on the other hand, has tried to cover and distort the seamy side of its life by highlighting its specific cultural and scientific achievements.

The cultural offensive has taken various forms. There have been periodic tours by Russia's justly renowned ballet troupes, choral groups, and folk dancers. There has been sponsorship of or participation in trade fairs where the latest Russian industrial accomplishments can be displayed. Traveling exhibits of Soviet science and technology—especially in the space field— have been designed to show the heights of communist achievement. Personal visits of Russian cosmonauts have generated much popular enthusiasm. The works of Russian writers, authors, and musicians (when not under the ideological ban) have been extolled and widely disseminated. Visiting lecturers and exchange professors have sought to elaborate the virtues of the Soviet system. At the same time, cultural groups of various kinds from all over the world have been invited to the Soviet Union as evidence of Moscow's friendship and understanding. Soviet information centers and Marxist bookshops have been established around the world to tell the communist story and to distribute communist literature. In many instances these sophisticated propaganda outlets have made distinct impacts on local populations, and Russian prestige has risen considerably.

Complementing cultural exchange has been the drastically increased effort to encourage tourism in the Soviet Union. While general tourism has not been ignored, emphasis has been placed on what might be called political tourism. Opinion leaders from other countries have been brought to the Soviet Union to be shown the architectural, scientific, industrial, agricultural, and cultural triumphs of the Soviet society. Executives, legislators, political party leaders, journalists, educators, trade unionists, and others have been treated to such expense-paid tours in the hope that they would be suitably impressed with the results of their guided tours and see the U.S.S.R. as the model to follow in their own countries. The effect of such efforts has not been uniform. While there is certainly much that is impressive in Russia, and while first hand observation communicates a sense of understanding which can be achieved in no other way, the tourists—political or otherwise—have occasionally been disappointed. They have objected to the lack of freedom to see what they wished; some of what they did see did not come up to expectations; and they were able to glimpse some of the drearier aspects of Soviet existence. In such instances, obviously, tourism had unfortunate repercussions for the Russian hosts.

Either in conjunction with its information centers, at the United Nations, at international conferences, or as pronouncements from Moscow, the Soviet Union has periodically initiated intensive propaganda campaigns. Such outbursts have emphasized slogans designed to have particular appeal to selected audiences and have not necessarily been consistent with Russia's intent or actions. For instance, one repeated theme has been anti-imperialism, a strange stand coming from the world's most active contemporary imperialist. On the other hand, the constant repetition of Soviet accomplishment in science and industry had basis in fact. Soviet dedication to peace has been another focus of Russian propaganda, though the sincerity of the Soviet position has occasionally been brought into question when the U.S.S.R. in seeking an objective has resorted to "bomb rattling." If Soviet propaganda efforts have sometimes been crude or comical, there is still no denying the potential impact of a well-designed program, and there is no doubt that Russian activities in this area have made numerous converts to the communist cause.

The Latin American stage gives us further insight into current communist strategy. The U.S.S.R. has long viewed Latin America as a fertile field for implantation of communist ideas, but it has shrewdly avoided making blunt approaches in its own name. Instead it has utilized the more subtle technique of indirect action and influence to give the appearance of indigenous origin and autonomous decision to local communist groups. For one thing, it has given surreptitious support to the organization of Communist Parties in the states of Central and South America and then has relied heavily on action by these local organs to implement plans formulated in Moscow. For another, it has provided Moscow training for Latin Party leaders who then returned to their native lands thoroughly indoctrinated and supplied with the practical knowledge for forwarding the communist program. More recently, in the new era of coexistence, the Soviet Union has sought to increase its contacts and its influence in Latin America by delegating to its satellites the specific task of offering assistance, negotiating trade agreements, and demonstrating communist interest in Latin affairs. Especially as some of the satellites have reached a level of moderate autonomy in their own affairs, their overtures represent an independent tender of opportunity which might not be as carefully scrutinized as if such offer came directly from Moscow. The most striking development, however, is the relation of world communism's leaders with Castro's Cuba. When Castro effected his revolution and subsequently announced that he was a Marxist, Soviet assistance and Soviet advisers were quickly arranged. On the basis of mutual benefit, Castro spouted the Moscow line and Moscow responded with large amounts of aid eventually leading to the provision of missiles which produced the crisis previously described. Though Khrushchev's political retreat led to something of an estrangement and Castro's flirtation with the Chinese communists, the important item to note was the long range advantage which the Russo-Cuban relationship might give to Moscow. Castro's stature as a successful revolutionary against the forces of reaction was high in Latin minds, and his apparent ability to "confront" the mighty United States in his independence increased his prestige further. Therefore, for the Russians, Cuba could be a western base from which new intrigues would be hatched, new insurrections mounted, new unrest stimulated—in short, the "export of revolution" from a geographically convenient position. This was a new variation on the theme of wars of national liberation and one which would not bear the stigma of "outside" direction.

A final item of interest as regards tactics in the new international setting is what may be called "junketing diplomacy and summitry." Diplomacy is normally conducted within the context of the embassy structure mutually agreed upon by two or more nations. Political relations may be supplemented by economic, cultural, and even military activities, but all arrangements are generally supervised by the ambassador as the chief representative of his country in a host nation. The principals whom the ambassador represents—heads of state or heads of government—usually remain at home and do not involve themselves directly in the actual transactions between their countries and others. In this new era that pattern has been changed. Today presidents, premiers, vice presidents, and foreign ministers travel and consult with much greater frequency than previously. The presence of such dignitaries gives a sense of importance to the mission on which they embark and is surrounded by a ceremonial protocol which naturally calls attention to the purpose of a visit. Furthermore, it can be assumed that any agreements reached in a "summit conference"—a meeting between or among the highest political personages in the countries involved—will have a greater certainty of acceptance and implementation than those arrived at through negotiation by intermediaries. There is, however, a certain degree of risk in these practices. They are exhausting for the principals; they may create a belief in the significance of a visit which is not intended; they offer an occasion for inadvertent affront. Most important, should any visit or conference at the highest level fail to produce accord, the resulting animosity is greater than that resulting from exchanges at lower diplomatic levels. Junkets of this sort are by no means a monopoly of the communist camp, but the frequent travels of Khrushchev and Bulganin, the 1963 tour of Chou En-lai through Africa, and the more recent state visits of Brezhnev and Kosygin give ample evidence of the importance which communist leaders attach to the practice.

The implications for the West of the communist strategy in the new period of coexistence are fairly obvious. The use of force has not been completely abandoned, and the free world must stand ready to counter overt aggression should it occur, but it must also be alert to the more subtle and devious practices which communist forces now utilize to influence, entangle, infiltrate, and subvert other societies. The ability of communist leaders to use effectively techniques also employed by the free nations and acceptable because of their legal and humanitarian nature requires an intensified watchfulness to insure the integrity of states subject to communist blandishments. It also places a burden on free societies to play the game of coexistence better than their opponents. If economic assistance can influence new states or developing societies, then the free world must be active in this field with realistic programs, greater efficiency, and a sincere concern for the welfare of the people concerned; it must demonstrate that it acts from unselfish motives and a firm belief in the open world society of which it speaks. If education is a key to national development, it must be offered to aspiring students without strings, free from indoctrination and exploitation, and on a totally non-discriminating basis. If mutual understanding of diverse societies is held to be a factor in creating a tranquil world, then honesty must remain the point of departure, and cultural exchange must be encouraged as a means of appreciating dissimilar culture patterns. To the extent that propaganda is employed it must have a foundation in fact, and its intent must be to attract by the simple expedient of proclaiming the truth. And if summit diplomacy is to achieve its objective, western leaders must accept the heavy responsibility of acting intelligently, patiently, and carefully.

STUDY QUESTIONS AND PROJECT SUGGESTIONS

1. Outline the origin and major facets of the "cold war" from 1945 to 1962.

2. Describe the significant cold war tactics employed by the Soviet Union from the end of World War II to the rise of Khrushchev.

3. What is the essential meaning of "coexistence" as applied to Soviet-American relations?

4. Discuss in detail the origin, evolution, and disposition of the "Cuban missile crisis" of 1962. Assess the significance of this episode.

5. Discuss the foreign policy tactics of the Soviet Union from Khrushchev's ascendancy to the present, emphasizing the implications of novel techniques for American policy-makers.

6. Prepare an essay on the theme "How World Communism Views the Vietnam War."

CHAPTER 9

COMMUNISM IN AMERICA

Communism as an ideology or a political movement has made little headway in the United States, but the communist attempt to attract an American following and the tactics employed constitute an interesting illustration of communist methodology in a democratic capitalist society. Originating in 1919 in the organization of left-wing socialists and undergoing various reorganizations and appellations from that time, the CPUSA (Communist Party, USA) persists to the present day. While its fortunes rose for a time in the 1930s and its members were moderately acceptable during the temporary alliance of the U.S. and the U.S.S.R. during the Second World War, on the whole the American Communist Party has never had any substantial status among the American people. Various aspects of the Party's structure and operations in the United States are, however, illuminating from the viewpoint of inspecting the variety of communist approaches and techniques in this particular setting and in terms of assessing American reaction to the presence of what most Americans considered an alien menace in their midst.

Political Party or International Conspiracy

From its beginning the Communist Party in America has been faced with the problem of establishing an identity. Given the stricture of Marxist doctrine that communism is an international class movement unrestrained by national loyalties, should the Party identify itself with internationalism to gain the theoretical strength attributable to the breadth of solidarity, but at the same time risk the loss of status as a legitimate political party on the American scene? Or, should the Party eschew the international affiliation in order to benefit from the position of an indigenous political party operating within the confines of traditional politics which would be advantageous in establishing its acceptability along democratic lines? The latter course might have been more desirable, but such a pose offered problems in the light of American antagonism to the ideology which the Party proposed to espouse. Therefore, while proclaiming periodically its legitimate and independent nature, the CPUSA by its enunciations and its actions has more or less consistently shown itself to be committed to an affiliation with the international communist movement led from Moscow.

The prime index of this commitment can be seen in the Party's relation to the Comintern. Despite differences of opinion within the Party and, for a while, even the existence of two branches of the Party—the Communist Party and the Communist Labor Party, by 1921 the Party had unified and accepted the twenty-one conditions for inclusion in the Comintern. Thus, not only did the CPUSA accept the dictum of legal and illegal operations within the United States, but it similarly accepted the unique position of the Soviet Union as the leader of the international communist movement. This initial subscription to alien direction was continued for twenty years at the end of which time the American Party sought to establish an independent identity as a means of avoiding the legal restrictions enacted relative to political organizations subject to foreign control. When the Comintern was succeeded by the Cominform in 1947, the American Party did not affiliate in order to continue conveying the impression of independence.

On some occasions there were literal attempts on the part of American communists to make of the CPUSA a true, autonomous, leftist political party working within the traditional bounds of the American party system, but each such effort was defeated by the Soviet-oriented leaders. The CPUSA remained then, if not a captive of the CPSU, at least a group amenable to accepting the guidance of the senior member of the world communist conspiracy. This fact was reflected in the Party's organization which closely paralleled that in Russia and in the readiness of American communists to parrot the Moscow line with all its shifts and changes. Additional evidence of Soviet influence could be discovered in the sporadic and successful attempts to discipline American Party members whose loyalty, ideological correctness, or efficiency was in question. Observations of these phenomena were forcefully confirmed by the affirmations of disillusioned members who, for one reason or another, finally broke with the Party.

Despite the more or less conclusive evidence of alien influence in the American Communist Party, and the fact that it based its activities on a theory which was anathema to the political and economic ideology of the American people, the Party's acceptance of the idea of a legal as well as an illegal apparatus gave it an opportunity to enjoy the privileges of any political party in the United States. In late 1921 the Workers Party of America was formed ostensibly to serve as a legal outlet for communist activities. Under the auspices of that party William Z. Foster and Benjamin Gitlow were nominated as presidential and vice presidential candidates in 1924. Other candidacies followed for national, state, and local offices either under the Communist Party banner or with the sponsorship of such groups as the People's Rights Party. The American tradition of party activity and early uncertainty regarding the indigenous nature of the Communist Party in America thus allowed the Party to behave as though it were a legitimate political organ and to campaign for its cause in typical political fashion.

The American emphasis on individual rights—especially freedom of speech and of the press—has likewise served to "legitimize" the working of the CPUSA. The spirit of the Bill of Rights implies that any person or group has the right—within reasonable limits—to express opinions which are totally unorthodox. (If mouthing the orthodox was all that was permitted, the rights would be meaningless.) Therefore, denial to communists of the right to argue their case would be an affront to the command of the Bill of Rights even though experience made it clear that the communists themselves permitted no such privilege where they were in control. But the case was not as clear cut as might at first be assumed. Freedom of speech and press are precious rights, but their exercise has never been guaranteed absolute. No one would argue seriously that the right of freedom of expression authorized the transmission of military secrets to the enemy in war time. Libel and slander laws are predicated on the belief that an unfettered use of free speech irrespective of truth and accuracy can grievously infringe the rights of other individuals. Free speech, like other rights, may be exercised only relative to time, and place, and circumstance. Therefore, the question ultimately arose whether the apostles of an ideology dedicated to the overthrow of the politico-economic system within which they operated, possessed of an underground apparatus committed to the same cause, receiving direction from a foreign power, and bound on a course which would translate words into deeds could legitimately claim the protection of the Bill of Rights. A premature denial of rights might bear out the communist contention that the state is a tool in the hands of the exploiting economic class which permits only expressions of conformity; undue extension of the right of free speech—which could incite to violent *action* against which any state has a right to protect itself—might jeopardize the security of the republic. It was in this vein that the dual posture of the CPUSA raised a most important problem for the American citizen and the American lawmaker. As a political party operating according to the rules it was entitled to the same prerogatives of other parties though its platform might not be popular. As a conspiratorial group working for the violent overthrow of the government of the United States it could claim no legal protection. The problem was not easily solved, and, to the extent that a solution has emerged, it has not been completely free from the emotionally motivated fear which communism generated in the American public. Drawing the line between permissible and impermissible speech, or between speech in the abstract and speech designed to promote action, is a difficult proposition. In the final analysis, the American answer has been prompted by a growing conviction that the CPUSA from its inception has never been a truly legitimate political party, that the influence of the Soviet Union in its councils has always been overriding, that its overt activities have been primarily a cover for its more important covert actions, and that its aim is the dissolution of the American government by revolutionary rather than evolutionary methods.

Legal Restraints

The first significant legal setback for the CPUSA came in the U.S. Supreme Court's decision in the case of *Gitlow v. New York*, 268 U.S. 652 (1925). The question involved was the extent to which the publication of communist doctrine was protected under the right of free speech and press. The state of New York had passed a law prohibiting the advocacy of criminal anarchy which was defined as "the doctrine that organized government should be overthrown by force or violence." Benjamin Gitlow was prosecuted and convicted under this law for publishing and distributing various pamphlets which purportedly advocated such overthrow. He appealed his conviction on the ground that the law infringed his liberty as protected by the fourteenth amendment to the Constitution. The U.S. Supreme Court had to decide first whether free speech was among those liberties protected by the amendment and second, if so, had New York's law been a violation of such protected right. The Court held that the fourteenth amendment did indeed protect free speech and free press from state infringement, but it went on to uphold Gitlow's conviction on the ground that "utterances inciting to the overthrow of government by unlawful means present a sufficient danger of substantive evil to bring their punishment within the range of legislative discretion." The Court dismissed the contention that the pamphlets were not an incitement to action but merely the exposition of an idea by saying that the state could not "reasonably be required to defer the adoption of measures for its own peace and safety until the revolutionary utterances lead to actual disturbances of the public peace or imminent and immediate danger of its own destruction; but it may, in the exercise of its judgment, suppress the threatened danger in its incipiency." Justices Holmes and Brandeis dissented from the holding on the basis that the publications did not constitute a "clear and present danger" to the state—the guide line that had been established six years earlier in *Schenck v. United States,* 249 U.S. 47, as a determinant of the circumstances under which freedom of speech might be legitimately curtailed. Thus, only a few years after its origin, the Communist Party in America was emburdened with the proposition that the core of its dogma was unpresentable as a normal exercise in free speech.

From that time forward the legal assault on communism in the United States has continued intermittently with the communists not always the losers. Various states passed or invigorated laws similar to the New York statute and initiated prosecutions against Party members. Legislative investigating committees at both the national and state levels conducted hearings periodically on "un-American" activities which, while they did not necessarily culminate in new restrictive statutes had the effect of exposing communist activities and stimulating the American people to a continuing opposition to the CPUSA. The notorious "McCarthy Committee" of the U.S. Senate was the most conspicuous of these investigating bodies—and raised the question in American minds of the propriety of such procedures. The Attorney General's office published a list of "communist front" organizations thus making it more difficult for the Party to enlist non-communist support for communist causes by the use of attractive and even patriotic titles for the organs they created to assist in implementing their various objectives. In time the national government, too, got around to passing restrictive legislation which, in turn, led to further judicial proceedings before the nation's highest court.

The Alien Registration (Smith) Act was passed in 1940—the first peace time sedition act since 1798—which, among other things, prohibited the advocacy of the overthrow of the government of the United States by force or violence. Ten years later this act was to serve as the basis for the prosecution of Eugene Dennis and ten other top communist leaders which led in turn to the Supreme Court's famous decision in *Dennis v. United States*, 341 U.S. 494 (1951). In 1950 the Internal Security Act was passed over a presidential veto with the major objective of forcing communist and communist front organizations to register with the Attorney General and disclose their membership lists and finances. The Communist Control Act followed in 1954 designed to withdraw from the Party and its affiliates the privileges of legal bodies operating in the United States. While none of this legislation made individual membership in the Communist Party illegal, the collective impact was to impose distinct limitations on the freedom of Party members. Their freedom of travel was curtailed as was their right to propagandize openly for the violent overthrow of government; their pose as legitimate political participants was denied; and they were prevented from holding government jobs, becoming part of the armed forces, or working in private industries which held defense contracts. While the laws showed clearly a congressional intent to limit the prerogatives of the CPUSA—and seemed to reflect the wishes of the general public, it was the judicial interpretation of the application of the statutes which clarified the position of the Party in America.

The *Dennis* case involved a prosecution of communist chiefs under the Smith Act for conspiring to advocate the forceful overthrow of the government of the United States. In appealing their conviction to the Supreme Court the communists contended that the decision contravened their rights under the first and fifth amendments to the U.S. Constitution. The crux of the matter was whether freedom of speech—as previously interpreted by the Court—permitted the exposition of the Marxist doctrine of overthrow of government by force and violence. The justices, conscious of the "clear and present danger" precedent—and the criticism which the Gitlow decision generated—phrased their conclusions within its context, but they interpreted the doctrine in a broader way. Relying on the words of Judge Learned Hand of the Court of Appeals, the Supreme Court accepted this formula: "In each case [courts] must ask whether the gravity of the 'evil,' discounted by its improbability, justifies such invasion of free speech as is necessary to avoid the danger." Finding that the communist "evil" was grave and that the petitioners intended to overthrow the government "as speedily as circumstances would permit" the Court upheld the conviction and the constitutionality of the Smith Act. Justices William O. Douglas and Hugo Black offered vigorous dissents distinguishing between speech and action and arguing that the protection offered to free speech is meaningless if it can be casually brushed aside because the content of the speech is broadly disliked. (Whatever one's opinion of the decision the query remains whether "present" equates with "as speedily as circumstances would permit"?) The majority opinion, at any rate, suggested a further restraint on the potential for the dissemination of communist dogma.

Six years later the Court had an opportunity to reconsider its interpretation of the Smith Act. In *Yates v. United States,* 354 U.S. 298 (1957) second rank communist leaders from California appealed their conviction under the "advocacy" provision of the federal law. It should be noted that by this time the popular anti-communist emotionalism of the McCarthy period had subsided, a development which may have had some bearing on the decision. In acquitting five of the petitioners and ordering new trials for the rest, the justices (by a 6–1 vote) distinguished between "advocacy of abstract doctrine and advocacy directed at promoting unlawful action" and concluded that only the latter was prohibited by the Smith Act and that there was inadequate evidence to uphold the conviction in these terms. While one might be disgruntled over such "leniency" for communists in our country, it must be conceded that the decision restored luster to the right of free speech—somewhat tarnished by the earlier interpretation, clarified the traditional distinction between speech (which deserves protection) and action (which may warrant prohibition), and implied—though it nowhere stated—that the Court might have been a bit impetuous in its prior loose interpretation of imminency in the "clear and present danger" doctrine. To be sure, delineating speech which is calculated to incite to action from that which is not is no simple task; any speech may contain an inherent incitement for some audience. The Court, nevertheless, obviously believed that some attempt had to be made to draw that line.

These two important decisions, contradictory in their general outlook as regards the Communist Party and its propaganda activities, depict the continuing difficulty of defining the rights of a despised minority in a society which presumably offers the maximum scope for the exposition of the unorthodox. Subsequent decisions by the Supreme Court provide no clearer picture as the highest judicial body appears at one time to narrow and at the next to increase the latitude permitted the Party and its members. This seeming vacillation should not be construed as indecision (or, as some have contended, leftist leanings) on the part of the jurists; rather, they should be considered an index of the difficulty of interpreting restrictive legislation as applied to an unpopular group without doing violence to the framework of liberty on which the republic rests.

Scales v. United States, 367 U.S. 203 (1961) saw the Court holding (5–4) that knowing, active membership in the Communist Party constitutes *per se* illegal advocacy of the overthrow of government by force and violence prohibited by the Smith Act. (There was ample evidence of the "active" nature of Scales' membership.) The judges carefully emphasized that nominal, passive, inactive, or purely technical membership in an organization which engaged in illegal advocacy was not of itself evidence of participation in such advocacy, but that knowledge of and intent to cooperate in the illegitimate action was. Despite this distinction the *Scales* decision appeared to be more of a return to the *Dennis* position than a continuation of the *Yates* interpretation. A change in outlook was signalled when in 1964 the Court (6–3) invalidated a section of the 1950 Subversive Activities Control Act which prohibited the issuance of passports to Communist Party members (*Aptheker v. Secretary of State,* 378 U.S. 500, 1964). Speaking for the majority Justice Arthur Goldberg described the section as too broadly and indiscriminately restrictive of the right to travel thus abridging a liberty prescribed by the due process clause of the fifth amendment. During its 1964–65 term the Supreme Court called a violation of free speech a 1962 section of the postal regulations which required withholding communist political propaganda unless and until the addressee requested delivery. (*Lamont v. Postmaster General,* 381 U.S. 301, 1965.) In *United States v. Brown,* 381 U.S. 437 (1965) the judges struck down (5–4) a 1959 act which made it illegal for communists to serve as labor union officials because they saw it as a bill of attainder—legislative action inflicting punishment without trial—prohibited by the Constitution.

These decisions moderating legal restraints on communists because they conflicted with fundamental rights guaranteed by the Constitution were soon to be supplemented with others in which the Supreme Court seemed to be reconsidering the implications of its earlier "anti-communist" holdings. The Internal Security Act of 1950 required, among other things, that the Communist Party (as a communist action group) should register annually with the Attorney General, and the Court had upheld this provision (5–4) in *Communist Party of the U.S. v. Subversive Activities Control Board,* 367 U.S. 1 (1961). The majority believed that the provision was regulatory rather than punitive, and that the foreign-dominated nature of the organization justified this special treatment and did not violate first amendment freedoms. In 1965, however, when the specifics of registration were examined by the Court in *Albertson v. Subversive Activities Control Board,* 382 U.S. 70, a serious problem presented itself. How was "the Party" to register? Practically it had to do so through its officers and members; but the individuals insisted that such procedure violated the fifth amendment privilege against self-incrimination since they could be punished for knowing membership. In a unanimous decision the justices agreed. And in 1967 the Court of Appeals of the District of Columbia held that the registration requirement even as applied to organizations violated the fifth amendment. As a result attempts to enforce this provision seem to have been abandoned.

Several developments on the educational front are also of interest. Concern with communist infiltration of the educational field where they might use their positions for indoctrination of youth has prompted various kinds of state action to forestall this possibility ranging from loyalty oaths to outright prohibition of communist teachers. The judicial history of these efforts is too long to be detailed here; suffice it to say that judicial decisions on the issues have been inconsistent and have frequently turned on the phrasing and specificity of the laws. In one prominent case, *Adler v. Board of Education,* 342 U.S. 485 (1952), the Court upheld New York's Feinberg Law which declared that membership in a subversive organization was *prima facie* evidence of unfitness to teach. With Justices Black and Douglas dissenting, the majority felt that the state had a vital interest in the school's function of shaping young minds and that it could utilize past or present associations as a criterion of teacher fitness. In 1967, however, this matter was reconsidered. The Supreme Court held (5–4) in *Keyishian v. Board of Regents of New York*, 385 U.S. 589 (1967), that the New York statute was unconstitutional. While conceding the state's interest in education the justices insisted that it could not stifle fundamental personal liberties when the end can be more narrowly achieved. The majority warned that such words as "seditious" and "treasonable" if left undefined are dangerously uncertain, and that one cannot be left to "guess" what conduct or utterance may lose him his position. Academic freedom, said the Court, is all important and laws cannot cast a pall of orthodoxy over the classroom. A year earlier the Court had invalidated an Arizona loyalty oath as a violation of the first amendment in that no exclusion was made for a person who might have been a member of a proscribed organization but did not subscribe to the organization's unlawful ends. (*Elfbrandt v. Russell*, 86 S. Ct. 1238, 1966.)

These decisions of the mid-1960s would appear to offer greater freedom to American communists than could be inferred from the intent of legislative acts of the prior two decades. This is no reason to conclude that the members of the Supreme Court are unaware of the objectives of the CPUSA, the close connection of the Party with the Soviet Union, its illegal activities, the danger inherent in its activities, and the opposition of Americans to communists generally. The Court has a most important and delicate task. It must interpret the Constitution and laws of the land consistently and carefully—often in an atmosphere of intense popular emotionalism—so that the fine balance between majority rule and protection of minority rights, upon which our democracy depends, will be retained. It must give its rulings on first amendment freedoms out of a serious recognition of the importance of free speech, press, assembly, and religion in American society and a sure knowledge that the denial of these privileges, even to a despised group, is the first step in depriving these precious guarantees of their vitality. It can be argued that a Court responding in its decisions to a momentary popular emotional outcry is not living up to its obligations.

Communist Tactics

That the CPUSA has made no more headway than it has in America is not because the indigenous communists have not tried. The Party's efforts have been continuous, varied, and intense. While its early attempts to gain adherents and spread its doctrines were awkward and fumbling, it quickly became more adept and devised a wide range of legal and illegal tactics designed to attract followers, subvert democratic institutions, and accomplish the overthrow of the American government. Many of these practices were cloaked in legitimate democratic format, thus giving them a deluding respectability, and all were interrelated for maximum progression toward communist goals.

One of the first and most persistent of the tactics has been the establishment of a "united front" between the communists and other groups or organizations. The effectuation of such unity has several advantages. It tends to put the communists "on the side of the angels" in allying them with more respectable groups seeking legitimate objectives; it offers a unique opportunity to contact and influence members of the affiliated groups; it may permit infiltration of those organs associated in the front; it disguises the unvarying communist goals; it suggests a communist willingness to work within a legal framework for reasonable ends; it gives the Party a broader audience than it could attract on its own; and it familiarizes the communists with those issues which may be utilized to foment discord. Thus we find the CPUSA seeking to create a united front with other left-wing parties, with labor unions, with civil rights organizations, and with other groups attempting to work for specific objectives. Through the years the nature of the fronts and the objects of unity have varied. For the first ten years of its existence the Party sought to achieve "union from above," an appeal to the leaders of the left to make common cause with the communists. Between 1928 and 1935 there was a shift in approach as the communists sought to appeal to the masses, especially in the labor ranks, by-passing their leaders. International developments ushered in a third phase of front activity between 1935 and 1939. Hitler's rise and the resurgence of a militarist Germany offered a beautiful opportunity to develop a front against fascism. The Nazi menace could be loudly condemned without betraying the particular interest of the Soviet Union in combatting the German potential for aggression. The abrupt change in international politics occasioned by the Russo-German non-aggression pact of 1939 forced the CPUSA into an equally abrupt about face and a new effort to develop a front for peace which would deter American participation in World War II. When two years later Hitler reneged on the agreement with the Soviet Union and turned his attack to the east, the Party—which by this time had become practically a whirling dervish—once again shifted its policy and essayed the creation of a front to win the war. From that point until the end of the war communist status was probably as high as it ever got in the United States as all mutual efforts were concentrated on achieving victory, and mutual antagonisms were pushed into the background. With the end of World War II and the advent of the cold war communist front efforts have been dedicated to occasional specific issues and the general theme of peace in which the U.S.S.R. is normally pictured as the prime advocate of a peaceful world.

Closely related to the "united front" tactics has been that of creating individual "communist front" organs. The effort here has been less combination than it has been the establishment of organizations with attractive titles which might entice unwary non-communist members and serve as contexts for communist indoctrination and the pursuit of specific aims. Again the intent is to secure a degree of respectability and to disguise communist direction and control of such organs. Among the alluringly titled organizations appearing on the U.S. Attorney General's list of groups having significance in connection with national security are the Abraham Lincoln Brigade, the American League Against War and Fascism, the American League for Peace and Democracy, the American-Russian Fraternal Society, the Committee to Uphold the Bill of Rights, and many others (not exclusively pro-communist). Membership in front organs may be innocent, but it allows communists to argue their cause subtly—and possibly to make converts, and sizeable memberships may be propagandized into signs of growing support for the communist position on any specific issue.

A third tactic is seeking support from non-communists for legitimate causes which the communists can utilize for devious purpose. No "front" action may be involved here. Instead an appeal may be made for funds and/or moral support (including the signing of petitions) to those known to be truly concerned about some problem but who are not pro-communist. Such items as peace, improved living standards for workers, and civil rights are among those which could be counted on to elicit non-communist backing. From the communist viewpoint—and appeals were frequently made in such manner as to disguise communist sponsorship—aid received was not to be dedicated to the solution of the problem involved but was to be used to dramatize, perhaps disproportionately, the flaws in contemporary American society as a means of upgrading proposed communist "solutions" to existing problems. Thus the CPUSA was able to capitalize on legitimate grievances and popular concern by enlisting the assistance of those genuinely interested in working for reasonable practical solutions and by perverting such aid to communist ends.

In each of the above schemes there is an additional tactical advantage for the Party; they enable the communists to introduce their particular jargon into legitimate group usage. Popularization of an idea can be advanced by acceptance of a seemingly descriptive phrase and its frequent use. Though the phrase may be too simplified to be adequately descriptive of the idea, its continued repetition implies understanding and acceptance. "Economic democracy," for example, means something quite different to communists and non-communists, but use of the term by non-communists allows communists—by similar usage —to pose as backers of an acceptable idea. The greater the introduction of communist clichés into widespread communication the less the communists appear to be "different" and suspect.

Much of communist activity has been strategically aimed at generating class tensions and exacerbating real discontent. Negroes, Puerto Ricans, Jews, industrial workers, itinerant farmers, and other groups have been special targets of communist propaganda. The traditional communist claim has, of course, been that capitalist society is split into bourgeois and proletarian classes which are naturally antagonistic. In the United States the same approach has been made, and all the ills of a free enterprise economy (depression, collusion, monopoly, etc.) have received wide publication. But those who sought to remedy these ills have received similar condemnation. To the extent that the Progressive Movement, the New Deal, or other programs sought to rectify faults rather than discard the system they came under fire from the communists for deterring the violent upheaval which Marxism-Leninism insists is the prerequisite for the "ideal" society. As long as it could be demonstrated that renovation was possible and that cooperation between supposedly opposed groups could benefit both, communist claims of the inability of the system to produce a good life for all— calling for its overthrow—would appear crude and unappealing.

The thwarting of the CPUSA in its effort to picture the ills of the American economic system as requiring the total eradication of laissez-faire economics has not, however, prevented the Party from using continuing sources of discontent for their own purposes. It must be admitted that with all the progress the American society has made, there remain significant pockets of poverty, inequities of opportunity, denials of equal rights, and disturbing degrees of intolerance and suspicion. In any of these there is a fertile field for communist plowing, because dissatisfaction can be worked to create dissension, increase animosities, and produce violence—all of which work to the Party's advantage. *The point to be emphasized is* that wherever the communists interest themselves in a disadvantaged group *there is no intention of seeking to improve the circumstances of that group.* A problem solved offers no benefit to the Marxists. Only as long as discontent and frustration can be preserved is the communist cause served. No matter what posture the CPUSA assumes, the welfare of non-communists is its last concern. The plight of the American Negro and communist "milking" of this problem are illustrative of the tactic. For too long the Negro has been a second class citizen; for too long he has been denied those political and civil rights which were superficially granted after the Civil War; he has been too little a beneficiary of the economic and social gains in America. Quite naturally the Negro minority has been dissatisfied, disenchanted, and increasingly frustrated, and unfulfilled aspirations can lead to violent action. Knowing this, communists have devoted considerable energy to stimulating Negro self-expression—especially in violent fashion. (It should be noted that most Negro leaders were sophisticated enough to recognize the hypocritical nature of communist support and to reject it, contenting themselves with fighting their own battles.) As gains in equality of rights and opportunities for Negroes were made, the communists were then not above fostering the prejudices of whites who felt themselves economically or socially threatened by the new movement. Discord, animosity, disorder—these are the grist for the communist mills even when they proceed from causes unrelated to communism, and the communists are quick to make what contribution they can to produce or prolong strife. American communists are even prompt to condemn any evidence of prejudicial activity toward those of the Hebrew faith despite the ample record of anti-Semitism in the Soviet Union.

Next in the list of tactical maneuvers of the CPUSA is its long program of peace campaigning. Typical and most prominent of these efforts was the World Peace Congress of 1950 and the circulation of the Stockholm peace petition which followed, to which American communists gave wide support. While nominally committed to the meritorious tasks of condemning aggression, calling for the outlawing of atomic weapons, and even advocating general disarmament, these peace movements have been really nothing more than a criticism of the United States and its allies. The Soviet Union is always the "peace loving" state, and its enemies are "war mongers" and aggressors. "Western" imperialism is a constant claim, and no notice is taken of the fact that since the end of World War II the western nations have disbanded their empires and that it is the U.S.S.R. which has worked feverishly to create and maintain an empire and to extend the tentacles of its influence around the globe. It is always, for the communists, the freedom bloc which is militaristic, and no attention is directed to the fact that the NATO defensive alliance was a direct result of the Soviet Union's failure to disarm after the Second World War and its conscious effort to bring all Europe under its sway through the use or threat of military force. Once again it is abundantly clear that the CPUSA in conjunction with other communist parties seeks to deprecate American policies and positions by the most blatant hypocrisy, hopeful that enough people are sufficiently concerned about peace that they will fail to realize the inaccuracies of the Marxist charges.

In furtherance of its aims the American Communist Party has utilized the whole range of propaganda processes available in a democratic society but has never balked at resorting to illegal activities to achieve its purposes. Public speeches, publication of a newspaper, production and distribution of leaflets, organization of "study groups," and seeking of converts have all been steady tools of the communist effort; but certain attention-getting techniques have received special emphasis. Demonstrations and the circulation of petitions are in this category. We should note immediately that it would be highly inaccurate to conclude that all demonstrations against the existing order are the result of communist instigation and organization. It may well be true that the CPUSA may try to "capture" the leadership of any demonstration issuing from legitimate causes or attempt to turn a peaceful demonstration into a violent one, but we should not assume, therefore, that there is no reasonable complaint involved—only a "communist plot"—and fail to ascertain the motives which prompt the demonstrators. This kind of confusion and intensification of difference is exactly what the communists seek, so a careful analysis of the issues involved is always necessary. Similarly, a circulated petition which receives the support of the CPUSA should not be summarily dismissed as unworthy simply because the Party has sought to enhance its stature through affiliation with a genuine cause. On the other hand, knowing the propaganda value, the Party has often mounted demonstrations or circulated petitions to try to create an aura of popular support for its dogma and has been successful on occasion in attracting non-communists to its side by careful phrasing of its position. The publicity thus gained is, of course, beneficial to the Party's total scheme.

Another maneuver of the American communists has been the effort to turn one of America's greatest virtues against it. Freedom of speech, press, and religion, and the other rights protected by the United States Constitution are cornerstones of the American system; without them American democracy could not exist. Ignoring the fact that all rights are relative and may be exercised only so long as they do not infringe the rights of others or jeopardize the safety and stability of the society, communists have stretched the exercise of individual rights beyond the limits of permissibility and have then cried "persecution" when they were restrained. The obvious irony of this situation is found in a comparison of the American and Soviet systems with respect to rights, but the stratagem of communist activities nevertheless presents a serious dilemma to the American people. The denial of fundamental rights to communists would make a mockery of our contentions; too lenient an interpretation of what is allowable could aid the communist goal of overthrow of government. What is particularly intriguing about the communist actions in this regard is that the Party does not really want equality of treatment. It is much more interested in picturing itself as a persecuted minority denied the essential privileges because of the unpopularity of its doctrine and suffering martyrdom in pursuit of justice. This posture is more conducive to the establishment of its claim that the American government is controlled by the capitalists who will brook no opposition to their will. And this is all the more reason why every effort must be made to permit communists to use to the fullest extent—but subject to the same restraints—those rights exercised by non-communists.

Perhaps the most persistent—and at times the most valuable —tactic of the CPUSA has been infiltration. From its inception the Party has recognized the importance of gaining a voice in special segments of the American society and has sought ceaselessly to insinuate its members into influential positions in various organizations and groups in order to use them as the communist leadership thought best. Target groups or organs included the governmental apparatus, the armed forces, the educational system, trade unions, veterans organizations, the Negro community, youth groupings, intellectual circles, and religious affiliations. Each of these offered some special attraction for the communists. The governmental agencies provided an opportunity to influence policy or engage in espionage; the armed forces were a ground for the sowing of discontent, lowering morale, and, in the extreme, inciting to mutiny; the schools and youth groups were the ideal locations for introducing Marxist ideology and molding immature minds along communist lines; trade unions were the natural habitat for those who proclaimed themselves the champions of the working masses and might be manipulated for disruptive purposes in collective bargaining, strikes, and violence; racial, ethnic, and religious groups might be shaped so as to give overtly hostile expression to their discontent or enlisted in support of the Party's supposedly humanitarian ventures. What made the infiltration effort moderately successful was the Party's pose of legality and its claim of indigenous status, the sophisticated presentation of its "reasonable" position, and the accuracy of many of its criticisms of American society. It was aided further by the economic depression of the 1930s and the degree of harmony achieved between the United States and the Soviet Union during the war years. Trade unionists were not too likely to question the ultimate motives of those who apparently sought the economic elevation of the masses; ideological conflict was naturally subordinated to the combined military action necessary to achieve victory in the 1940s. That the communists were successful in the infiltration try is attested by trade union records, FBI reports, congressional investigations, Supreme Court cases, and the results of state governmental inquiries. Though at times governmental agents may have been too fervent—or politically motivated—in ferreting out "communist supporters," the investigative activities leave no doubt of the extent and partial success of the Party's infiltration game. The dividends of the effort were not great, however. Disclosure brought a new awareness of the threat and alertness in denying communists further inroads. Trade unions began the job of cleansing themselves of communist influence; a new series of loyalty-security programs was initiated by governmental agencies; examination of teacher qualifications was intensified. As a matter of fact, the reaction was almost too strong; the zealousness displayed in weeding out communists affected adversely many individuals about whom only certain vague suspicions were aroused or who were too quickly judged on the principle of "guilt by association." In time fortunately a greater passionless objectivity was restored in applying the legal devices of restraint on communists, and this end was fostered while the rights of non-communists began to receive the protection they deserved.

There remain, then, to be noted two illegal tactics which the American communists have employed in their total plan of subversion—espionage and sabotage. Spying is not, of course, a uniquely communist tactic; it is practiced by agents of all nations in the interest of their respective societies. But it is a revealing commentary on a group that claims legal political party status and an independent indigenous nature that it should commit itself to a program of espionage in behalf of a foreign state. As in the case of infiltration, espionage activities achieved some results, but their exposure led to tightened security measures. Sabotage seems to have remained more a potential than an actual tactic of the CPUSA primarily because of the common effort in World War II and because the ensuing circumstances did not warrant its extensive use as a practical weapon. The instances of sabotage which did come to light, however, suggest the danger inherent in the potential and offer a further indication of the importance the Party attaches to penetrating the industrial complex in key positions.

The pattern of communist tactics here described clarifies the variety of weapons in the Party's arsenal as it seeks to subvert the government and the established institutions of the American society and the developing sophistication of the leaders who direct their use. Especially noteworthy is the utilization of legitimate avenues of democratic expression for communist purposes. The atmosphere of freedom in the United States has given the CPUSA more leeway in expounding its doctrine and pursuing its aims. Cognizance of this fact must not, nevertheless, lead to a diminution of the area of freedom; this would only play into communist hands. Instead Americans must accept the responsibility of guarding its free environment for all while remaining constantly alert to its perversion for illegal ends; restraint must be applied only after careful consideration and only in the flagrant cases of the abuse of guaranteed freedoms. Despite the advantage taken by the Party of the free spirit of America it has failed essentially in its mission. The reason for this failure is to be found primarily in the inability of the CPUSA to sell its doctrine to the American people. Marxism's deceptive attraction has never replaced America's faith in its own system. With all of its faults the democratic-capitalist structure seemed to offer a better context within which to resolve problems and conflicts than did the communist alternative. Even for those who felt themselves deprived of the benefits which our politico-economic-social scheme presumably offered, the communist society remained less attractive. Coupled with this failure was the zeal of the Party in seeking its goals which awakened Americans to the nature of the threat which they faced. As they became aware of the existence of a well-organized, highly dedicated, foreign-oriented organization operating to overthrow the government of the United States, Americans took the necessary steps and developed the alertness required to insure the defeat of the communist effort.

STUDY QUESTIONS AND PROJECT SUGGESTIONS

1. Discuss the status of the American Communist Party as a legitimate political group in the United States.
2. On what bases has the CPUSA attracted adherents in this country?
3. Outline the major tactics utilized by the communists to further their program in America.
4. Discuss briefly the legal restraints imposed on American communists in the last half-century.
5. Why is the imposition of legal restrictions on communists a sensitive matter in the United States?
6. Distinguish carefully between the U.S. Supreme Court's decisions in *Dennis v. U.S.* and *Yates v. U.S.* indicating the extent to which existing circumstances may have had an influence on the Court's reasoning.

CHAPTER 10

COMMUNISM—AN APPRAISAL

The attempt to appraise honestly and objectively the merits and defects of communism is necessarily difficult for one reared in a democratic-capitalist society whose principles are so diametrically opposed to those of Marxism-Leninism. The matter is complicated further by the necessity of distinguishing between communism as a theory and communism as a movement with all of its political as well as economic ramifications. If a more complete understanding of this ideology and its practical manifestations is to be achieved, however, the effort must be made, and the reader should try insofar as possible to dispel his own emotional opposition and resist the temptation to dismiss communism simply as "something" equatable with the pernicious policies of the Soviet Union or Red China—and therefore "bad" by definition. That the conclusion may be reached that communism's vices outweigh its virtues should not blind us to a recognition of whatever worth may be found in communist doctrine or practice.

The Pros

The first acknowledgment which must be made is that over a billion people today live under regimes which for one reason or another classify themselves as communistic, and they live in a spirit of relative satisfaction or even of contentment in terms of what they enjoyed previously. From the free world's viewpoint the shortcomings of communist societies often obscure the fact that the mass of the population lives and works in a tolerable environment in which the harsher aspects of communist rule may not be noticed in the normal course of events. Goods and services are produced, distributed, and consumed, and living standards may be more than minimal even though they may not compare with those of the free societies. Indeed, for the Russian and Chinese peasants it may be argued that their economic situation is improved—or at least not worsened—compared with that of the previous regimes under which they lived. The Soviet Union has demonstrated, as it developed and matured, that it is capable of producing consumer goods on an increasing scale while meeting its self-defined levels of heavy industrialization. In the sense of daily routine, then, the presence of a communist system does not automatically condemn citizens to a life of utter economic deprivation.

Nor can it be shown that the typical communist regime has been completely negligent of the welfare of the people. In the first place, the repressive tactics which are so familiar are normally directed at those who oppose the system, who criticize and seek change. The average citizen does not become so politically involved, and while he may resent limits on free choice and the direction of controlled media of communication, he accommodates to them and goes about his business. More importantly, communist governments do make some effort to curry public favor by providing basic social services (health and welfare) and recreational facilities. A great deal of energy is also expended to give the citizen a sense of participation in public affairs and to inculcate a sense of pride in the achievements of his society. If these tactics are successful, the citizen is less conscious of the advantages of others and more content with his lot. Keeping these things in mind it is not difficult to realize. that the average inhabitant in a communist state is not as unhappy as we would like to believe.

More than this it must be remembered that the communist ideology has been sufficiently attractive to millions of people to enlist their support in the communist cause and to lead them to fight to overthrow the prevailing political and economic institutions of their own societies. Though this development may have resulted in part from self-delusion and lack of understanding it does not eliminate the allure of the ideology or the compulsion of its reasoning. The vibrancy and attraction of Marxism is further substantiated by the continued affiliation of many who learned through experience the discrepancies in the theory and the cynicism of the leaders. In other words, communist dogma and practice possess the ability to recruit and retain the support of large numbers of individuals who find its precepts appealing and its accomplishments praiseworthy.

Another "plus" which communism can claim—in refutation of its critics—is that, within limits, it works. It can naturally be argued that the ultimate communist economic ideal cannot even be assessed for it does not exist. This is true. But if we accept the Soviet Union as the prime example of "scientific socialism" in action, embracing the basic tenets of public ownership, elimination of the profit motive, state planning, etc., we can assay that system. Proponents of capitalism have argued that the elimination of the profit motive must deprive the society of the incentive required for economic progress, that public ownership and centralized planning would suffocate the economic process. Shunting aside for the moment considerations of freedom, state ownership has not been incompatible with economic progress, and, despite the errors made in politicizing economic decisions, centralized planning has been successful in directing the course of the economy into productive channels. As a matter of fact, "mass ownership" has been the most practical approach to financing and productivity. For example, large scale farming has proved to be more effective than small plot agriculture—with its varying degrees of efficiency in which the advantages of mechanization and other technical expertise cannot be brought to bear.

Some motive—probably a simple desire for at least a minimum living standard or fear of punishment—has proved an adequate replacement for wage competition as labor incentive, and in a society where the individual entrepreneur has disappeared, consideration of profits as an entrepreneurial incentive is irrelevant and capital accumulation is effected by governmental fiat and selective allocation of resources. This does not mean that there is no pressure for successful achievement—measured in monetary terms—in any economic enterprise, but the motivation is not the enrichment of individual capitalists; rather, the motive and the index of success is the extent to which the total projected economic plan is fulfilled. The inescapable reality is, then, that though shot through with many unsavory features and operating on radically different principles the Soviet economy has made remarkable economic strides and its *rate* of economic growth has frequently surpassed that of the capitalist countries. (Its total production, however, has remained considerably below that of the United States.) The surprising accomplishments of the Soviet scientific and industrial establishment in weaponry and space exploration are further illustrations of the capacity of a regimented non-capitalist society to match the feats of the free world.

In the process of devising and improving its industrial complex the Soviet Union has derived an additional benefit which has given the economic system a firmer base—which may in time work a significant theoretical modification in the communist society. This benefit has been the evolution of a managerial cadre—a scientific and technological elite—whose capabilities are so essential to economic success. These individuals, forged in the fire of experience where success brings great rewards and failure warrants considerable economic or physical punishment, have sharpened their skills and improved their techniques in a manner which naturally contributes to the upgrading of the whole economic process. Such men and women have found their way into the military establishment and the government as well as industry, and, while "professionalizing" performances in these areas, their "pseudo-capitalist" orientation to success could well undermine the communist concept of classlessness within the society and the dictum of opposition to capitalist incentives.

A related benefit has accrued to the U.S.S.R. in the field of education. Spurred by necessity and motivated by desire to match or exceed the standards of the more advanced countries the Soviet leaders have placed great emphasis on developing the educational system. Though marred—from the western view —by heavy doses of Marxist indoctrination and a student selection based in part on political orthodoxy, Russia's scheme of higher education over the last forty years has trained more engineers, physicists, agricultural specialists, and physicians than American colleges and universities. It might be suggested that quality of performance and productive research still excel in the free world, but the communist achievement cannot be discounted—particularly in the aerospace field. As in the case of the professional elite, it may be a legitimate speculation that the broadening of the spirit of inquiry fostered by advanced educational training will ultimately bring into serious question some of communism's shaky premises and lead to doctrinal modification.

The actual existence of a number of viable politico-economic communist entities in which economic progress is significant and in which the average citizen enjoys a tolerable existence is surely not an absolute virtue, because the question can always be raised regarding the price in freedom which had to be paid for this reality. Neither should we ignore the failures of the communists in the economic realm. The opposition of the Russian peasants to socialization of the land, the collapse of Red China's peoples' communes, the lack of adequate agricultural production in both countries, and the general scarcity of consumer goods even after decades of experience are all indices of communism's shortcomings as an economic panacea. We can also speculate that communist citizens would enjoy considerably greater benefits under some other system.

There is, however, a real constructiveness to communism which lies in its theory—in the truth and half-truth of its historical analysis. It is here that the non-communist can learn invaluable lessons. Whatever else may be said of the dialectic, its concept of change and accommodation should be adequate caution to any society of the dangers inherent in a too rigid attachment to the status quo. Whether or not the Marxist idea of historical progression is rejected, the notion that any version of societal organization persisting over a long period must inevitably produce tensions demanding institutional or ideological alteration is a truism whose implications cannot be ignored. In the face of this challenge, then, the society must recognize and accept the pressure for change, channeling it to reasonable goals through peaceful compromise and modification, or run the risk of violent upheaval to effect the desired transformation. Complete intransigence on the part of those in power will, in time, only fulfill the Marxist prophecy of revolutionary necessity. In this same vein, the communist belief that economic motives underlie all human activity and dictate the nature of all of society's institutions requires careful scrutiny. It is not enough to dismiss this interpretation as being too facile and failing to take into account other motivations; we must give attention to the extent of validity of the contention. A conviction that economic concerns are not overriding for many individuals cannot invalidate the pragmatic observation that economic status is a major concern for most people most of the time, and that political and social arrangements reflect in large measure the basic economic stratification of society. The inference to be drawn, therefore, is that a society's organization and policies must demonstrate an awareness of the importance of economics in the lives of its citizens and must insure a basic satisfaction of the needs of all, otherwise the society—as the communists predict—will find itself embroiled in the destructive competition among its members for a reasonable slice of the economic pie. In this regard, the Marxian outline of class conflict takes on added importance. Even though it can be demonstrated that class conflict is not inevitable, the potential for such a contest must be a prime consideration of policy-makers. To the degree that a nation is class structured along economic lines, every effort must be made to assure that the classes do not conceive of themselves as arrayed against each other in economic battle; every energy must be expended to provide that economic satisfaction to the lower class which will minimize its antipathy toward the more affluent, and to foster the practice of cooperation among classes which will advance the economic interests of all. If the economic self-interest of the upper classes is made the principal criterion of public policy, then the communist projection of eventual conflict will in all probability ensue.

Interestingly, Marxist doctrine provides the insight for avoiding the logical implications of its own prognosis. Communist theory makes some strikingly accurate indictments of the free enterprise system. The charge that the profit motive in capitalism promotes a feverish chase for the dollar which tends to become an end in itself must be conceded; that this chase promotes cutthroat competition and unscrupulous business tactics is likewise too readily observable. It is a recognized fact that legitimate healthy competition has frequently given way to monopoly and price fixing thereby denying the consumer the supposed advantage of the producer's drive to improved product and lower cost. It is undeniable that the unbridled operation of laissez-faire economics has produced periodically the economic boom and bust of the business cycle with its attendant miseries. The surplus value theory of worker exploitation—though questionable on its premises—at least raises the question of whether laborers receive a fair income for their contribution to the productive process and opens the door to the broader question of labor's treatment by management in the era of the industrial

revolution. When Marxists call attention to the obvious gulf between the wealth of the few and the poverty of the many under
capitalism, they not only emphasize a distressing inequity but
sound a call to arms to rectify it. The communist condemnation
of the ideal of private property, while overdrawn, should also
give pause for reconsideration of the ramifications of capitalist
commitment to the precept. Even such a defender of the private property concept as John Locke had reservations about the
kinds and amounts of private property which might be amassed
by individuals as a "natural" right. Though private property as
an abstract concept may well be justified, as the core of an
economic system which developed so many flaws it is not a precept of undiluted virtue.

The verity of this collection of communist accusations offers
a distinct benefit to non-communists *if* the verity is accepted
rather than rebuffed. If the free enterprise response is to dispute
the technicalities of the charges and engage in semantic debate
little practical advantage will be gained. If, instead, a candid
concession of the faults is made and a conscious effort follows
to seek out and remedy the causes, the capitalist system will be
strengthened through the removal of legitimate bases of criticism. In other words, regardless of the motives of Marxist critics
the nature of the analysis they make of the free enterprise system presents an excellent opportunity for stock-taking in the
capitalist camp and an occasion for remedial action before repairs come too late to save the worthy structure.

One final comment might be made about a development
which, though it is not an inherently virtuous characteristic of
communism, suggests a modification of communist principles
from which the non-communist world may draw some satisfaction. An initial appraisal of Marxist-Leninist dogma may lead
to the conclusion that communism and capitalism are embarked
on an inevitable collision course. The reality of the evolution of
communist societies intimates that this inference may not be
fully warranted. As the Soviet Union moved from the status of
a backward agrarian society to that of world power a subtle—

and still inconclusive—change could be noted in its outlook and policies. Its leaders persisted in their condemnation of capitalism and leveled periodic charges at the free world, but their actions displayed a new character of moderation which did not match the fire of their pronouncements. There has been no complete renunciation of probing for soft spots in the free world's armor or of seeking to extend Soviet power and influence into new geographic areas; but when confronted with a firm opposition Russian officials have not forced the issue to the point where a military contest would have become inevitable. There appears to be, in other words, a growing recognition that great power and high stature in the international community create an obligation not to act irresponsibly, that the immaturity of national adolescence must be abandoned in the sober world of national adulthood. The U.S.S.R., of course, shows no intention of permitting the disintegration of its empire or surrendering fully its aggressive designs. But in recent years its general demeanor has given new hope that its growing maturity as a senior member in the family of nations may submerge the rashness of its fledgling years and may permit a rapprochement with non-communist countries in the interest of a peaceful world.

The Cons

Whatever the validity of the Marxist attack on laissez-faire economics and whatever the allure of the communist appeal, a careful analysis of the doctrine of scientific socialism reveals a number of theoretical inconsistencies and a wide disparity between theory and practice. Rigorous examination suggests not only that the communist ideal is unattainable, but that, if it were, the tactics advocated by the Marxists are probably the least likely to produce the desired results. The invalidity of Marx's prophecy, the consistent deviation from dogma by communist leaders, the egocentric competition for power among the communist elite, the demonstrated perfectibility of the capitalist system, and the cost of securing even an approximation of the idealized vision of the Marxist-Leninists should make it perfectly clear that the continued exposition of communist views is nothing more than a gigantic hoax perpetrated by a handful of power seekers and calculated to attract the support of the underprivileged by conscious deception. An appreciation of this fact should point the way to the most effective means of combatting the threat posed by the so-called communist camp and should allay the unreasoning fear which communism seems capable of producing in the minds of citizens of the free world.

The first jarring inconsistency is apparent in the relation of two basic premises in Marxist philosophy—the dialectic and the necessity for revolutionary activity. The dialectic analysis prescribes the *inevitable* downfall of capitalism and its succession by a communist economy. If this be so, why is such elaborate revolutionary planning and action necessary? If capitalism is doomed by the irrepressible march of historical forces, it would appear that the proletariat need only await the ultimate collapse rather than risk a revolutionary uprising. On the other hand, if the dialectic is merely a theoretical working hypothesis, as Engels maintained, and requires instigation by the conscious effort of the proletariat, the communists are necessarily deprived of the force of historical imperative inherent in the concept of dialectical materialism. The potential rebuttal that revolutionary upheaval is a way of hastening the inevitable is unsatisfactory in that Marx insisted that the capitalist system would have to run its full evolutionary course before the succeeding era of communism could be inaugurated. The communistic theme thus begins on a contradictory note—a claim of historic inevitability and simultaneously an insistence that revolutionary action is necessary to implement the inevitable. In this same vein we can ask why, in view of the dialectic, the communists should argue that their system will necessarily be the ultimate end of historical evolution. Even granting that minimizing class friction might modify the urge to conflict, the logic of the dialectic suggests that a communist economic system must in time breed opposing tendencies which would cause change. If Marxists would have us accept the unrelenting pressure of history, they cannot expect us to disregard the drive to change when their own ideal is implemented.

Are the tactics of revolution compatible with the characteristics of the ideal communist society? The late Professor Harold Laski—a British socialist—pointed out that large scale violence was conducive to the release of exactly those passions whose restraint was required for the establishment of a communist community. Physical combat, hatred, suspicion, anger, and kindred emotions do not contribute to the creation of the co-operative serenity essential to the Marxist-Leninist utopia. And once unleashed these human qualities are not easily rechained; once mortal competition has been undertaken and the struggle for power joined, it cannot be expected that, upon the cessation of hostilities, those in the forefront of this battle will quietly surrender themselves to the equality of a classless society, or that erstwhile foes will contain their antagonisms and gladly embark on a course of peaceful mutuality. The communists, it would then seem, place obstacles in the path to the millenium by their selection of the tactic of revolution.

The next question which might be raised about Marx's theory is whether economic influences are all controlling in human activity. If they are not, it follows that the Marxist interpretation of history is fallacious. We can acknowledge the influence of economics in life and still dispute the emphasis Marx places. Certainly such ideals as personal liberty, national patriotism, and religious beliefs can be seen to override economics at various stages in the sweep of history; the search for power and glory often seems to outweigh the pursuit of material gain as leadership motivations; innumerable instances of self-sacrifice and service appear to bring into question the surpassing dominance of economic motives in human action. The relegation of other than economic inducements to human action to subordinate positions and the analysis which pictures all ideals as stemming from an economic base look, more than anything else, like a forced arrangement of historical factors to substantiate Marxian interpretation. Economic competition and the scramble for higher living standards cannot be erased from the human equation, but an historical computation which centers on only a single factor is distinctly warped.

Does human nature allow for the communist ideal of a classless society? As an answer to the problem of economic inequities under capitalism and as a rejoinder to the contention that the dialectic process would not end with communism the Marxists propose the creation of a classless society in which economic gain would be equalized and the spirit of class competition eliminated. Granting for the moment that narrowing the gulf between wealth and poverty is a worthy objective and that modification of the economic class structure is a legitimate means to that end, can classlessness be attained? Agreeing that the provision of economic security for all is a desirable aim and assuming that there is a spirit of cooperation in most people which could be evoked in this effort, it is still inconceivable that a truly classless society could be developed. Each individual possesses a personality which, though pliable, ultimately rejects being put in a common mold. The drive to be different —to excel—supersedes any tendency to accept superficial similarities or to espouse a general orthodoxy. The observable "herd" instinct which courts uniformity and distrusts nonconformity is not a permanent phenomenon or innate human addiction. It is, rather, an inherent eccentric egoism which propels the human organism. Classlessness, therefore, in the sense of leveling individuals to a common norm would have to be achieved against the onslaught of basic human drives.

To be sure, to accuse communists of desiring to create a society in which each individual is identical to the next is to warp communist theory. The Marxists would insist that the concept of classlessness means simply a disruption of the class system of capitalism and a more equitable distribution of society's economic produce to all. Even on the basis of this definition, however, the classless society of the communists can be challenged.

The economic organization of the community, even if we accept Marx's version of the "withering away" of the state, will require that some persons order and others obey; this requirement alone will perpetuate a class structure in which policy-makers will claim a disproportionate economic return. Further, if classlessness as an ideal is characterized only by a general equality and rising living standards for the lower economic groups, and if the Soviet Union and the United States are chosen as prime examples of scientific socialist and capitalist systems, it might well be asked whether the communist or free enterprise system has come closer to reaching the ideal.

Can a planned society of economic equalitarianism such as the communists envision be established without destroying initiative and ambition? We have already noted that economic incentives are not the only practical stimulants to the exercise of individual initiative. However, if the communists were able to establish the practice of "from each according to his ability, to each according to his needs" and each person's economic status became relatively static with no expectation of extra compensation for the exertion of extra effort or initiative, would the society not lose the advantage of the collective impetus which could be fostered by the promise of greater economic rewards? Would not the entrepreneurial drive to improved productive process—urged by the hope of increased profits—likewise be a casualty? The stick may replace the carrot as inducement to minimum economic activity, but an observation of human nature induces the inference that the more able, the more industrious, the more inventive will have no compulsion to exert themselves unduly so long as they know that those less able may receive as much or more economic return if their "needs" are deemed to equal or exceed those of the more capable. The zest of the organizer, the developer, the salesman, and the potential entrepreneur would be diminished. In the final analysis, the tendency to minimum and mediocre productive effort may well create a national environment in which the marginally productive worker becomes the norm, leading to a progressive stagnation of economic production. The very nature of governmental enterprise is a further commentary on this same theme. Since the organizers and directors of public corporations operate on fixed incomes, and since, theoretically, the aim of government is service rather than profit, there is little inducement in this context to improve productivity, invent new processes, streamline organization, or develop novel and better techniques out of a desire for increased monetary gain.

As a rebuttal to this projection of deterioration Marxists may argue that the utopian ideal will be reached only after a long period of experience and education, and that any speculation on its ultimate nature is premature. In the interim the communists would point to the implementation of the Leninist principle of "from each according to his ability, to each according to his work" as adequate incentive to production during the transition period. But the very fact of graduated compensation being offered as an incentive completely invalidates the communist principle of economic equality and substitutes one group of economic classes for another. It is simply the profit motive operating in a different guise—the precise capitalist tenet which the communists claim they wish to destroy.

What will be the living standard in the communist society? Communistic philosophy gives no precise answer to this question. It speaks about "economic democracy" and "economic security" but avoids mention of how the "needs" of individuals will be ascertained or of specific levels of income which will be sought. Again we are in an area of speculation, and we cannot predict with certainty a complete failure of ideal realization, but an examination of living standards in the U.S.S.R. since the inception of the communist regime—during which time monetary incentives have been utilized for increased productivity—would suggest that the Marxist concept of individual economic needs is not a particularly enticing promise.

What will be the duration of the temporary period of proletarian dictatorship? Recalling the communist dictum that the uprising of the masses must be succeeded *temporarily* by a dictatorship of the proletariat, it may reasonably be asked when such dictatorship will terminate and a popular regime providing liberty and equality take its place. It is needless to labor the point that the prototype of such dictatorship established in the Soviet Union is not a "popular," workers' dictatorship, but is the imposed regime of a self-selected and self-perpetuating "elite" and is hardly concerned with expanding individual freedoms. Nor can it be said that recent events in the U.S.S.R. itself or in its satellite empire augur well for a shift in the direction of relaxed controls on the citizenry. This "temporary" dictatorship has now persisted for half a century and shows no signs of releasing its grip on the reins of political power. This fact should give serious pause for thought to those attracted to communism as a "humanitarian" philosophy who might be willing to undergo a momentary period of political autocracy as a necessary price for the attainment of an ideal.

A related question, of course, is whether the political state can "wither away" as Marxists claim. Even if a modification of the proletarian dictatorship could be secured, some group would still have to remain responsible for determining economic policies and defining the public good. Goals must be set, allocations made, processes adopted, and plans implemented. At least a minimum degree of authority and power would be necessary for carrying out economic decisions. To what extent the exercise of such power would differ from the political authority now wielded is certainly not clear. It would also seem too much to expect that those accustomed to positions of power would voluntarily relinquish those positions and the attached privileges. Instead the steady hold of the elite communist bureaucracy indicates its determination to perpetuate the class structure of the Soviet society, to maintain its privileged position, and to ignore the implications of dogma regarding its ultimate self-effacement. The intrigues and periodic purges within the Party illustrate the intense competition for the perquisites of leadership and the jealousy with which the leadership positions are guarded.

Cannot there be cooperation rather than conflict between economic classes? Marxist theory insists that the competition for economic resources makes class conflict inevitable. It prescribes that there can be no détente, that one class must triumph over another. Though Americans perceived the imperfections of their own system, they were not willing to reject it outright and to accept the ideas of class conflict; they sought another way out. The way was to create a governmentally supervised process of *cooperation* between labor and management—a scheme of collective bargaining and mutual restraint, in which the welfare of all might be protected. This was coupled with a system of legal restrictions designed to eliminate the abuses of capitalist freedom while retaining the worthy elements in the system. That the whole development was largely involuntary is true; that the cooperation it established was grudging is also true. Various types of competition and conflict remain, but they have been overlaid by a spirit of cooperative mutuality which has produced tremendous economic benefits for the entire society. In short, the path to economic satisfaction and equality does not inevitably entail the massive class conflict of Marxist musings. Compromise and cooperation can achieve better results while maintaining the essential virtues of laissez-faire which the communists fail to acknowledge.

Further theoretical contradictions and practical inconsistencies can be found in a closer examination of the Chinese version of communism and in the relations between the Soviet Union and its communist associates. The discussions of the philosophic leaders of Red China on democratic centralism are a case in point. Superficially it might appear that this shibboleth is not a contradiction in terms, that democratic processes can be combined with highly centralized control. Potentially, information and advice can filter from the bottom to the top of the governmental hierarchy as the basis for decisions which, once made at the highest echelon, must be unquestioningly implemented. The doctrinal debates and experiences of the Chinese communists leave no doubt, however, that centralism overrides democracy. Only "correct" advice can be pushed upward; critics of the leaders are not tolerated; faulty decisions are invariably attributed to subordinates; suggested improvements in centrally approved plans run the risk of being classed as deviationism. The nice, neat balance implied in the term is a fiction.

The principles of "collective leadership" and "individual responsibility" are likewise deceptive. They serve to preserve the infallibility of the leadership and provide scapegoats for errors. Once a general policy has been outlined by the collective leadership, individuals must decide on the specifics of implementation. If the execution is faulty, the individual can be called to account. If, in his defense, he pleads the ideological correctness of his position, his prosecutors will charge him with inflexibility; should he claim a pragmatic flexibility for his actions, he will be subject to the charge of deviationism or lacking ideological steadfastness. Even those in the top echelons are not safe from the implications of individual responsibility should they incur the ire of the Party leader. And given the deviousness of doctrinal phrasing and the alternatives which must be faced in the practical execution of a general policy, the potential for error and punishment is great.

The "mass line" and the "Party line" concepts are also contradictory. The mass line idea—much like democratic centralism —implies a balance between Party initiative and guidance on the one hand and popular support on the other. Correct ideas and policies, according to Mao, must reflect the will of the masses, but they must be refined and popularized by the Party. Therefore it is the duty of cadres to elicit public opinion and generate public support for official policies; alienation of the masses is a cardinal sin. At the same time, the Party line prescribes the dogma and policies which must be accepted by the rank and file to insure the Party's continuing leadership and to effectuate political and economic plans. Theoretically there should be no divergence between the two, but actually the differences may be great, and subordinates are caught in the trap of having to enforce Party decisions which may be highly unpopular or of relaying mass opinions which run contrary to Party stands. In either case it is difficult if not impossible for cadre members to validate fully and simultaneously both concepts.

The image of an ideological and cooperative unity throughout the "communist world" which the Soviet Union tries to project is another myth. Even a superficial examination discloses the falseness of the façade and underscores the reality of Soviet imperialism which the CPSU attempts to mask with its contention of solidarity among all socialist states and their commitment to Marxist doctrine as an ideal. This deception is designed not only to hide the dissension which exists, but to picture the communist camp as an ideological and military monolith whose attraction is irresistible and whose march cannot be restrained. It is intended to confuse and to frighten non-communists, and it is intended to lure the unwary. When the mask is stripped away, the Soviet Union is seen as a typically imperialist state whose actions and aspirations can be dealt with in a more forthright and practical manner.[1]

The evidence that the fostering of communism *per se* is a subordinate goal of Soviet policy and that communist unity is a fiction is plentiful. In the first place, little effort has been made within the U.S.S.R. to inaugurate the political and economic utopia of classlessness and equality which is the supposed goal of the communist movement. The government is certainly not withering away, and the population is highly disciplined. Doctrinal debates in the Soviet Union are not dedicated to purifying dogma, but are maneuvers in the incessant struggle for power. While it may be conceded that the top Party leaders hold some reverence for communism, it is distinctly questionable whether their commitment is born of ideological dedication. Communism is a thought system in which they are immersed and it is a politico-economic system through which they have risen to power. Yet, should they have to make a choice between

[1] See Emile B. Ader, "Soviet Imperialism or Communist Ideology—the Real Threat," *Social Science,* Vol. 38, #2 (April, 1963), 75–82.

self-perpetuation in authority and defense of communism at the cost of their own positions, it ls unlikely that ideological devotion would triumph over political opportunism.

On the international front there is a long history of dissidence within the communist group and a clear picture of the Soviet Union's attempt to build a new empire. That at least a portion of the Communist Party leadership and membership in the Western world is disillusioned and cynical is bountifully attested by the spate of writings of disenchanted ex-communists. For such apostates neither the sense of power derived from Party hierarchical status nor the remuneration received as Party functionaries has blurred the observance of the discouraging gulf between communist theory and achievement or mitigated the pressure of the Soviet demand for loyalty to Moscow as the price of continuing support. Behind the "iron curtain" the relations between the U.S.S.R. and its satellites lend credence to the idea that the leaders of international communism are not satisfied with the existence of an independent communist state but require instead political subservience to Moscow. In the 1950s the grudging rapprochement with the Polish communists and the ruthless suppression of the Hungarian uprising indicate that ideological affinity is an insufficient substitute for subjugation as the basis for satisfactory relations with the Soviet Union. At the same time Palmiro Togliatti's proposal of a "polycentric system" of full autonomy for national communist movements illustrated the wide variety of interpretations of world communism made in the personal interest of communist leaders outside the U.S.S.R. And Moscow's slightly veiled denunciations of the Togliatti approach is another example of Soviet insistence on calling the tune for communists in all countries as a means of furthering its imperialist aspirations. The 1968 invasion of Czechoslovakia by Russian troops is a more recent illustration of Moscow's determination to retain its control over satellite regimes and to utilize ideology as a rationalization for exercising its authority in military form. But it is the Sino-Soviet rift which depicts most clearly the absence of unity in the commu-

nist camp and the competition among the leaders. The prolonged ideological debate between the Russian and Chinese
Party chieftains is properly interpreted not as an effort to refine
doctrine or as proof of the significance of dogma in the communist scale of values but rather as a device to assure the maintenance of Moscow's position as the Mecca of communism and,
simultaneously, its channels of control over communists everywhere. When Liu Shao-ch'i was still in power, he expressed the
Chinese resentment over Soviet tactics by cautioning his Russian
neighbor that "in our relations with all fraternal parties . . . we
must resolutely oppose any dangerous inclination toward great-
nation chauvinism or bourgeois nationalism"—a caveat which was
not given a cordial reception in the Kremlin. The reality of the
conflict between the communist giants and the inadequacy of
ideology as a restraint on conflicting national ambitions was
concisely expressed by Harrison Salisbury when he wrote in
The New York Times (August 4, 1959) that "neither camouflage
nor verbiage can conceal the fact that here in Central Asia
Soviet and Chinese policies are competitive and directed to
divergent goals."

The numerous doctrinal discussions, the defections, and the
open leadership contests within the communist orbit really raise
the question of whether there is even a nucleus of theory to
which Soviet and other communists subscribe unanimously and
freely. Do the constant theoretical shifts and resorts to "tactical
flexibility" suggest a search for contemporary modification of
traditional doctrine—a reexamination of Marxism-Leninism for
current applicability? Or do these deliberations suggest the absence of any core belief and the prevalence of merely a nebulous
conglomeration of ideas, phrases, catchwords, and excuses which
may be used for the advantage of the erstwhile leaders and as a
smoke screen for the new imperialism? The failure of the world
society to conform to Marx's predictions, the changed circumstances of capitalist economics, the evolution of the Soviet society itself, the neo-imperialism of the U.S.S.R., and the internecine conflicts among communist countries argue for the latter

interpretation. Even if dissent were permitted by the Soviet Union and individualized interpretations of communism tolerated, it is apparent that a doctrine affording such latitude in conception and application could hardly serve as a meaningful cohesive force acceptable to all parties. Against the background of differences in national traditions and cultural heritages, it is difficult to visualize communism serving as the cement for a structure housing the common interests of the U.S.S.R., Red China, France, Italy, Indonesia, and other countries around the world.

Recognition of the lack of cohesion among communist states and the secondary nature of ideology as a unifying factor is important not only as a further demonstration of communism's fallacies but as a guide to the way in which the imperialist thrust of the Soviet Union or Red China should be met. Communist doctrine is definitely a *tool* in Russian and Chinese colonial ventures. It is a basis of appeal to the economically underprivileged as a means of penetration; the "communist system" is presented as the key to the comparatively rapid industrialization of the U.S.S.R.—a model for emulation by underdeveloped countries; dogma is cited to create a sense of historic inevitability for the victory of world communism; and a Party apparatus provides a convenient opportunity for the politically ambitious individual in a newly emergent nation or one in the midst of change. But communist theory is only a tool; it is not a mystical phenomenon of such force and attractiveness as to insure its own invincibility, and we of the free world must not treat it as such. Armed with this knowledge we should not fear the irresistible advance of a dread scourge against which we are trying to erect makeshift defenses. We must not attribute to communists the steadfastness of purpose and single-minded pursuit of their world objectives as to suggest the impossibility of deterring the avalanche more than temporarily. We must not act as though the only alternatives were total capitulation or a final indulgence in nuclear holocaust.

Relations with communist states can be conducted much more

pragmatically when a rational appraisal of the international situation is made and we divest ourselves of the hysterical emotionalism which the communists consciously foster. Changes in Soviet policy should not be construed exclusively as exercises in tactical flexibility, but as forced responses to free world policy or involuntary deviations caused by changed circumstances. Communist foreign policy failures must be assessed for what they are—losses in the game of international politics, and should not be viewed as shrewd maneuvers ingeniously calculated to confuse the free world and guarantee subsequent gains. The communists are certainly not unbeatable at the conference table, and the search for a *modus vivendi* in this arena should not be abandoned out of unreasoning fear. Free world programs of technical aid and economic assistance have been eminently more successful than those of the communist bloc, and even communist propaganda has lost much of its initial impact.

Free world foreign policy—particularly American—must be predicated on the certain knowledge we possess about the opposition. We know that communism as a theory is replete with inconsistencies; we know that there is little coincidence between theory and practice; we know that communism is not monolithic; we know that we have been victims of a certain amount of self-deception and self-induced apprehensiveness; we know that the Soviet Union embarked on a course of more or less traditional imperialism using communist theory as a theme of justification. Our responsibility then is to broadcast the facts, the fallacies, the hypocrisy. We must exploit the schisms in communist ranks. We must patiently await and work for changes in the communist societies themselves. We must demonstrate by example the superiority of our own system and values. In our dealings with underdeveloped nations and those recently emerged from colonial status we must be careful to avoid pushing them into the arms of the communists. We must recognize that neutralism or non-alignment does not constitute "siding with the communists"; we must appreciate that all states will not pattern their politico-economic systems after our own;

we must accept the fact that nations seeking rapid economic development will turn to almost any source of assistance; we must be willing to help less fortunate peoples while refraining from any action which might suggest the imposition of a new and more subtle colonial yoke; we must caution against the dangers of Soviet imperialist penetration and point out the incompatibility of truly nationalist movements and international communism under Soviet hegemony, but we must avoid any seeming intent to dictate their national policies.

In the end, the most telling criticism which can be leveled against communism is the extent to which it restricts individual freedom. Even without considering the ramifications of a dictatorial totalitarian state, the very nature of the projected economic arrangements of a communized society requires severe limitations on personal liberty. Should it be possible to develop a plan insuring economic stability, the regimentation necessary to implement such a program would drastically limit freedom of choice in the economic sphere. Any deviation from the plan affecting its outcome would have to be curtailed. Employment changes, collective bargaining, strikes or other voluntary employee actions adversely impinging on the economic blueprint would necessarily have to be restrained or prohibited. Very little, if any, criticism of the plan (or the planners) could be tolerated. Individual desires would have to be subordinated to the "common good" as defined by the planning elite. In short, centralized economic planning might be able to make a contribution to stabilizing economic activity and to equalizing income distribution, but it could do so only at the cost of eliminating a vast area of individual freedom.

It is not, however, this aspect of restriction which is the greatest concern. Instead, it is the demonstrated destruction of overall liberty which accompanies the installation of the dictatorship of the Communist Party leadership. However justified, all the individual freedoms which are so highly prized in democratic societies seem to vanish under the aegis of the "vanguard of the proletariat." Free speech, free press, free assembly, freedom of religion, and the protections established for persons accused of crimes all go by the board; they are replaced by state-controlled communications media, attacks on all traditional religions, and summary judicial procedures. Criticism and dissent are not acceptable and may be severely punished. Spying, terrorism, purges, forced labor, and execution become a way of life. The arts and even the sciences become subject to political direction, and creativity withers. For those accustomed to the general liberty of a free society it may be difficult to visualize the sudden extinction of all the rights and privileges they possess and use, as they are taken for granted. But a few moments' contemplation can begin to depict the extent to which even minor restraints on free expression would begin to gnaw at one's spirit, to create a sense of frustration, to build a cell of despair. Multiplying this sensation many times will give some idea of the magnitude of the loss which, experience teaches, communism imposes. These are the stakes of the game. The existence of some kind of communist-oriented society does not necessarily require the obliteration of all personal freedom, but empirical analyses of existing regimes confirm that restraint is the rule and permissiveness the exception. Whenever the muzzle on free speech has been loosened, extensive criticism of both the system and the leaders has followed, with the result that restrictions have been reinstituted. Dictatorships require popular enthusiasm or enforced quiescence, and should the ruling clique feel its position threatened by public discontent it will forcibly close the avenues of expression to restore submissiveness.

In conclusion, we may again acknowledge that something called communism does exist in the world and has worked within limits. But in accepting that fact we should ask whether what has worked is communism. Ideal economic goals remain unachieved; the governmental apparatus of the state remains very much in evidence; class structures are prominent; the temporary dictatorship seems destined to persist indefinitely. In other words, except for public ownership and central planning, the major characteristics of Marxism are absent from those societies designating themselves communist. Actually, from Lenin's New Economic Policy to Khrushchev's "individual economic incentives," economic progress in the U.S.S.R. has been related in large measure to the capitalist profit motive. "From each according to his ability, to each according to his work" is merely another way of phrasing the traditional laissez-faire concept of higher pay for greater productivity. Communist "success," in short, relies heavily on a basic doctrine of the economic system which communism condems so vociferously. Finally, we should note that "communist" gains do not represent the growing attraction of communist philosophy or even the development and expansion of a unified communist camp. Rather, we must recognize that the "spread of communism" is, in reality, only the institution of a series of authoritarian regimes using communist theory as a vehicle for gaining and holding power. Our efforts in opposition, then, should be directed against authoritarianism and against the ignorance which permits the deceptiveness of Marxist theory to serve as a tool in establishing dictatorships.

STUDY QUESTIONS AND PROJECT SUGGESTIONS

1. On what bases can communism be defended theoretically or practically?
2. What criticisms can be made of communist ideology?
3. Outline the major discrepancies between communist theory and the practice of "communism" in the Soviet Union and Red China.
4. What meaning do you attach to the term "classless society"? Is it a desirable goal to be sought? Explain.
5. What are the implications of disunity in communist ranks for the formulation of American foreign policy?
6. Prepare an essay on the theme "Freedom in a Communist Society."

THE COMMUNIST MANIFESTO*

KARL MARX AND FRIEDRICH ENGELS

A spectre is haunting Europe — the spectre of Communism. All the Powers of old Europe have entered into a holy alliance to exorcise this spectre: Pope and Czar, Metternich and Guizot, French Radicals and German police-spies.

Where is the party in opposition that has not been decried as Communistic by its opponents in power? Where the Opposition that has not hurled back the branding reproach of Communism, against the more advanced opposition parties, as well as against its reactionary adversaries?

Two things result from this fact.

I. Communism is already acknowledged by all European Powers to be itself a Power.

II. It is high time that Communists should openly, in the face of the whole world, publish their views, their aims, their tendencies, and meet this nursery tale of the Spectre of Communism with a Manifesto of the party itself.

To this end, Communists of various nationalities have assembled in London, and sketched the following Manifesto, to be published in the English, French, German, Italian, Flemish and Danish languages.

* From the English translation edited by Frederich Engels, 1888.

I

BOURGEOIS AND
PROLETARIANS

The history of all hitherto existing society is the history of class struggles.

Freeman and slave, patrician and plebeian, lord and serf, guild-master and journeyman, in a word, oppressor and oppressed, stood in constant opposition to one another, carried on an uninterrupted, now hidden, now open fight, a fight that each time ended, either in a revolutionary re-constitution of society at large, or in the common ruin of the contending classes.

In the earlier epochs of history, we find almost everywhere a complicated arrangement of society into various orders, a manifold gradation of social rank.   In ancient Rome we have patricians, knights, plebeians, slaves; in the Middle Ages, feudal lords, vassals, guild-masters, journeymen, apprentices, serfs; in almost all of these classes, again, subordinate gradations.

The modern bourgeois society that has sprouted from the

ruins of feudal society has not done away with class antagonisms. It has but established new classes, new conditions of oppression, new forms of struggle in place of the old ones.

Our epoch, the epoch of the bourgeoisie, possesses, however, this distinctive feature: it has simplified the class antagonisms. Society as a whole is more and more splitting up into two great hostile camps, into two great classes directly facing each other: Bourgeoisie and Proletariat.

From the serfs of the Middle Ages sprang the chartered burghers of the earliest towns. From these burgesses the first elements of the bourgeoisie were developed.

The discovery of America, the rounding of the Cape, opened up fresh ground for the rising bourgeoisie. The East-Indian and Chinese markets, the colonisation of America, trade with the colonies, the increase in the means of exchange and in commodities generally, gave to commerce, to navigation, to industry, an impulse never before known, and thereby, to the revolutionary element in the tottering feudal society, a rapid development.

The feudal system of industry, under which industrial production was monopolised by closed guilds, now no longer sufficed for the growing wants of the new markets. The manufacturing system took its place. The guild-masters were pushed on one side by the manufacturing middle class; division of labour between the different corporate guilds vanished in the face of division of labour in each single workshop.

Meantime the markets kept ever growing, the demand ever rising. Even manufacture no longer sufficed. Thereupon, steam and machinery revolutionized industrial production. The place of manufacture was taken by the giant, Modern Industry, the place of the industrial middle class, by industrial millionaires, the leaders of whole industrial armies, the modern bourgeois.

Modern industry has established the world market, for which the discovery of America paved the way. This market has given an immense development to commerce, to navigation, to communication by land. This development has, in its turn, reacted on the extension of industry; and in proportion as industry, commerce, navigation, railways extended, in the same proportion the bourgeoisie developed, increased its capital, and pushed into the background every class handed down from the Middle Ages.

We see, therefore, how the modern bourgeoisie is itself the product of a long course of development, of a series of revolutions in the modes of production and of exchange.

Each step in the development of the bourgeoisie was accompanied by a corresponding political advance of that class. An oppressed class under the sway of the feudal nobility, an armed and self-governing association in the mediaeval commune; here independent urban republic (as in Italy and Germany), there taxable "third estate" of the monarchy (as in France), afterwards, in the period of manufacture proper, serving either the semi-feudal or the absolute monarchy as a counterpoise against the nobility, and, in fact, corner stone of the great monarchies in general, the bourgeoisie has at last, since the establishment of Modern Industry and of the world market, conquered for itself, in the modern representative State, exclusive political sway. The executive of the modern State is but a committee for managing the common affairs of the whole bourgeoisie.

The bourgeoisie, historically, has played a most revolutionary part.

The bourgeoisie, wherever it has got the upper hand, has put an end to all feudal, patriarchal, idyllic relations. It has pitilessly torn asunder the motley feudal ties that bound man to his "natural superiors," and has left remaining no other nexus between man and man than naked self-interest, than callous "cash payment." It has drowned the most heavenly ecstasies of religious fervour, of chivalrous enthusiasm, of philistine sentimentalism, in the icy water of egotistical calculation. It has resolved personal worth into exchange value, and in place of the numberless indefeasible chartered freedoms, has set up that single, unconscionable freedom — Free Trade. In one word, for exploitation, veiled by religious and political illusions, it has substituted naked, shameless, direct, brutal exploitation.

The bourgeoisie has stripped of its halo every occupation hitherto honoured and looked up to with reverent awe. It has converted the physician, the lawyer, the priest, the poet, the man of science, into its paid wage-labourers.

The bourgeoisie has torn away from the family its sentimental veil, and has reduced the family relation to a mere money relation.

The bourgeoisie has disclosed how it came to pass that the brutal display of vigour in the Middle Ages, which Reactionists so much admire, found its fitting complement in the most slothful indolence. It has been the first to show what man's activity can bring about. It has accomplished wonders far surpassing Egyptian pyramids, Roman aqueducts, and Gothic cathedrals; it has conducted expeditions that put in the shade all former Exoduses of nations and crusades.

The bourgeoisie cannot exist without constantly revolutionising the instruments of production, and thereby the relations of production, and with them the whole relations of society. Conservation of the old modes of production in unaltered form, was, on the contrary, the first condition of existence for all earlier industrial classes. Constant revolutionising of production, uninterrupted disturbance of all social conditions, everlasting uncertainty and agitation distinguish the bourgeois epoch from all earlier ones. All fixed, fast-frozen relations, with their train of ancient and venerable prejudices and opinions, are swept away, all new-formed ones become antiquated before they can ossify. All that is solid melts into air, all that is holy is profaned, and man is at last compelled to face with sober senses, his real conditions of life, and his relations with his kind.

The need of a constantly expanding market for its products chases the bourgeoisie over the whole surface of the globe. It must nestle everywhere, settle everywhere, establish connexions everywhere.

The bourgeoisie has through its exploitation of the world market given a cosmopolitan character to production and consumption in every country. To the great chagrin of Reactionists, it has drawn from under the feet of industry the national ground on which it stood. All old-established national industries have been destroyed or are daily being destroyed. They are dislodged by new industries, whose introduction becomes a life and death question for all civilised nations, by industries that no longer work up indigenous raw material, but raw material drawn from the remotest zones; industries whose products are consumed, not only at home, but in every quarter of the globe. In place of the old wants, satisfied by the productions of the country, we find new wants, requiring for their satisfaction the products of distant lands and climes. In place of the old local and national seclusion and self-sufficiency, we have intercourse in every direction, universal inter-dependence of nations. And as in material, so also in intellectual production. The intellectual creations of individual nations become common property. National one-sidedness and narrow-mindedness become more and more impossible, and from the numerous national and local literatures there arises a world-literature.

The bourgeoisie, by the rapid improvement of all instruments of production, by the immensely facilitated means of communication, draws all, even the most barbarian, nations into civilisation. The cheap prices of its commodities are the heavy artillery with which it batters down all Chinese walls, with which it forces the barbarians' intensely obstinate hatred of foreigners to capitulate. It compels all nations, on pain of extinction, to adopt the bourgeois mode of production; it compels them to introduce what it calls civilisation into their midst, *i.e.*, to become bourgeois themselves. In one word, it creates a world after its own image.

The bourgeoisie has subjected the country to the rule of the towns. It has created enormous cities, has greatly increased the urban population as compared with the rural, and has thus rescued a considerable part of the population from the idiocy of rural life. Just as it has made the country dependent on the towns, so it has made barbarian and semi-barbarian countries dependent on the civilised ones, nations of peasants on nations of bourgeois, the East on the West.

The bourgeoisie keeps more and more doing away with the scattered state of the population, of the means of production, and of property. It has agglomerated population, centralised means of production, and has concentrated property in a few hands. The necessary consequence of this was political centralisation.   Independent, or but loosely connected provinces, with separate interests, laws, governments and systems of taxation, became lumped together into one nation, with one government, one code of laws, one national class-interest, one frontier and one customs-tariff.

The bourgeoisie, during its rule of scarce one hundred years, has created more massive and more colossal productive forces than have all preceding generations together.   Subjection of Nature's forces to man, machinery, application of chemistry to industry and agriculture, steam-navigation, railways, electric telegraphs, clearing of whole continents for cultivation, canalisation of rivers, whole populations conjured out of the ground — what earlier century had even a presentiment that such productive forces slumbered in the lap of social labour?

We see then: the means of production and of exchange, on whose foundation the bourgeoisie built itself up, were generated in feudal society.   At a certain stage in the development of these means of production and of exchange, the conditions under which feudal society produced and exchanged, the feudal organisation of agriculture and manufacturing industry, in one word, the feudal relations of property became no longer compatible with the already developed productive forces; they became so many fetters.   They had to be burst asunder; they were burst asunder.

Into their place stepped free competition, accompanied by a social and political constitution adapted to it, and by the economical and political sway of the bourgeois class.

A similar movement is going on before our own eyes. Modern bourgeois society with its relations of production, of exchange and of property, a society that has conjured up such gigantic means of production and of exchange, is like the sorcerer, who is no longer able to control the powers of the nether world whom he has called up by his spells. For many a decade past the history of industry and commerce is but the history of the revolt of modern productive forces against modern conditions of production, against the property relations that are the conditions for the existence of the bourgeoisie and of its rule. It is enough to mention the commercial crises that by their periodical return put on its trial, each time more threateningly, the existence of the entire bourgeois society. In these crises a great part not only of the existing products, but also of the previously created productive forces, are periodically destroyed. In these crises there breaks out an epidemic that, in all earlier epochs, would have seemed an absurdity — the epidemic of over-production. Society suddenly finds itself put back into a state of momentary barbarism; it appears as if a famine, a universal war of devastation had cut off the supply of every means of subsistence; industry and commerce seem to be destroyed; and why? Because there is too much civilisation, too much means of subsistence, too much industry, too much commerce. The productive forces at the disposal of society no longer tend to further the development of the conditions of bourgeois property; on the contrary, they have become too powerful for these conditions, by which they are fettered, and so soon as they overcome these fetters, they bring disorder into the whole of bourgeois society, endanger the existence of bourgeois property. The conditions of bourgeois society are too narrow to comprise the wealth created by them. And how does the bourgeoisie get over these crises? On the one hand by enforced destruction of a mass of productive forces; on the other, by the conquest of new markets, and by the more thorough exploitation of the old ones. That is to say, by paving the way for more extensive and more destructive crises, and by diminishing the means whereby crises are prevented.

The weapons with which the bourgeoisie felled feudalism to the ground are now turned against the bourgeoisie itself.

But not only has the bourgeoisie forged the weapons that bring death to itself; it has also called into existence the men who are to wield those weapons — the modern working class — the proletarians.

In proportion as the bourgeoisie, *i.e.*, capital, is developed, in the same proportion is the proletariat, the modern working class, developed — a class of labourers, who live only so long as they find work, and who find work only so long as their labour increases capital. These labourers, who must sell themselves piecemeal, are a commodity, like every other article of commerce, and are consequently exposed to all the vicissitudes of competition, to all the fluctuations of the market.

Owing to the extensive use of machinery and to division of labour, the work of the proletarians has lost all individual character, and, consequently, all charm for the workman. He becomes an appendage of the machine, and it is only the most simple, most monotonous, and most easily acquired knack, that is required of him. Hence, the cost of production of a workman is restricted, almost entirely, to the means of subsistence that he requires for his maintenance, and for the propagation of his race. But the price of a commodity, and therefore also of labour, is equal to its cost of production. In proportion, therefore, as the repulsiveness of the work increases, the wage decreases. Nay more, in proportion as the use of machinery and division of labour increases, in the same proportion the burden of toil also increases, whether by prolongation of the working hours, by increase of the work exacted in a given time or by increased speed of the machinery, etc.

Modern industry has converted the little workshop of the patriarchal master into the great factory of the industrial capitalist. Masses of labourers, crowded into the factory, are organised like soldiers. As privates of the industrial army they are placed under the command of a perfect hierarchy of officers and sergeants. Not only are they slaves of the bourgeois class, and of the bourgeois State; they are daily and hourly enslaved by the machine, by the over-looker, and, above all, by the individual bourgeois manufacturer himself. The more openly this despotism proclaims gain to be its end and aim, the more petty, the more hateful and the more embittering it is.

The less the skill and exertion of strength implied in manual labour, in other words, the more modern industry becomes developed, the more is the labour of men super-seded by that of women. Differences of age and sex have no longer any distinctive social validity for the working class. All are instruments of labour, more or less expensive to use, according to their age and sex.

No sooner is the exploitation of the labourer by the manufacturer, so far, at an end, that he receives his wages in cash, than he is set upon by the other portions of the bourgeoisie, the landlord, the shopkeeper, the pawnbroker, etc.

The lower strata of the middle class — the small trades-people, shopkeepers, and retired tradesmen generally, the handicraftsmen and peasants — all these sink gradually into the proletariat, partly because their diminutive capital does not suffice for the scale on which Modern Industry is carried on, and is swamped in the competition with the large capitalists, partly because their specialised skill is rendered worthless by new methods of production. Thus the proletariat is recruited from all classes of the population.

The proletariat goes through various stages of development. With its birth begins its struggle with the bourgeoisie. At first the contest is carried on by individual labourers, then by the workpeople of a factory, then by the operatives of one trade, in one locality, against the individual bourgeois who directly exploits them. They direct their attacks not against the bourgeois conditions of production, but against the instruments of production themselves; they destroy imported wares that compete with their labour, they smash to pieces machinery, they set factories ablaze, they seek to restore by force the vanished status of the workman of the Middle Ages.

At this stage the labourers still form an incoherent mass scattered over the whole country, and broken up by their mutual competition. If anywhere they unite to form more compact bodies, this is not yet the consequence of their own active union, but of the union of the bourgeoisie, which class, in order to attain its own political ends, is compelled to set the whole proletariat in motion, and is moreover yet, for a time, able to do so. At this stage, therefore, the proletarians do not fight their enemies, but the enemies of their enemies, the remnants of absolute monarchy, the landowners, the non-industrial bourgeois, the petty bourgeoisie. Thus the whole historical movement is concentrated in the hands of the bourgeoisie; every victory so obtained is a victory for the bourgeoisie.

But with the development of industry the proletariat not only increases in number; it becomes concentrated in greater masses, its strength grows, and it feels that strength more. The various interests and conditions of life within the ranks of the proletariat are more and more equalised, in proportion as machinery obliterates all distinctions of labour, and nearly everywhere reduces wages to the same low level. The growing competition among the bourgeois, and the resulting commercial crises, make the wages of the workers ever more fluctuating. The unceasing improvement of machinery, ever more rapidly developing, makes their livelihood more and more precarious; the collisions between individual workmen and individual bourgeois take more and more the character of collisions between two classes. Thereupon the workers begin to form combinations (Trades' Unions) against the bourgeois; they club together in order to keep up the rate of wages; they found permanent associations in order to make provision beforehand for these occasional revolts. Here and there the contest breaks out into riots.

Now and then the workers are victorious, but only for a time. The real fruit of their battles lies, not in the immediate result, but in the ever-expanding union of the workers. This union is helped on by the improved means of communication that are created by modern industry, and that place the workers of different localities in contact with one another. It was just this contact that was needed to centralise the numerous local struggles, all of the same character, into one national struggle between classes. But every class struggle is a political struggle. And that union, to attain which the burghers of the Middle Ages, with their

miserable highways, required centuries, the modern proletarians, thanks to railways, achieve in a few years.

This organisation of the proletarians into a class, and
consequently into a political party, is continually being upset
again by the competition between the workers themselves.
But it ever rises up again, stronger, firmer, mightier. It
compels legislative recognition of particular interests of the
workers, by taking advantage of the divisions among the
bourgeoisie itself. Thus the ten-hours' bill in England was
carried.

Altogether collisions between the classes of the old society
further, in many ways, the course of development of the
proletariat. The bourgeoisie finds itself involved in a constant battle. At first with the aristocracy; later on, with
those portions of the bourgeoisie itself, whose interests have
become antagonistic to the progress of industry; at all times,
with the bourgeoisie of foreign countries. In all these battles it sees itself compelled to appeal to the proletariat, to
ask for its help, and thus, to drag it into the political arena.
The bourgeoisie itself, therefore, supplies the proletariat
with its own elements of political and general education,
in other words, it furnishes the proletariat with weapons
for fighting the bourgeoisie.

Further, as we have already seen, entire sections of the
ruling classes are, by the advance of industry, precipitated
into the proletariat, or are at least threatened in their conditions of existence. These also supply the proletariat with
fresh elements of enlightenment and progress.

Finally, in times when the class struggle nears the decisive
hour, the process of dissolution going on within the ruling
class, in fact within the whole range of old society, assumes

such a violent, glaring character, that a small section of the ruling class cuts itself adrift, and joins the revolutionary class, the class that holds the future in its hands. Just as, therefore, at an earlier period, a section of the nobility went over to the bourgeoisie, so now a portion of the bourgeoisie goes over to the proletariat, and in particular, a portion of the bourgeois ideologists, who have raised themselves to the level of comprehending theoretically the historical movement as a whole.

Of all the classes that stand face to face with the bourgeoisie to-day, the proletariat alone is a really revolutionary class. The other classes decay and finally disappear in the face of modern industry; the proletariat is its special and essential product.

The lower middle class, the small manufacturer, the shopkeeper, the artisan, the peasant, all these fight against the bourgeoisie, to save from extinction their existence as fractions of the middle class. They are therefore not revolutionary, but conservative. Nay more, they are reactionary, for they try to roll back the wheel of history. If by chance they are revolutionary, they are so only in view of their impending transfer into the proletariat, they thus defend not their present, but their future interests, they desert their own standpoint to place themselves at that of the proletariat.

The "dangerous class," the social scum, that passively rotting mass thrown off by the lowest layers of old society, may, here and there, be swept into the movement by a proletarian revolution; its conditions of life, however, prepare it far more for the part of a bribed tool of reactionary intrigue.

In the conditions of the proletariat, those of old society

at large are already virtually swamped. The proletarian is without property; his relation to his wife and children has no longer anything in common with the bourgeois family-relations; modern industrial labour, modern subjection to capital, the same in England as in France, in America as in Germany, has stripped him of every trace of national character. Law, morality, religion, are to him so many bourgeois prejudices, behind which lurk in ambush just as many bourgeois interests.

All the preceding classes that got the upper hand, sought to fortify their already acquired status by subjecting society at large to their conditions of appropriation. The proletarians cannot become masters of the productive forces of society, except by abolishing their own previous mode of appropriation, and thereby also every other previous mode of appropriation. They have nothing of their own to secure and to fortify; their mission is to destroy all previous securities for, and insurances of, individual property.

All previous historical movements were movements of minorities, or in the interest of minorities. The proletarian movement is the self-conscious, independent movement of the immense majority, in the interest of the immense majority. The proletariat, the lowest stratum of our present society, cannot stir, cannot raise itself up, without the whole superincumbent strata of official society being sprung into the air.

Though not in substance, yet in form, the struggle of the proletariat with the bourgeoisie is at first a national struggle. The proletariat of each country must, of course, first of all settle matters with its own bourgeoisie.

In depicting the most general phases of the development of the proletariat, we traced the more or less veiled civil war, raging within existing society, up to the point where that war breaks out into open revolution, and where the violent overthrow of the bourgeoisie lays the foundation for the sway of the proletariat.

Hitherto, every form of society has been based, as we have already seen, on the antagonism of oppressing and oppressed classes. But in order to oppress a class, certain conditions must be assured to it under which it can, at least, continue its slavish existence. The serf, in the period of serfdom, raised himself to membership in the commune, just as the petty bourgeois, under the yoke of feudal absolutism, managed to develop into a bourgeois. The modern labourer, on the contrary, instead of rising with the progress of industry, sinks deeper and deeper below the conditions of existence of his own class. He becomes a pauper, and pauperism develops more rapidly than population and wealth. And here it becomes evident, that the bourgeoisie is unfit any longer to be the ruling class in society, and to impose its conditions of existence upon society as an over-riding law. It is unfit to rule because it is incompetent to assure an existence to its slave within his slavery, because it cannot help letting him sink into such a state, that it has to feed him, instead of being fed by him. Society can no longer live under this bourgeoisie, in other words, its existence is no longer compatible with society.

The essential condition for the existence, and for the sway of the bourgeois class, is the formation and augmentation of capital; the condition for capital is wage-labour. Wage-labour rests exclusively on competition between the labourers. The advance of industry, whose involuntary promoter is the bourgeoisie, replaces the isolation of the labourers, due to competition, by their revolutionary combination, due to association. The development of Modern Industry, therefore, cuts from under its feet the very foundation on which the bourgeoisie produces and appropriates products. What the bourgeoisie, therefore, produces, above all, are its own grave-diggers. Its fall and the victory of the proletariat are equally inevitable.

II

PROLETARIANS AND
COMMUNISTS

In what relation do the Communists stand to the proletarians as a whole?

The Communists do not form a separate party opposed to other working-class parties.

They have no interests separate and apart from those of the proletariat as a whole.

They do not set up any sectarian principles of their own, by which to shape and mould the proletarian movement.

The Communists are distinguished from the other working-class parties by this only: 1. In the national struggles of the proletarians of the different countries, they point out and bring to the front the common interests of the entire proletariat, independently of all nationality. 2. In the various stages of development which the struggle of the working class against the bourgeoisie has to pass through, they always and everywhere represent the interests of the movement as a whole.

The Communists, therefore, are on the one hand, practically, the most advanced and resolute section of the working-class parties of every country, that section which pushes forward all others; on the other hand, theoretically, they have over the great mass of the proletariat the advantage of clearly understanding the line of march, the conditions, and the ultimate general results of the proletarian movement.

The immediate aim of the Communists is the same as that of all the other proletarian parties: formation of the proletariat into a class, overthrow of the bourgeois supremacy, conquest of political power by the proletariat.

The theoretical conclusions of the Communists are in no way based on ideas or principles that have been invented, or discovered, by this or that would-be universal reformer.

They merely express, in general terms, actual relations springing from an existing class struggle, from a historical movement going on under our very eyes. The abolition of existing property relations is not at all a distinctive feature of Communism.

All property relations in the past have continually been subject to historical change consequent upon the change in historical conditions.

The French Revolution, for example, abolished feudal property in favour of bourgeois property.

The distinguishing feature of Communism is not the abolition of property generally, but the abolition of bourgeois property. But modern bourgeois private property is the final and most complete expression of the system of producing and appropriating products, that is based on class antagonisms, on the exploitation of the many by the few.

In this sense, the theory of the Communists may be summed up in the single sentence: Abolition of private property.

We Communists have been reproached with the desire of abolishing the right of personally acquiring property as the fruit of a man's own labour, which property is alleged to be the ground work of all personal freedom, activity and independence.

Hard-won, self-acquired, self-earned property! Do you mean the property of the petty artisan and of the small peasant, a form of property that preceded the bourgeois form? There is no need to abolish that; the development of industry has to a great extent already destroyed it, and is still destroying it daily.

Or do you mean modern bourgeois private property?

But does wage-labour create any property for the labourer? Not a bit. It creates capital, *i.e.*, that kind of property which exploits wage-labour, and which cannot increase except upon condition of begetting a new supply of wage-labour for fresh exploitation. Property, in its present form, is based on the antagonism of capital and wage-labour. Let us examine both sides of this antagonism.

To be a capitalist, is to have not only a purely personal, but a social *status* in production. Capital is a collective product, and only by the united action of many members, nay, in the last resort, only by the united action of all members of society, can it be set in motion.

Capital is, therefore, not a personal, it is a social power.

When, therefore, capital is converted into common property, into the property of all members of society, personal property is not thereby transformed into social property. It is only the social character of the property that is changed. It loses its class character.

Let us now take wage-labour.

The average price of wage-labour is the minimum wage, *i.e.*, that quantum of the means of subsistence, which is absolutely requisite to keep the labourer in bare existence as a labourer. What, therefore, the wage-labourer appropriates by means of his labour, merely suffices to prolong and reproduce a bare existence. We by no means intend to abolish this personal appropriation of the products of labour, an appropriation that is made for the maintenance and reproduction of human life, and that leaves no surplus wherewith to command the labour of others. All that we want to do away with is the miserable character of this appropriation, under which the labourer lives merely to increase capital, and is allowed to live only in so far as the interest of the ruling class requires it.

In bourgeois society, living labour is but a means to increase accumulated labour. In Communist society, accumulated labour is but a means to widen, to enrich, to promote the existence of the labourer.

In bourgeois society, therefore, the past dominates the present; in Communist society, the present dominates the past. In bourgeois society capital is independent and has individuality, while the living person is dependent and has no individuality.

And the abolition of this state of things is called by the bourgeois, abolition of individuality and freedom! And rightly so. The abolition of bourgeois individuality, bourgeois independence, and bourgeois freedom is undoubtedly aimed at.

By freedom is meant, under the present bourgeois conditions of production, free trade, free selling and buying.

But if selling and buying disappears, free selling and buying disappears also. This talk about free selling and buying, and all the other "brave words" of our bourgeoisie about freedom in general, have a meaning, if any, only in contrast with restricted selling and buying, with the fettered traders of the Middle Ages, but have no meaning when opposed to the Communistic abolition of buying and selling, of the bourgeois conditions of production, and of the bourgeoisie itself.

You are horrified at our intending to do away with private property. But in your existing society, private property is already done away with for nine-tenths of the population; its existence for the few is solely due to its non-existence in the hands of those nine-tenths. You reproach us, therefore, with intending to do away with a form of property, the necessary condition for whose existence is, the non-existence of any property for the immense majority of society.

In one word, you reproach us with intending to do away with your property. Precisely so; that is just what we intend.

From the moment when labour can no longer be converted into capital, money, or rent, into a social power capable of being monopolised, *i.e.,* from the moment when individual property can no longer be transformed into bourgeois property, into capital, from that moment, you say, individuality vanishes.

You must, therefore, confess that by "individual" you mean no other person than the bourgeois, than the middle-class owner of property. This person must, indeed, be swept out of the way, and made impossible.

Communism deprives no man of the power to appropriate the products of society; all that it does is to deprive him of the power to subjugate the labour of others by means of such appropriation.

It has been objected that upon the abolition of private property all work will cease, and universal laziness will overtake us.

According to this, bourgeois society ought long ago to have gone to the dogs through sheer idleness; for those of its members who work, acquire nothing, and those who acquire anything, do not work. The whole of this objection is but another expression of the tautology: that there can no longer be any wage-labour when there is no longer any capital.

All objections urged against the Communistic mode of producing and appropriating material products, have, in the same way, been urged against the Communistic modes of producing and appropriating intellectual products. Just as, to the bourgeois, the disappearance of class property is the disappearance of production itself, so the disappearance of class culture is to him identical with the disappearance of all culture.

That culture, the loss of which he laments, is, for the enormous majority, a mere training to act as a machine.

But don't wrangle with us so long as you apply, to our intended abolition of bourgeois property, the standard of your bourgeois notions of freedom, culture, law, etc. Your very ideas are but the outgrowth of the conditions of your bourgeois production and bourgeois property, just as your jurisprudence is but the will of your class made into a law for all, a will, whose essential character and direction are determined by the economical conditions of existence of your class.

The selfish misconception that induces you to transform into eternal laws of nature and of reason, the social forms springing from your present mode of production and form of property — historical relations that rise and disappear in the progress of production — this misconception you share with every ruling class that has preceded you. What you see clearly in the case of ancient property, what you admit in the case of feudal property, you are of course forbidden to admit in the case of your own bourgeois form of property.

Abolition of the family! Even the most radical flare up at this infamous proposal of the Communists.

On what foundation is the present family, the bourgeois family, based? On capital, on private gain. In its completely developed form this family exists only among the bourgeoisie. But this state of things finds its complement in the practical absence of the family among the proletarians, and in public prostitution.

The bourgeois family will vanish as a matter of course when its complement vanishes, and both will vanish with the vanishing of capital.

Do you charge us with wanting to stop the exploitation of children by their parents? To this crime we plead guilty.

But, you will say, we destroy the most hallowed of relations, when we replace home education by social.

And your education! Is not that also social, and determined by the social conditions under which you educate, by the intervention, direct or indirect, of society, by means of schools, etc.? The Communists have not invented the intervention of society in education; they do but seek to alter the character of that intervention, and to rescue education from the influence of the ruling class.

The bourgeois clap-trap about the family and education, about the hallowed co-relation of parent and child, becomes all the more disgusting, the more, by the action of Modern

Industry, all family ties among the proletarians are torn asunder, and their children transformed into simple articles of commerce and instruments of labour.

But you Communists would introduce community of women, screams the whole bourgeoisie in chorus.

The bourgeois sees in his wife a mere instrument of production. He hears that the instruments of production are to be exploited in common, and, naturally, can come to no other conclusion than that the lot of being common to all will likewise fall to the women.

He has not even a suspicion that the real point aimed at is to do away with the status of women as mere instruments of production.

For the rest, nothing is more ridiculous than the virtuous indignation of our bourgeois at the community of women which, they pretend, is to be openly and officially established by the Communists. The Communists have no need to introduce community of women; it has existed almost from time immemorial.

Our bourgeois, not content with having the wives and daughters of their proletarians at their disposal, not to speak of common prostitutes, take the greatest pleasure in seducing each others' wives.

Bourgeois marriage is in reality a system of wives in common and thus, at the most, what the Communists might possibly be reproached with, is that they desire to introduce, in substitution for a hypocritically concealed, an openly legalised community of women. For the rest, it is self-evident that the abolition of the present system of production must bring with it the abolition of the community of women springing from that system, *i.e.*, of prostitution both public and private.

The Communists are further reproached with desiring to abolish countries and nationality.

The working men have no country. We cannot take from them what they have not got. Since the proletariat must first of all acquire political supremacy, must rise to be the leading class of the nation, must constitute itself *the* nation, it is, so far, itself national, though not in the bourgeois sense of the word.

National differences and antagonisms between peoples are daily more and more vanishing, owing to the development of the bourgeoisie, to freedom of commerce, to the world market, to uniformity in the mode of production and in the conditions of life corresponding thereto.

The supremacy of the proletariat will cause them to vanish still faster. United action, of the leading civilised countries at least, is one of the first conditions for the emancipation of the proletariat.

In proportion as the exploitation of one individual by another is put an end to, the exploitation of one nation by another will also be put an end to. In proportion as the antagonism between classes within the nation vanishes, the hostility of one nation to another will come to an end.

The charges against Communism made from a religious, a philosophical, and, generally, from an ideological standpoint, are not deserving of serious examination.

Does it require deep intuition to comprehend that man's ideas, views and conceptions, in one word, man's consciousness, changes with every change in the conditions of his material existence, in his social relations and in his social life?

What else does the history of ideas prove, than that intellectual production changes its character in proportion

as material production is changed?   The ruling ideas of
each age have ever been the ideas of its ruling class.

When people speak of ideas that revolutionise society,
they do but express the fact, that within the old society,
the elements of a new one have been created, and that the
dissolution of the old ideas keeps even pace with the dissolution of the old conditions of existence.

When the ancient world was in its last throes, the ancient
religions were overcome by Christianity.   When Christian
ideas succumbed in the 18th century to rationalist ideas, feudal society fought its death-battle with the then revolutionary
bourgeoisie.   The ideas of religious liberty and freedom of
conscience, merely gave expression to the sway of free competition within the domain of knowledge.

"Undoubtedly," it will be said, "religious, moral, philosophical and juridical ideas have been modified in the course
of historical development.   But religion, morality, philosophy,
political science, and law, constantly survived this change."

"There are, besides, eternal truths, such as Freedom, Justice, etc., that are common to all states of society.   But Communism abolishes eternal truths, it abolishes all religion, and
all morality, instead of constituting them on a new basis; it
therefore acts in contradiction to all past historical experience."

What does this accusation reduce itself to?   The history
of all past society has consisted in the development of class
antagonisms, antagonisms that assumed different forms at
different epochs.

But whatever form they may have taken, one fact is common to all past ages, viz., the exploitation of one part of
society by the other.   No wonder, then, that the social con-

sciousness of past ages, despite all the multiplicity and variety it displays, moves within certain common forms, or general ideas, which cannot completely vanish except with the total disappearance of class antagonisms.

The Communist revolution is the most radical rupture with traditional property relations; no wonder that its development involves the most radical rupture with traditional ideas.

But let us have done with the bourgeois objections to Communism.

We have seen above, that the first step in the revolution by the working class, is to raise the proletariat to the position of ruling class, to win the battle of democracy.

The proletariat will use its political supremacy to wrest, by degrees, all capital from the bourgeoisie, to centralise all instruments of production in the hands of the State, *i.e.,* of the proletariat organised as the ruling class; and to increase the total of productive forces as rapidly as possible.

Of course, in the beginning, this cannot be effected except by means of despotic inroads on the rights of property, and on the conditions of bourgeois production; by means of measures, therefore, which appear economically insufficient and untenable, but which, in the course of the movement, outstrip themselves, necessitate further inroads upon the old social order, and are unavoidable as a means of entirely revolutionising the mode of production.

These measures will of course be different in different countries.

Nevertheless in the most advanced countries, the following will be pretty generally applicable.

1. Abolition of property in land and application of all rents of land to public purposes.

2. A heavy progressive or graduated income tax.

3. Abolition of all right of inheritance.

4. Confiscation of the property of all emigrants and rebels.

5. Centralisation of credit in the hands of the State, by means of a national bank with State capital and an exclusive monopoly.

6. Centralisation of the means of communication and transport in the hands of the State.

7. Extension of factories and instruments of production owned by the State; the bringing into cultivation of waste lands, and the improvement of the soil generally in accordance with a common plan.

8. Equal liability of all to labour. Establishment of industrial armies, especially for agriculture.

9. Combination of agriculture with manufacturing industries; gradual abolition of the distinction between town and country, by a more equable distribution of the population over the country.

10. Free education for all children in public schools. Abolition of children's factory labour in its present form. Combination of education with industrial production, etc., etc.

When, in the course of development, class distinctions have disappeared, and all production has been concentrated in the hands of a vast association of the whole nation, the public power will lose its political character. Political power, properly so called, is merely the organised power of one class for oppressing another. If the proletariat during its contest with the bourgeoisie is compelled, by the force of circumstances, to organise itself as a class, if, by means of a revolution, it makes itself the ruling class, and, as such, sweeps away by force the old conditions of production, then it will, along with these conditions, have swept away the conditions for the existence of class antagonisms and of classes generally, and will thereby have abolished its own supremacy as a class.

In place of the old bourgeois society, with its classes and class antagonisms, we shall have an association, in which the free development of each is the condition for the free development of all.

III

SOCIALIST AND
COMMUNIST
LITERATURE

---

1. REACTIONARY SOCIALISM

a. Feudal Socialism

Owing to their historical position, it became the vocation of the aristocracies of France and England to write pamphlets against modern bourgeois society. In the French revolution of July, 1830, and in the English reform agitation, these aristocracies again succumbed to the hateful upstart. Thenceforth, a serious political contest was altogether out of the question. A literary battle alone remained possible. But even in the domain of literature the old cries of the restoration period had become impossible.

In order to arouse sympathy, the aristocracy were obliged to lose sight, apparently, of their own interests, and to formulate their indictment against the bourgeoisie in the interest of the exploited working class alone. Thus the aristocracy took their revenge by singing lampoons on their new master, and whispering in his ears sinister prophecies of coming catastrophe.

In this way arose feudal Socialism: half lamentation, half lampoon; half echo of the past, half menace of the future; at times, by its bitter, witty and incisive criticism, striking the bourgeoisie to the very heart's core; but always ludicrous in its effect, through total incapacity to comprehend the march of modern history.

The aristocracy, in order to rally the people to them, waved the proletarian alms-bag in front for a banner. But the people, so often as it joined them, saw on their hindquarters the old feudal coats of arms, and deserted with loud and irreverent laughter.

One section of the French Legitimists and "Young England" exhibited this spectacle.

In pointing out that their mode of exploitation was different to that of the bourgeoisie, the feudalists forget that they exploited under circumstances and conditions that were quite different, and that are now antiquated. In showing that, under their rule, the modern proletariat never existed, they forget that the modern bourgeoisie is the necessary offspring of their own form of society.

For the rest, so little do they conceal the reactionary character of their criticism that their chief accusation against the bourgeoisie amounts to this, that under the bourgeois *régime* a class is being developed, which is destined to cut up root and branch the old order of society.

What they upbraid the bourgeoisie with is not so much that it creates a proletariat, as that it creates a *revolutionary* proletariat.

In political practice, therefore, they join in all coercive measures against the working class; and in ordinary life, despite their high-falutin phrases, they stoop to pick up the golden apples dropped from the tree of industry, and to barter truth, love, and honour for traffic in wool, beetroot-sugar, and potato spirits.

As the parson has ever gone hand in hand with the landlord, so has Clerical Socialism with Feudal Socialism.

Nothing is easier than to give Christian asceticism a Socialist tinge. Has not Christianity declaimed against private property, against marriage, against the State? Has it not preached in the place of these, charity and poverty, celibacy and mortification of the flesh, monastic life and Mother Church? Christian Socialism is but the holy water with which the priest consecrates the heart-burnings of the aristocrat.

b. Petty-Bourgeois Socialism

The feudal aristocracy was not the only class that was ruined by the bourgeoisie, not the only class whose conditions of existence pined and perished in the atmosphere of modern bourgeois society. The mediaeval burgesses and the small peasant proprietors were the precursors of the modern bourgeoisie. In those countries which are but little developed, industrially and commercially, these two classes still vegetate side by side with the rising bourgeoisie.

In countries where modern civilisation has become fully developed, a new class of petty bourgeois has been formed, fluctuating between proletariat and bourgeoisie, and ever renewing itself as a supplementary part of bourgeois society. The individual members of this class, however, are being constantly hurled down into the proletariat by the action of competition, and, as modern industry develops, they even see the moment approaching when they will completely disappear as an independent section of modern society, to be replaced, in manufactures, agriculture and commerce, by overlookers, bailiffs and shopmen.

In countries like France, where the peasants constitute far more than half of the population, it was natural that writers who sided with the proletariat against the bourgeoisie, should use, in their criticism of the bourgeois *régime,* the standard of the peasant and petty bourgeois, and from the standpoint of these intermediate classes should take up the cudgels for the working class. Thus arose petty-bourgeois Socialism. Sismondi was the head of this school, not only in France but also in England.

This school of Socialism dissected with great acuteness the contradictions in the conditions of modern production. It laid bare the hypocritical apologies of economists. It proved, incontrovertibly, the disastrous effects of machinery and division of labour; the concentration of capital and land in a few hands; overproduction and crises; it pointed out the inevitable ruin of the petty bourgeois and peasant, the misery of the proletariat, the anarchy in production, the crying inequalities in the distribution of wealth, the industrial war of extermination between nations, the dissolution of old moral bonds, of the old family relations, of the old nationalities.

In its positive aims, however, this form of Socialism aspires either to restoring the old means of production and of exchange, and with them the old property relations, and the old society, or to cramping the modern means of production and of exchange, within the framework of the old property relations that have been, and were bound to be, exploded by those means. In either case, it is both reactionary and Utopian.

Its last words are: corporate guilds for manufacture; patriarchal relations in agriculture.

Ultimately, when stubborn historical facts had dispersed all intoxicating effects of self-deception, this form of Socialism ended in a miserable fit of the blues.

c. German, or "True," Socialism

The Socialist and Communist literature of France, a literature that originated under the pressure of a bourgeoisie in power, and that was the expression of the struggle against this power, was introduced into Germany at a time when the bourgeoisie, in that country, had just begun its contest with feudal absolutism.

German philosophers, would-be philosophers, and *beaux esprits,* eagerly seized on this literature, only forgetting, that when these writings immigrated from France into Germany, French social conditions had not immigrated along with them. In contact with German social conditions, this French literature lost all its immediate practical significance, and assumed a purely literary aspect. Thus, to the German philosophers of the Eighteenth Century, the demands of the first French Revolution were nothing more than the demands of "Practical Reason" in general, and the utterance of the will of the revolutionary French bourgeoisie signified in their eyes the laws of pure Will, of Will as it was bound to be, of true human Will generally.

The work of the German *literati* consisted solely in bringing the new French ideas into harmony with their ancient philosophical conscience, or rather, in annexing the French ideas without deserting their own philosophic point of view.

This annexation took place in the same way in which a foreign language is appropriated, namely, by translation.

It is well known how the monks wrote silly lives of Catholic Saints *over* the manuscripts on which the classical works of ancient heathendom had been written. The German *literati* reversed this process with the profane French literature. They wrote their philosophical nonsense beneath the French original. For instance, beneath the French criticism of the economic functions of money, they wrote "Alienation of Humanity," and beneath the French criticism of the bourgeois State they wrote, "Dethronement of the Category of the General," and so forth.

The introduction of these philosophical phrases at the back of the French historical criticisms they dubbed "Philosophy of Action," "True Socialism," "German Science of Socialism," "Philosophical Foundation of Socialism," and so on.

The French Socialist and Communist literature was thus completely emasculated. And, since it ceased in the hands of the German to express the struggle of one class with the other, he felt conscious of having overcome "French one-sidedness" and of representing, not true requirements, but the requirements of Truth; not the interests of the proletariat, but the interests of Human Nature, of Man in general, who belongs to no class, has no reality, who exists only in the misty realm of philosophical fantasy.

This German Socialism, which took its school-boy task so seriously and solemnly, and extolled its poor stock-in-trade in such mountebank fashion, meanwhile gradually lost its pedantic innocence.

The fight of the German, and, especially, of the Prussian

bourgeoisie, against feudal aristocracy and absolute monarchy, in other words, the liberal movement, became more earnest.

By this, the long-wished-for opportunity was offered to "True" Socialism of confronting the political movement with the Socialist demands, of hurling the traditional anathemas against liberalism, against representative government, against bourgeois competition, bourgeois freedom of the press, bourgeois legislation, bourgeois liberty and equality, and of preaching to the masses that they had nothing to gain, and everything to lose, by this bourgeois movement. German Socialism forgot, in the nick of time, that the French criticism, whose silly echo it was, presupposed the existence of modern bourgeois society, with its corresponding economic conditions of existence, and the political constitution adapted thereto, the very things whose attainment was the object of the pending struggle in Germany.

To the absolute governments, with their following of parsons, professors, country squires and officials, it served as a welcome scarecrow against the threatening bourgeoisie.

It was a sweet finish after the bitter pills of floggings and bullets with which these same governments, just at that time, dosed the German working-class risings.

While this "True" Socialism thus served the governments as a weapon for fighting the German bourgeoisie, it, at the same time, directly represented a reactionary interest, the interest of the German Philistines. In Germany the *petty-bourgeois* class, a relic of the 16th century, and since then constantly cropping up again under various forms, is the real social basis of the existing state of things.

To preserve this class is to preserve the existing state of things in Germany. The industrial and political supremacy of the bourgeoisie threatens it with certain destruction; on the one hand, from the concentration of capital; on the other, from the rise of a revolutionary proletariat. "True" Socialism appeared to kill these two birds with one stone. It spread like an epidemic.

The robe of speculative cobwebs, embroidered with flowers of rhetoric, steeped in the dew of sickly sentiment, this transcendental robe in which the German Socialists wrapped their sorry "eternal truths," all skin and bone, served to wonderfully increase the sale of their goods amongst such a public.

And on its part, German Socialism recognised, more and more, its own calling as the bombastic representative of the petty-bourgeois Philistine.

It proclaimed the German nation to be the model nation, and the German petty Philistine to be the typical man. To every villainous meanness of this model man it gave a hidden, higher, Socialistic interpretation, the exact contrary of its real character. It went to the extreme length of directly opposing the "brutally destructive" tendency of Communism, and of proclaiming its supreme and impartial contempt of all class struggles. With very few exceptions, all the so-called Socialist and Communist publications that now (1847) circulate in Germany belong to the domain of this foul and enervating literature.

2. CONSERVATIVE, OR BOURGEOIS, SOCIALISM

A part of the bourgeoisie is desirous of redressing social grievances, in order to secure the continued existence of bourgeois society.

To this section belong economists, philanthropists, humanitarians, improvers of the condition of the working class, organisers of charity, members of societies for the prevention of cruelty to animals, temperance fanatics, hole-and-corner reformers of every imaginable kind. This form of Socialism has, moreover, been worked out into complete systems.

We may cite Proudhon's *Philosophie de la Misère* as an example of this form.

The Socialistic bourgeois want all the advantages of modern social conditions without the struggles and dangers necessarily resulting therefrom. They desire the existing state of society minus its revolutionary and disintegrating elements. They wish for a bourgeoisie without a proletariat. The bourgeoisie naturally conceives the world in which it is supreme to be the best; and bourgeois Socialism develops this comfortable conception into various more or less complete systems. In requiring the proletariat to carry out such a system, and thereby to march straightway into the social New Jerusalem, it but requires in reality, that the proletariat should remain within the bounds of existing society, but should cast away all its hateful ideas concerning the bourgeoisie.

A second and more practical, but less systematic, form of this Socialism sought to depreciate every revolutionary movement in the eyes of the working class, by showing that no mere political reform, but only a change in the material conditions of existence, in economical relations, could be of any advantage to them. By changes in the material conditions of existence, this form of Socialism, however, by no means understands abolition of the bourgeois relations of production, an abolition that can be effected only by a revolution, but administrative reforms, based on the continued existence of these relations; reforms, therefore, that in no respect affect the relations between capital and labour, but, at the best, lessen the cost, and simplify the administrative work, of bourgeois government.

Bourgeois Socialism attains adequate expression, when, and only when, it becomes a mere figure of speech.

Free trade: for the benefit of the working class. Protective duties: for the benefit of the working class. Prison Reform: for the benefit of the working class. This is the last word and the only seriously meant word of bourgeois Socialism.

It is summed up in the phrase: the bourgeois is a bourgeois — for the benefit of the working class.

3. CRITICAL-UTOPIAN SOCIALISM AND COMMUNISM

We do not here refer to that literature which, in every great modern revolution, has always given voice to the demands of the proletariat, such as the writings of Babeuf and others.

The first direct attempts of the proletariat to attain its own ends, made in times of universal excitement, when feudal society was being overthrown, these attempts necessarily failed, owing to the then undeveloped state of the proletariat, as well as to the absence of the economic conditions for its emancipation, conditions that had yet to be produced, and could be produced by the impending bourgeois epoch alone. The revolutionary literature that accompanied these first movements of the proletariat had necessarily a reactionary character. It inculcated universal asceticism and social levelling in its crudest form.

The Socialist and Communist systems properly so called, those of St. Simon, Fourier, Owen and others, spring into existence in the early undeveloped period, described above, of the struggle between proletariat and bourgeoisie (see Section I. Bourgeois and Proletarians).

The founders of these systems see, indeed, the class antagonisms, as well as the action of the decomposing elements in the prevailing form of society. But the proletariat, as yet in its infancy, offers to them the spectacle of a class without any historical initiative or any independent political movement.

Since the development of class antagonism keeps even pace with the development of industry, the economic situation, as they find it, does not as yet offer to them the material conditions for the emancipation of the proletariat. They therefore search after a new social science, after new social laws, that are to create these conditions.

Historical action is to yield to their personal inventive action, historically created conditions of emancipation to fantastic ones, and the gradual, spontaneous class-organisation of the proletariat to an organisation of society specially contrived by these inventors. Future history resolves itself, in their eyes, into the propaganda and the practical carrying out of their social plans.

In the formation of their plans they are conscious of caring chiefly for the interests of the working class, as being the most suffering class. Only from the point of view of being the most suffering class does the proletariat exist for them.

The undeveloped state of the class struggle, as well as their own surroundings, causes Socialists of this kind to consider themselves far superior to all class antagonisms. They want to improve the condition of every member of society, even that of the most favoured. Hence, they habitually appeal to society at large, without distinction of class; nay, by preference, to the ruling class. For how can people, when once they understand their system, fail to see in it the best possible plan of the best possible state of society?

Hence, they reject all political, and especially all revolutionary, action; they wish to attain their ends by peaceful means, and endeavour, by small experiments, necessarily doomed to failure, and by the force of example, to pave the way for the new social Gospel.

Such fantastic pictures of future society, painted at a time when the proletariat is still in a very undeveloped state and has but a fantastic conception of its own position, correspond with[58] the first instinctive yearnings of that class for a general reconstruction of society.

But these Socialist and Communist publications contain also a critical element. They attack every principle of existing society. Hence they are full of the most valuable materials for the enlightenment of the working class. The practical measures proposed in them — such as the abolition of the distinction between town and country, of the family, of the carrying on of industries for the account of private individuals, and of the wage system, the proclamation of social harmony, the conversion of the functions of the State into a mere superintendence of production, all these proposals point solely to the disappearance of class antagonisms which were, at that time, only just cropping up, and which, in these publications, are recognised in their earliest, indistinct and undefined forms only. These proposals, therefore, are of a purely Utopian character.

The significance of Critical-Utopian Socialism and Communism bears an inverse relation to historical development. In proportion as the modern class struggle develops and takes definite shape, this fantastic standing apart from the contest, these fantastic attacks on it, lose all practical value and all theoretical justification. Therefore, although the originators of these systems were, in many respects, revolutionary, their disciples have, in every case, formed mere reactionary sects. They hold fast by the original views of their masters, in opposition to the progressive historical development of the proletariat. They, therefore, endeavour, and that consistently, to deaden the class struggle and to reconcile the class antagonisms. They still dream of experimental realisation of their social Utopias, of founding isolated *"phalanstères,"* of establishing "Home Colonies," of setting up a "Little Icaria" — duodecimo editions of the New Jerusalem — and to realise all these castles in the air, they are compelled to appeal to the feelings and purses of the bourgeois. By degrees they sink into the category of the reactionary conservative Socialists depicted above, differing from these only by more systematic pedantry, and by their fanatical and superstitious belief in the miraculous effects of their social science.

They, therefore, violently oppose all political action on the part of the working class; such action, according to them, can only result from blind unbelief in the new Gospel.

The Owenites in England, and the Fourierists in France, respectively oppose the Chartists and the *Réformistes*.

IV

POSITION OF THE COMMUNIST IN RELATION TO THE VARIOUS EXISTING OPPOSITION PARTIES

Section II has made clear the relations of the Communists to the existing working-class parties, such as the Chartists in England and the Agrarian Reformers in America.

The Communists fight for the attainment of the immediate aims, for the enforcement of the momentary interests of the working class; but in the movement of the present, they also represent and take care of the future of that movement. In France the Communists ally themselves with the Social-Democrats, against the conservative and radical bourgeoisie, reserving, however, the right to take up a critical position in regard to phrases and illusions traditionally handed down from the great Revolution.

In Switzerland they support the Radicals, without losing sight of the fact that this party consists of antagonistic elements, partly of Democratic Socialists, in the French sense, partly of radical bourgeois.

In Poland they support the party that insists on an agrarian revolution as the prime condition for national emancipation, that party which fomented the insurrection of Cracow in 1846.

In Germany they fight with the bourgeoisie whenever it acts in a revolutionary way, against the absolute monarchy, the feudal squirearchy, and the petty bourgeoisie.

But they never cease, for a single instant, to instil into the working class the clearest possible recognition of the hostile antagonism between bourgeoisie and proletariat, in order that the German workers may straightway use, as so many weapons against the bourgeoisie, the social and political conditions that the bourgeoisie must necessarily introduce along with its supremacy, and in order that, after the fall of the reactionary classes in Germany, the fight against the bourgeoisie itself may immediately begin.

The Communists turn their attention chiefly to Germany, because that country is on the eve of a bourgeois revolution that is bound to be carried out under more advanced conditions of European civilisation, and with a much more developed proletariat, than that of England was in the seventeenth, and of France in the eighteenth century, and because the bourgeois revolution in Germany will be but the prelude to an immediately following proletarian revolution.

In short, the Communists everywhere support every revolutionary movement against the existing social and political order of things.

In all these movements they bring to the front, as the leading question in each, the property question, no matter what its degree of development at the time.

Finally, they labour everywhere for the union and agreement of the democratic parties of all countries.

The Communists disdain to conceal their views and aims. They openly declare that their ends can be attained only by the forcible overthrow of all existing social conditions. Let the ruling classes tremble at a Communistic revolution. The proletarians have nothing to lose but their chains. They have a world to win.

WORKING MEN OF ALL COUNTRIES, UNITE!

SELECTED BIBLIOGRAPHY

General Works

Almond, Gabriel. *The Appeals of Communism*. Princeton University, 1954.

Browder, Earl. *What Is Communism*. Vanguard, 1936.

Christman, H. *Communism in Action*. Bantam, 1969.

Daniels, Robert V. *The Nature of Communism*. Random House, 1962.

Gyorgy, Andrew. *Communism in Perspective*. Allyn & Bacon, 1964.

Meyer, Alfred G. *Communism*. Random House, 1967.

Ulam, Adam B. *The Unfinished Revolution*. Random House, 1960.

Marx and Engels

Berlin, Isaiah. *Karl Marx*. Oxford, 1963.

Engels, Friedrich. *Selected Writings*. Edited by W. O. Henderson. Penguin, 1967.

Lichtheim, George. *Marxism*. Praeger, 1962.

Marx, Karl. *Capital, the Communist Manifesto, & Other Writings*. Edited by Max Eastman. Modern Library, 1932.

Mayer, Gustav. *Friedrich Engels*. Fertig, 1936.

Mayo, Henry B. *Introduction to Marxist Theory*. Oxford, 1960.

Mehring, Franz. *Karl Marx, The Story of His Life*. University of Michigan, 1962.

Tucker, Robert C. *Philosophy & Myth in Karl Marx*. Cambridge University, 1961.

Lenin & the Russian Revolution

Anderson, Thornton. *Masters of Russian Marxism*. Appleton-Century Crofts, 1963.

Deutscher, Issac. *The Prophet Armed*. Oxford, 1954.

———. *The Prophet Unarmed*. Oxford, 1959.

———. *The Prophet Outcast*. Oxford, 1963.

Lenin, V. I. *State & Revolution.* International, 1932.
Meyer, Alfred. *Leninism.* Praeger, 1962.
Moorehead, Alan. *The Russian Revolution.* Harper, 1958.
Wolfe, Bertram. *Three Who Made a Revolution.* Dial, 1948.

Stalinism & After

Deutscher, Issac. *Stalin.* Oxford, 1967.
Linden, Carl. *Khrushchev & the Soviet Leadership, 1957–1964.* Johns Hopkins University, 1966.
Payne, Robert. *The Rise & Fall of Stalin.* Avon, 1966.
Stalin, Joseph. *Problems of Leninism.* International, 1934.
Werth, Alexander. *Russia Under Khrushchev.* Fawcett, 1962.
Wolfe, Bertram. *Khrushchev & Stalin's Ghost.* Praeger, 1957.

The Soviet System

Brzezinski, Z. *Ideology & Power in Soviet Politics.* Praeger, 1967.
Fainsod, Merle. *How Russia Is Ruled.* Harvard University, 1963.
Hendel, Samuel, ed. *The Soviet Crucible.* Van Nostrand, 1967.
Inkeles, Alex and R. A. Bauer. *The Soviet Citizen.* Harvard University, 1959.
Nove, Alec. *The Soviet Economy.* Praeger, 1969.
Pomeroy, W. J. *Half a Century of Socialism.* International, 1967.
Rostow, W. W. and E. J. Rozek. *Dynamics of Soviet Society.* Norton, 1967.
Schapiro, Leonard. *The Communist Party of the Soviet Union.* Random House, 1960.

Chinese Communism

Clubb, O. E. *Communism in China.* Columbia University, 1968.
Crankshaw, Edward. *The New Cold War, Moscow v. Peking.* Penguin, 1963.
Hinton, Harold. *Communist China in World Politics.* Houghton Mifflin, 1966.
Lifton, Robert. *Revolutionary Immortality.* Random House, 1968.
Liu, William T., ed. *Chinese Society Under Communism.* Wiley, 1967.
Pye, Lucien W. *The Spirit of Chinese Politics.* M.I.T. Press, 1968.

Schram, Stuart. *The Political Thought of Mao Tse-tung.* Praeger, 1969.

Tang, Peter S. H. *Communist China Today.* Research Institute, Sino-Soviet Bloc, 1961.

——— and Joan Maloney. *Communist China: The Domestic Scene, 1949–1967.* Seton Hall University, 1968.

Zagoria, Donald. *The Sino-Soviet Conflict, 1956–1961.* Princeton University, 1962.

Communist Internationalism

Aspaturian, Vernon. *The Soviet Union in the World Communist System.* Hoover Inst., Stanford University, 1966.

Borkenau, Franz. *World Communism.* University of Michigan, 1962.

Braunthal, Julius. *History of the International,* 2 vols. Praeger, 1967.

Brzezinski, Z. *The Soviet Bloc, Unity & Conflict.* Praeger, 1961.

Dallin, Alexander, ed. *Diversity in International Communism.* Columbia University, 1963.

Drachkovitch, M. M. & B. Lazitch, eds. *The Comintern: Historical Highlights.* Praeger, 1966.

Gruber, H. *International Communism in the Era of Lenin.* Cornell University, 1967.

Laquer, Walter & L. Labedz, eds. *Polycentrism.* Praeger, 1962.

Mayer, Peter. *Cohesion & Conflict in International Communism.* Nijhoff, 1968.

Staar, Richard. *The Communist Regimes in Eastern Europe.* Hoover Inst., Stanford University, 1967.

Triska, Jan. *Communist Party-States: International & Comparative Studies.* Bobbs-Merrill, 1969.

Cold War & Coexistence

Barghoorn, Frederick. *The Soviet Cultural Offensive.* Princeton University, 1960.

———. *Communist China & Asia: Challenge to American Policy.* Harper, 1960.

Boyd, R. G. *Communist China's Foreign Policy.* Praeger, 1962.

Brzezinski, Z. *Africa & the Communist World.* Stanford University, 1963.

Gurian, Waldemar. *Soviet Imperialism: Its Origins & Tactics*. Notre Dame University, 1953.

Jackson, Bruce. *Castro, the Kremlin, & Communism in Latin America*. Johns Hopkins University, 1968.

Mamatey, Victor. *Soviet Russian Imperialism*. Van Nostrand, 1964.

Morris, Bernard S. *International Communism & American Policy*. Atherton, 1966.

Scalapino, Robert, ed. *The Communist Revolution in Asia*. Prentice-Hall, 1965.

Schatten, Fritz. *Communism in Africa*. Praeger, 1965.

Seton-Watson, Hugh. *Neither War Nor Peace, The Struggle for Power in the Postwar World*. Praeger, 1960.

Suarez, Andres. *Cuba*. M.I.T. Press, 1967.

Ulam, Adam B. *Expansion & Coexistence*. Praeger, 1968.

Communism in America

Draper, Theodore. *American Communism & Soviet Russia*. Viking, 1960.

Ernst, Morris L. & D. Loth. *Report on the American Communist*. Putnam, 1962.

Hoover, J. Edgar. *Masters of Deceit*. Holt, 1958.

Howe, Irving. *The American Communist Party*. Beacon, 1957.

Latham, Earl. *The Communist Controversy in Washington*. Harvard University, 1966.

Luce, Phillip. *Road to Revolution*. Viewpoint, 1967.

Oneal, James & G. A. Werner. *American Communism*. Dutton, 1947.

Overstreet, Harry & Bonaro. *What We Must Know about Communism*. Norton, 1958.

Philbrick, Herbert. *I Led Three Lives*. McGraw-Hill, 1952.

Rossiter, Clinton. *Marxism: The View from America*. Harcourt, 1965.

Communism—An Appraisal

Acton, H. B. *The Illusion of the Epoch*. Dufour, 1955.

Burnham, James. *The Coming Defeat of Communism*. Greenwood, 1968.

Cole, G. D. H. *The Meaning of Marxism*. University of Michigan, 1964.

Crossman, Richard, ed. *The God That Failed*. Bantam, 1959.

Djilas, Milovan. *The New Class*. Praeger, 1957.

Drachkovitch, M. M., ed. *Marxist Ideology in the Contemporary World*. Praeger, 1966.

Hunt, R. N. Carew. *The Theory & Practice of Communism*. Macmillan, 1957.

Katakowski, L. *Toward a Marxist Humanism*. Grove, 1968.

Marcuse, Herbert. *Soviet Marxism, A Critical Analysis*. Columbia University, 1958.

Meyer, Alfred. *Marxism, The Unity of Theory & Practice*. Harvard University, 1954.

Petrovic, G. *Marx in the Mid-Twentieth Century*. Anchor, 1967.

INDEX